Bazooka Charlie

Bazooka Charlie

THE UNBELIEVABLE STORY OF MAJOR CHARLES CARPENTER AND ROSIE THE ROCKETER

JAMES P. BUSHA

WITH CAROL (CARPENTER) APACKI

SCHIFFER MILITARY
4880 Lower Valley Road   Atglen, PA 19310

Other Schiffer books on related subjects

B-26 "Flak-Bait": The Only American Aircraft to Survive 200 Bombing Missions during the Second World War, Alan F. Crouchman, 978-0-7643-6343-6

The Aviation Pioneers Of McCook Field: Candid Interviews with American Aeronautical Visionaries of the 1920s, Jerry Koszyk, 978-0-7643-6352-8

Type set in Cambria/Times New Roman

ISBN: 978-0-7643-6636-9 HB
ISBN: 978-0-7643-6870-7 PB
Printed in China
5 4 3 2

Published by Schiffer Publishing, Ltd.
4880 Lower Valley Road
Atglen, PA 19310
Phone: (610) 593-1777; Fax: (610) 593-2002
Email: Info@schifferbooks.com
Web: www.schifferbooks.com

FSC
www.fsc.org
MIX
Paper from
responsible sources
FSC® C167893

For our complete selection of fine books on this and related subjects, please visit our website at www.schifferbooks.com. You may also write for a free catalog.

Schiffer Publishing's titles are available at special discounts for bulk purchases for sales promotions or premiums. Special editions, including personalized covers, corporate imprints, and excerpts, can be created in large quantities for special needs. For more information, contact the publisher.

We are always looking for people to write books on new and related subjects. If you have an idea for a book, please contact us at proposals@schifferbooks.com.

This book is dedicated to the brave men and women of the United States armed forces, especially those who have paid the ultimate sacrifice to ensure that our freedoms are preserved and protected.
Godspeed to all of you!

Jim Busha 2022

Contents

Introduction

When I began writing this book, I remembered a quote from long ago and used it as my guidepost: "History without documentation is mythology." As incredible as this story is, some would argue that it's purely folklore, great folklore at that. Some would also say it's the story movies are made of—with heroes facing uncertainty and adversity around every corner while brittle freedoms and hope hang in the balance. Add in the journey of courage and despair, while the delicate strands of love between a husband and wife and their newborn child are pulled apart during a world war.

But what's even more unbelievable is the long-forgotten historic treasures that were lost and rediscovered along the way. As much as I would love to agree with you that what you are about to read and digest is historical fiction, and it would be preposterous to say differently, well my friends, you would be dead wrong. As the reader, you are in for a big surprise—this is a true story, lock, stock, and barrel as they say. For you the reader, I would like to begin with a disclaimer, but before I do, I want to share with you how this book came to fruition.

For more than twenty-five years I have been interviewing World War II veterans, mainly pilots, about their experiences during that significant time frame in history. I had been reading about them and their adventures for most of my fifty-eight years of life. They were my heroes, and the planes they flew were replicated in $\frac{1}{32}$ plastic scale models that filled my bedroom shelf as a kid.

The interviews I conducted were vast. From bomber pilots fending off swarms of German fighters high over Europe to a B-29 pilot carrying an atomic bomb across the vastness of the Pacific Ocean on his way to Japan, knowing that the chances were great it would be a one-way mission. Then there were the fighter pilots, both Allied and Axis, who realized that the only way to strap on a fighter and slug it out with the enemy day after day was to make a personal declaration with themselves that they were already dead.

But it was the liaison pilots that I felt a closer bond with. Maybe it was because I have been flying the same types of airplanes they did—albeit no one was shooting at me for the last twenty plus years at the controls of an Aeronca L-3 and Stinson L-5. It was intriguing to capture their stories and listen to them reenact both harrowing and, in some cases, very mundane missions of droning over the forests of Russia, Germany, and France, or the jungle islands of the Pacific looking for a well-concealed enemy or a fellow downed pilot or crew member to rescue. Some of them were "frustrated fighter pilots" who took potshots at the enemy with their .45-caliber sidearm, Thompson machine guns, and in some cases strapped bazookas to the struts of their wings and became the aggressor instead of the observer.

What was also interesting to note was the fact that on almost every interview I did, especially those I conducted early on, I would end the conversation with this statement, "I wish I would have interviewed you twenty years ago." There was always a long pause, the clearing of the throat, and a mimicked response. What the majority of them told me can be paraphrased like this: "I wouldn't have spoken to you then. The only reason I am telling you about my combat experiences now is so that my grandchildren understand what I did, and that they understand that there is no glory in war. The true heroes were the guys that never made it back."

During these last twenty-five years, I've had the honor and fortune of interviewing only about 350 of them, a mere pittance to the thousands of pilots, many of them transformed from "farm boys to fighter pilots" who flew and fought during the war. I've had hundreds of magazine articles published by over a dozen aviation/history magazines and have authored several books about these brave men.

But they were not my stories. I simply collected hundreds of hours of interviews, verified historic facts, and cross-referenced actual combat reports so that *their stories* could be shared and consumed as an extraordinary lesson during a very desperate time in history.

I created my own "hit list" of veterans I sought out to interview—guys like P-51 Mustang ace's Bud Anderson and Don Strait, Medal of Honor recipient, and F4F Wildcat pilot James Swett, to name just a few. But there was one pilot I had read about early on whose acts of bravery and in some cases unselfish, reckless behavior (necessary during wartime,) were legendary. Maj. Charles "Bazooka Charlie" Carpenter was at the top of my list. As I began researching him and the reputed exploits of his bazooka-toting Piper L-4 Cub he dubbed "Rosie the Rocketer," I knew from the little I read about him, his would make an incredible story.

But my quest to speak with him ended as quickly as it began. Charles Carpenter had died in 1966.

I knew his was another story, incredible as it was, that would never be shared in detail with the rest of the world. All any of us would read about Major Carpenter was sourced from some old newspaper articles that gave ambiguous speculation about several of his wartime adventures. But there was nothing written about the man, what made him tick, or *why* he did what he did. Strangely, I also found that no book was ever written about him or his Piper L-4 "Rosie the Rocketer." I quickly accepted defeat and realized his story would remain a mystery and forever placed into a category of World War II oddities and "urban legends."

But that all changed in 2016. As the editor in chief of *Warbirds*, *Vintage*, and *Sport Aviation* magazines for the Experimental Aircraft Association (EAA), I received a story inquiry from a woman named Carol Apacki in Ohio. Carol explained that she had been looking through some old boxes in her basement, boxes she inherited from her mother after her death. She went on to explain that it was mainly full of letters her dad had written home while training in the states and then when he was over in England and France and Luxembourg during World War II. My ears perked up a little, thinking her father might have been a crewmember on an airplane, a copilot, or maybe even a pilot.

Carol explained that it had been a while since she last looked through the family heirlooms because, as she stated, "I wanted to find out more about what my dad did during the war."

Carol then said she began researching on the internet and came across some disturbing forums where people were chatting back and forth saying that what her father did was all made up, and was simply "US war propaganda." Carol was aghast at those remarks; she had mounds of proof of her father's heroic acts and wartime memories. Carol then stated, "My father was Maj. Charles Carpenter and he flew a plane called 'Rosie the Rocketer.' Have you ever heard of him?"

There was stunned silence on my end. At one point, I'm sure Carol thought I had hung up on her. When I was able to shake the initial shock off, and coherently put words together, I remember muttering, "Charles Carpenter was your father?"

That initial phone conversation with Carol not only sparked an incredible journey, friendship, and quest into the obscure past of her father; it also unraveled not one but several mysteries about Major Carpenter and his L-4 "Rosie the Rocketer." It became evident early on, from the conservations I had with Carol about her father; her mother, Elda; and her family that there was much more to the story. But when she said she had "some" wartime letters written by her father that he had written to her mother, I assumed "some" meant a handful, or at the most a dozen. I assumed wrong.

What Carol shared with me on one of my early visits to see and interview her was like opening an undisturbed time capsule. Scattered across a large dining table, living room hutch, several end tables, couches, and the living room floor were hundreds of handwritten letters spanning the years from 1941 to 1965, assorted stacks of photo albums, scrapbooks, newspaper clippings, diaries, and personal effects of her father and family. To say I was dumbstruck is an understatement.

As the only living relative, Carol wanted her father's story shared with the world. Pouring over the letters, I quickly realized that Charles Carpenter was not only a prolific writer and poet, but one that had such an envious command of the English language, I felt completely out of his league.

That is why it was important to leave many of his letters—whether whole or excerpts—"as is" and not try to paraphrase his writings, lest we lose the true meaning behind his words.

I have to admit, even up to the day of the printing of this book, I wondered what Lt. Col. Charles Carpenter would think. Did I let him down? Did Carol and I capture the true essence and soul of his personal and sometimes tragic journey? Did we tell his story the way he would have told it?

I believe we did, but I will let you the reader make that final determination. With that, we are almost ready to turn you loose and let you devour this incredible journey of a multifaceted man and his aerial chariot of destruction—much of it in his own words and actions. But before I do, I need to end this portion with what I spoke about at the beginning—a disclaimer.

This book depicts actual events in the life of Charles M. Carpenter. But like anything over 110 years old, there are bound to be some missing pieces. Using a multitude of resources at our fingertips—including personal letters, diaries, photographs, period newspaper articles, military records, research periodicals, and personal interviews and recollections—we have attempted to fill in as many of those gaps as possible. To that end, the material presented before you is factual to the best of our knowledge.

Jim Busha
2021

Foreword

Reflections from a Daughter
by Carol Carpenter Apacki

Over the past few years, the war stories about my dad have been surging and swirling around my head in the form of online discussions, YouTube videos, newspaper articles, and more recently in the Smithsonian's *Air and Space* magazine with the heady title "Bazooka Charlie and the Grasshopper: A Tale of World War II—The most famous small airplane of the war is about to fly again."

Jim Busha's remarkable book about my dad brings all of this together in a coherent, thoroughly researched book that is accurate, highly personal, and deeply compelling. To me, it is far more than another military tale about my dad as a "hero," it is a moving love story that was greatly tested during wartime. There are many books on World War II, but this one includes a very close-up look at the unraveling of the human spirit and what war can do to a tender new marriage and a young soldier's idealism. I want to share it because there is much to learn from it—and it has such a happy ending.

While I grew up knowing a few scattered stories about my dad and his little cloth-covered L-4 plane, "Rosie the Rocketer," he seldom spoke about the war, and for most of my life, I was not that interested in the time before I knew him. But when I was seventy-three and read an online discussion questioning the realities of his wartime feats with comments like "Sorry, I don't believe it ever happened" and "Complete bollocks," I was rankled enough to bring out the boxful of old yellowed newspaper stories that I found in my mom's closet after her death and start going through them.

This was the beginning of an improbable chain of events that led to my writing an article for *EAA Warbirds* magazine about my dad, which led to Joseph Scheil finding "Rosie the Rocketer" plane in a small museum in Austria, which led to the Collings Foundation bringing back the plane to be fully restored by Colin Powers, which led to several newspaper articles about the plane's restoration, which led to Jim Busha putting all these stories together in this book. And more recently, another book is on its way, written by two former high school students of my dad who are writing about his enduring impact on their lives as young counselors at the boys' summer camp he started in the 1960s.

Now in this ninth decade of my life, I am learning about my parents in ways I never knew before. While I had always thought of my dad as a "hero," I was stunned to discover how my dad entered the war as an idealistic young man, and after a short summer as an artillery observer, destroying tanks with his small L-4 plane laden with bazookas, turned into a shattered and very sick man seemingly unable to return to my mom and lead a normal life again. I now realize that it was my mom who held things together, and through the power of love and forgiveness, I was able to grow up with two wonderful parents at my side.

So while Jim's book is providing a detailed look at my father and mother's lives both before, during, and after the war, I will give you a short, more personal description of what they were like from my perspective as their only child.

The image of my dad as "Bazooka Charlie," with stories in the newspaper clippings as both "mad" and as a legendary warrior, is very different from the person I knew. Family and friends knew him as someone charismatic, highly principled, articulate, and wise. He was a man of peace, a scholar, a book collector, a poet, a practical joker, and an athlete. He loved and sang operetta in the shower and carried on serious discussions about philosophy and history. He was a devoted husband and father who patiently taught me chess, tennis, and regularly took me on nature walks, and camping and canoe trips. He spent long hours with me in deep conversations about books and big ideas.

He was also a deeply respected high school history teacher who had the school yearbook dedicated to him several times. In the summers he ran a boys' camp in the Ozarks—a camp that focused on teaching outdoor skills and building character. I think what I'm trying to say is that his war deeds as Bazooka Charlie with "Rosie the Rocketer" were only a small part of who he was and the legacy he left.

While strikingly beautiful, my mom lacked the confidence that my dad always had. Because of a nervous condition that was diagnosed as Saint Vitus's dance, she dropped out of school in the ninth grade. This lack of education shaped her view of herself. And while she appeared to be shy and soft-spoken, she had a fierceness of spirit that carried her through eighty-eight years of life in which she pushed herself to lead of life of independence and well being. To educate herself, she got her high school degree through a correspondence program, often with my dad at her side guiding her through algebra problems. After my dad died, she took college courses, became a beloved teacher's assistant at a Montessori school, and continued working there until her mideighties.

She was a loving, gentle mother who modeled through her everyday actions the virtues of courage, forgiveness, integrity, and utmost honesty. She loved to dance and make fun—and when I was a child, she read to me from *The Book of Knowledge* to instill in me a curiosity about the world that is with me still. Most of all, she was always there for comfort and advice—and while she lacked the intellect of my dad, she brimmed with commonsense and a nonjudgmental, generous spirit. Later in life, she became a Christian Scientist, and she learned how to overcome her insecurities and health issues. She studied Christian Science teachings every morning and never went to doctors or took medicine again. On the day before she died at age eighty-eight, my daughter and I went to see her with my two small grandchildren. She held the baby, chatted happily with us, and served us summer strawberries. As she stood on the porch and waved goodbye, I said to my daughter, "Doesn't Grandma look beautiful?" The next day I found her lying on her bedroom floor. She had passed away on my father's birthday. I like to picture my father coming for her with outstretched hands and saying, "Bunny, it's time to come home." There were still some strawberries left in the refrigerator—and the boxes about my dad's war years in her closet.

For you as readers, my hopes for this book are many. I hope that it brings together all the disparate stories about my dad into one book that is chronological and historically accurate. As you will discover, it is also painfully honest and revealing, and I have been willing to share my father's letters home because I trust that you will see them in the context of war and its haunting effects on so many who serve on the battlefront, no matter how justified the war. I also see this as a legacy for my own five children and thirteen grandchildren who have a copy of my father's creed with goals for his life that he wrote as a young and fatherless man at age seventeen. I hope that they can take pride in their grandparents' story and see how love and forgiveness can overcome the trauma of the war and allow for recovery and a return to happy and productive lives. Most of all, I hope that you, the reader, get caught up in the exciting story of Bazooka Charlie, "Rosie the

Rocketer," and General Patton's Third Army, 4th Armored Division, sweeping through France in the summer, fall, and winter of 1944/1945.

"The 4th Armored Division does not need and will not have a nickname. They shall be known by their deeds alone."
—Maj. Gen. John S. Wood, commanding officer, 4th Armored Division, Third Army

CREED
My Creed

I have resolved to exert all my efforts toward being a nobler and stronger fellow, a gentleman, a scholar, a friend, and a real man. To the best of my ability, I will ever strive to self-control, self-improvement, freedom, wisdom, courage, generosity, truth, and true nobility before gods and men. I will be better.

Charles Marston Carpenter
1929

CHAPTER 1

Luck Runs Out

It had been almost two months since the Normandy invasion, and Maj. Charles M. Carpenter had only been in occupied France for less than two weeks. Less than four days ago, on August 1, 1944, he was a part of a herculean force of thousands of men whose main task, a task they had trained day and night for, for more than two years, was to destroy a ruthless enemy and rid them of lands that were not theirs to take. Not now and not in 1918, either. Those old scars both on the landscape and on the faces of those old enough to remember were still evident as they slugged it out with the Germans once again, on the land, in the air, and on the seas. As a history teacher, he studied men's faults, especially the wicked ones, and knew they were condemned to repeat history over and over again.

This was just one of the hundred or more thoughts that were racing through his head. But in his mind, he felt like no more than a common criminal, struggling as he tried to grasp why his actions in combat suddenly had hard and fast rules. What troubled him the most, though, was when his fellow soldiers, those that wore the same GI uniform but displayed a different armored division triangle on their shoulders, confiscated his leather flight jacket, which flaunted his hard-earned silver wings with a big "L" stamped on them, along with his .45-caliber sidearm and holster. But when the officer in charge threw the words "court-martial" at him, well now he felt that his luck had simply run out.

He recalled something he had written many years ago, back in Centre College, when life seemed so well defined. When a good sturdy pen and a small, dark-chocolate-colored spiral notebook were all a young, receptive man needed to conjure and capture the boundless philosophical insights that ran rampant in his mind.

He often found solace on those late summer nights in Kentucky, when the only sounds he heard were the shrill rapid drumbeat of an army of cicadas. That sound kept a rhythm between his thoughts and his pen. He recalled one of his random feelings that he jotted down that seemed very fitting for the situation.

"It is our foolish pride and little fears that make life so difficult at times." No truer words were written, he thought.

Closing his eyes for just a moment, he tried to imagine the sounds he was hearing outside were those of the big bands he enjoyed listening to at the Coliseum, just across the Mississippi River from his home in Moline. The bass drums were M7 self-propelled 105 mm howitzers, and the shells they fired whirred like woodwinds as they trailed off toward the front lines. The distinct harmonic sound of P-47 Thunderbolts, powered by huge 2,000 hp, Pratt & Whitney Double Wasp R-2800 radial engines echoed off the canvas tent walls like a wailing trumpet section as they zoomed low overhead searching for their next German targets only a few miles away. The large tanks and half-tracks rolling by his tent clanked like piano keys that nearly drowned out the chattering of machine-gun fire and rifle crack a half mile away.

"Major Carpenter, the sergeant said you wanted some paper?"

He sat upright on his cot, turned toward the voice, and squinted at the open flap as daylight invaded his sanctuary cell. He stared at the black-and-white armband stretched across the corporal's left bicep with the letters MP facing outward and noted the leather strap running down his right side that held the Thompson submachine gun upright, tight against his back.

He nodded and held out his hand. Taking the papers, he paused for a split second, sizing up the soldier who appeared not much older than one of his students back home. He was about to ask his name and where he was from but stopped himself. He didn't know if prisoners were allowed to talk.

As the corporal's footsteps faded away, he stared at the blank sheets of paper. How would he even begin to explain?

August 5, 1944

Dear Elda,
Brace yourself because this letter will probably jolt you like hell. At present, I am at a field medical unit, well and sound, but bearing a tag that says "battle fatigue and exhaustion" in line of duty. What it really means is "shooting my mouth off," and doing things that fall somewhat out of my duty as Division Artillery Air officer.

The last few days have been amazing ones. Our advance had been rapid and events have tumbled upon the other. Someday I shall tell you the whole story. Now, I only want to tell you that I shall probably come out of this situation as a common soldier or in some sort of noncombatant activity like driving an ambulance.

Frankly, right at present the Division authorities do not know what to do with me. As you would probably guess I have done nothing that would disgrace my friends, my reputation, or my country. If anything, it is probably an overzealousness of mine that has run rampant lately.

Be prepared as soon as possible to accept a monthly income, very much less than you have at present. You may even have to find employment of some kind to get by. As things appear from where I stand now, I shall probably not even return home at the end of the war. The old life is pretty much gone for me, although you and home are as lovely and sweet as ever.

All material possessions that are ours belong to you now. Be sure to immediately start taking such legal steps as are necessary to secure them in your own name.

From now on, I must be free to speak my mind and follow what I believe to be the true course for the most concerned.

In the future, if any of my old luck falls my way, I shall continue to share it with you. I am always under obligation to see that you and Carol Ann do not suffer from any lack of actual necessities of life itself. Other than that, much of your own destiny is in your own hands.

Our life together has been filled with happiness and growth. You have become a confidant and fine lady. The only way you can ever fail me is by not facing up bravely and proudly to what I am telling you.

I shall write my mother soon. She is like the Rock of Gibraltar in any storm this world can brew. Go to her. Let her tell you of the "crazy Carpenters" and take her advice.

Please do not read "battle fatigue" into this letter. I have always known what I've said. What the next few days, hold in store for me, I do not know. I shall write to you and let you know how things are with me.

You and I have some lovely memories to share. Do not lose them. I am not worthy of a broken heart. Your God will take care of you and I will take care of me. Feel quite free to write to any of my associates or superiors. Many men lose ideals in a war such as this. A few of mine have merely taken on new luster.

The war so far has been a glorious adventure for me, except for the burning homes and needlessly devastated cities and villages. Amid some scenes of confusion and panic, I have done what I thought was right. Although in all cases the situation has been helped, I have not done myself any good. However, the individual should no longer count for much when so much else is at stake.

Good-bye for now, and a lot of love from me to you and Carol Ann. Will I be proud of her too someday?

Sincerely with love,
Charles

CHAPTER 2

Poor and Proud

Charles Marston Carpenter did not barge into this world to become famous. In fact, by the time he was assisted into this world by Dr. Allen J. Miller, on August 29, 1912, many other world events would have overshadowed any birth announcement, had there been one. The sinking of the "unsink-able" Royal Mail Ship (RMS) *Titanic* had occurred four and a half months earlier on April 15 when the ship, four days into its maiden voyage, made its fateful run through the Iceberg Alley in the North Atlantic. Over 1,500 souls would never reach their intended destination of New York City, nor would they bear witness to the solar eclipse that occurred on their intended arrival date of April 17.

During the same month Wilber Wright, one-half of the famed aviation Wright brothers and the eldest of the two, became ill and was diagnosed with typhoid fever in April, while on a business trip to Boston. He was only forty-five years old when he died on May 30, at his home in Dayton, Ohio.

The Wrights had ignited world interest in aviation, so much so that on the very day Charles was born, the *Woodfield County Journal*, of Eureka, Illinois, a small town 100 miles southeast of Moline, announced "Aviation Events Big Fair Feature" as one of their headlines.[1] The story went on to proclaim that aviation would have top billing at the Illinois State Fair with an air race between two daredevils, one an American monoplane built by the fledgling Johnson Brothers of Terra Haute, Indiana, and piloted by the inventor Louis Johnson. The other entrant was a French-built Nieuport monoplane, flown by a record-setting Frenchman, named La Tournten, "who doesn't speak a word of English, will be the engineer on this machine."

A Curtiss biplane was also on the docket to make an appearance and compete against the monoplanes. "A Curtiss aeroplane has never exhibited in Springfield, the Wrights being the only machines in the air in 1910 and 1911."

Aviation was already growing by leaps and bounds with new technologies and designs surpassing the once unthinkable at breakneck speed. As a newborn, Charles had no idea about the impact that the Wright brothers would have on his future life with the advent of powered flight on the windswept dunes of Kill Devil Hills, North Carolina, in December 1903. But for Charles, those flying adventures were still twenty-five-plus years away. As the newest resident of Edgington, Illinois, an unincorporated township in Rock Island County, just a stone's throw away from Moline and the dark muddy waters of the Mississippi River, which slithered and sliced through the bluffs of Illinois and Iowa. Charles was one of 1,100 residents of the 424-square-mile county area.

Born into a family of farmers, Charles's father, Fred, and mother, Lois Mary (Marston), had been married for only four years when they welcomed their third child. Charles's sisters Mildred and Margaret preceded him by four and two years, respectively, as the growing family settled on the Henry B. Carpenter farm. Henry had been a pioneer resident of Rock Island County when he moved there with his parents at age three from Pennsylvania in 1854. By 1907, Henry had retired from farming and relied on his son, Fred, to take over the daily chores. Overseeing 1,000 acres and a large amount of stock, Fred oversaw what on the surface was a successful farming operation, but internally he struggled as a family man.

With a new wife and budding family, Fred by all accounts was not the epitome of a father figure. Fred's inclination was more toward alcohol and gambling. Not good company, especially when one would overcome the other, so much so that according to the decree for divorce filed by Lois:

> On or about the 15th day of January, A.D. 1919, The Defendant, Fred
> M. Carpenter willfully deserted and absented himself from the Plaintiff
> (Lois) without and reasonable cause for the space of one year and
> upward, and he has continued to absent himself from the said Plaintiff.

By then the Carpenter clan had grown by three, with the addition of Merle in 1913, Eugene (Gene) in 1915, and Helen in 1917. With six children to care for, Lois had simply had enough with her imperceptible husband and separated herself from the marriage. Lois's brother-in-law Mylo assisted in moving Lois and the children to Reynolds, Illinois, a mere 9 miles farther east. With a team of horses and a wagon, the family of seven piled what little possessions they had inside and focused their attention on the dirt road ahead, never looking back or speaking the name Fred Carpenter ever again. What seemed like an insurmountable challenge for any woman of 1920, let alone one with six children in tow, would by all accounts become another tragic story of a broken family. But Lois Carpenter was not like other women and had one thing going for her—she was a Marston.

Born in 1886 to Freeman and Emily Marston, the Marston name is of noble linage, tracing its roots in ancient English history to the time of the Conquest in 1066.

Described by others as "cold, rather rigid, tough but a proper group" or simply "the Wild Carpenters," the family was very frugal, hardworking, and extremely loyal to Lois. Outwardly, they did not eject a warmth immediately upon first meeting them. Religion was not a part of the family upbringing as they found salvation and harmony among the family corps. From an early age, all of the children became somewhat individualistic, but as a clan, the Carpenters were tighter than a steel drum.

Due to a lack of steady income, most of the children, especially the older ones, were sent off to other local farms in the summer months, where they tended to livestock or helped in the gardens and fields, earning whatever money they could to help support their mother.

Although the country was in the middle of prosperity and growth known as the "Roaring Twenties," the only thing Lois was concerned about was the "roaring and rumbling" stomachs of her growing children. Most summers the children were barefoot, with the boys in overalls and the girls in straw hats and knee-length dresses, all of them caked in Illinois dust and dirt.

By 1925, the entire Carpenter family moved into Lois's mother's three-bedroom house on Clark Street in Reynolds. A widow since 1903, when her husband, Freeman, passed away in the home at age fifty-four, Emily opened her home to her daughter Lois and six grandchildren. The interior of the home was very tidy and well kept, and to ensure that practice was obeyed, the children were taught discipline and respect for others' belongings at an early age. As a jokester, Charles had a wicked sense of humor, was fond of foolishness, and loved to laugh. On more than one occasion, his sense of adventure and wittiness caught the eye and disdain of his grandmother Emily, and in return, Charles received the wrath of a sharp tongue and a leather strap.

Outside, the yard was adorned with mature trees and grapevine crisscrossing and running up and down one side of the two-story whitewashed exterior. An outhouse was located nearby, and a water pump with a long rusty handle spit out cool water on a hot summer's day for young adolescents and soiled farmhands, was positioned prominently in the front yard.

At an early age, Charles enjoyed reading books, especially those about world history and philosophy. As a student, he was academically endowed and loved to learn. One newsworthy item that Charles probably never read about in late February 1925 was the story of an Austrian man by the name of Adolf Hitler, who had been released from a German prison. A day later, he attended a rally in Munich, Germany, and proclaimed the relaunching of the Nazi Party in Germany. By July he had published his autobiographical manifesto *Mein Kampf*, which began as an insignificant burning ember for his followers that would eventually engulf the entire world in the scorching fury of death and destruction twenty years later—a world of demise and devastation that Charles would experience firsthand.

But small-town life for a child, especially a young teenager like Charles, was not all work all the time. Halloween brought its own set of traditions for Charles and his friends. On one night, Charles and a friend dared one another to see who could walk through the nearby Reynolds Cemetery without breaking stride. As the boys tramped their way under the massive whitewashed metal archway, past gravestones and under rustling trees, they soon realized they were being followed. With heartbeats racing, and their throats bone dry with fear, the footsteps behind them grew louder with an eerie swishing sound. As the boys stopped to listen to determine where this person, phantom, or creature was approaching from, the sound stopped. But as soon as they began to walk, picking up their stride to match their rushing heartbeats, they heard the fearful swishing noise once again.

Both boys, filled with trepidation and taking what they thought was their final gasp of air, slowly turned toward their grim reaper and saw in the far distance a white, ethereal large shape. With panic paralyzing both of them, unable to convince their legs to move, they watched in horror as the creature began to move toward them once again. With a volley of "moos," and the whooshing of a large tail, a large white milk cow turned and paralleled two screaming, sprinting figures as it searched for a patch of cool, long grass to graze upon.

Another of the "games" Charles and the local boys use to play at night was to see how many outhouses they could tip over at the surrounding farms and houses in the Reynolds area. After several years of mischief, one of the local farmers had simply had enough. Not knowing who was responsible, but knowing Halloween was upon him, he simply pushed his outhouse several feet forward and waited. When Charles and his friends made their way in the dark toward their next target, several of them tumbled into the exposed hole below. By the stench they carried with them, there was no denying who had been responsible. Thus ended the "great outhouse tip-over."

One of Charles's best friends, who didn't accompany him on his gallant outhouse raids, was his dog, Jack. One part terrier, three parts mongrel, Jack would never be mistaken for a classy dog. With a full white stripe running from the tip of his snout vertically over his head, to a 4-inch-wide fluffy white "J" arching from left to right across his chest, Jack wore blacks and browns, and assorted burrs and grass stains on the rest of his unkempt coat. Jack was by all accounts a farm dog, but to Charles, Jack provided affection and loyalty—traits that Charles was craving from an absconded father figure in his life.

Part of what Charles was searching for could be found in the town of Reynolds, population 320 give or take. Full of lush green trees and well-kept yards with homes spread out comfortably, this area was a shining star compared to the dumpy-looking, minuscule downtown area. But for Charles, he found Shangri-La among one tired building situated among the other depressing-looking structures and grain elevators. O'Leary's Drug Store, later named Reynolds Drug store, became his haven. Proprietor J. H. O'Leary was a soft-spoken, gentle bachelor with two maiden sisters. Bespeckled, with thinning hair, O'Leary was slender, with a small build and very genteel. As a pharmacist, besides dispensing medication to the local customers, his storehouse was like many others of the times, with two aisles running down the middle with assorted merchandise hanging from the walls, supplying the locals with everything from "soup to nuts, to candy, and comics."

What Charles loved most about O'Leary though was the twinkle in his eye and the mutual respect O'Leary paid to him as a teenager. Considered a presence in his life, O'Leary recognized the maturity and seriousness of Charles and became an encouraging role model during his high school years.

Charles, like his siblings before and after, all attended Reynolds High School. Charles transferred to Rock Island High School in 1929, where he not only excelled academically in the classroom, but also outshined others on the football field, basketball court, and track. Perhaps it was his upbring-ing and early farm life demands of hard work and physical activity that allowed Charles to become a natural athlete. "Carp," as he was called by fellow teammates, was an all-star. During the Rock Island basketball season, Charles proved to be a valuable player and asset for the team. His high school yearbook stated, "Carp could fill the guard position in easy style. He was handicapped by playing an entirely new style of play under Coach Burgitt, but by the end of the season, he was one of the most consistent players on the team." A trait that would shadow him through life.

In the summer of 1929, right before his senior year was about to begin, Charles enlisted in the Citizens Military Training Camp (CMTC). The an-nouncement to join was irresistible and mesmerizing, especially for a seventeen-year-old:

Citizens Military Training Camps. Thirty days of healthful manly outdoor life—summer 1929. If you are over 17 and under 24 and physically fit, send for further information and application blank. Uncle Sam takes and feeds you, clothes you, sends you back home without cost to you!

The CMTC program was created to enhance national defense training and offer more than thirty thousand young, physically fit volunteers four weeks of military-style training each summer.

These camps emphasized good citizenship and national defense. In early 1920, General Lenihan from the War Department said:

The object of the camps was to bring together young men of high type from all sections of the country (of wealthy and poor parents alike) in the same uniform and on a common basis of equality, under the most favorable conditions of outdoor life; to stimulate and promote the most patriotism and Americanism and, through expert physical direction, athletic coaching, and military training to benefit the young men individually and lead them to be better realization of their obligations to their country.

The camp routine consisted of willing obedience to lawful authority, neatness, politeness, and reliability. To earn a reserve commission in the military with the rank of a second lieutenant, the candidate had to complete four stages of four-week training for the next four years. These consisted of Basic, Red, White, and Blue.

During the first year, cadets learned elementary drills. Most of this consisted of outdoor activities and sports, like track, wrestling, tennis, boxing, and football, to build up physical conditioning and overall strength. Charles Carpenter was in his element. Advanced courses taught the basics of infantry, cavalry, and field artillery, and how to utilize and properly maintain military equipment.

Because of these military standards of behavior, Charles's handwritten creed of 1929 was evidence enough of what kind of man he strove to become.

Charles graduated from Rock Island High school in 1930. After graduation, Charles bounced around from one odd job to another. He continued with his military reserve obligations in the summer but found it difficult at best to find steady work while millions like him, suffering the same plight, all struggling to survive a Great Depression that was raging across the nation. But Charles had one magnetism in life that became an insatiable hunger, one driven by excellence of one's self. Charles Carpenter thrived on discipline, education, and writing. After four successful summer courses, Charles was commissioned in the US Army Reserve in 1932 as a second lieutenant.

In 1932, Charles applied for and was accepted to attend the Roosevelt Military Academy in Aledo, Illinois, and for the next two years began his journey in preparing for eventual military service. The school, which had first opened in 1924, was named in honor of Theodore "Teddy" Roosevelt and the cadets became known as "Rough Riders."

For the next twenty-four months, consistency and military discipline reigned supreme as reveille was sounded at 6:40 a.m., followed by exercises, breakfast, an inspection of quarters, and chapel exercises. By 8:00 a.m., it was time for classes and study, followed by physical drill and lunch. The afternoon consisted of more classroom work followed by military drill and athletics and recreation before supper was served at 6:00 p.m. The study period followed forty-five minutes later with an hour of recreation beginning at 8:15 p.m. until the call to quarters sounded before a lone bugler played taps at 9:30 a.m.

Because of these military standards of behavior and because of his multitalented athletic prowess, Charles received an athletic scholarship to attend Centre College in February 1934. Centre was located in Danville, Kentucky, 36 miles from Lexington if you followed the twisting, turning, and double backtracking Kentucky River. This small town of around 6,700 residents would be his home for the next two years. As a liberal arts campus, Charles again exceeded expectations both in the classroom and on the field. His classes included English composition,astrology, philosophy, business law, banking (which earned him his lowest grade of B+), trigonometry, chemistry, and an abundance of history and English classes that included English, Victorian, and American literature, world, Greek, and modern European history—all of them his favorite topics. While in college he began reading and collecting the books written by Will Durant and his wife, Ariel. Their first title in their eleven-book series, *The Story of Civilization: Our Oriental Heritage*, whet the appetite of Charles as his hunger for world knowledge continued to grow. Charles, already known to expound on a variety of topics, especially those dealing with philosophy and history, could light up any room with his charisma and natural dispatching of facts.

But Charles, who was described by others as a "Renaissance man," enjoyed writing poetry. Just two days after Christmas in 1934 he wrote the following:

Fireside Contentment

A well-filled pipe, a wise old book,
An easy chair near a fireplace nook,
A lazy fires ruddy, flickering, glow
Music that's soft, and sweet, and slow
Memories dear of places, faces, and names
Dreams that leap and dance among the flames.
For these, surely a part of life was meant
With these, that part of my life is well content.

Charles wrote this poem while most if not all his classmates were home on holiday break. Without the financial means to travel back to his home in Illinois, Charles remained behind, along with the school's janitor as his only companion. Although Charles excelled in the upper class of academics, he remained in the lower class financially. Although dirt poor, Charles was still able to develop refinements that he did not have growing up in rural Illinois. He became a "gentleman's, gentleman" and lived life with gusto. While in college Charles wrote, "In what I am I can be rich. In what I have I may always be poor. My body and my mind are my best investments."

Besides his growing achievements in academia, he also carried a burning competitive acuity within him. He played halfback as part of the Centre College "Colonels," a guard on the basketball court, and a multipurpose member of the track team. His specialty was the half-mile and discus, and as a letterman, his coaches quipped, "Carp is so versatile that they have to hold up events for him to place in one and compete in the other."

But when he hung up his cleats or set his basketball down, he focused on his priorities at hand—earning a college degree. As a member of the "Ye Rounde Table," an honorary scholarship society on the Centre campus with a focus on cultural subjects beyond the classroom, Charles by all accounts was an extremely gifted and well-rounded student. And as a reserve military officer, his self-discipline, tenacity, and the ability to overcome any obstacle thrown at him allowed him to become anything he wanted to. Graduating on June 1, 1936, with a bachelor of arts degree, Charles Carpenter set out to change the world—he elected to become a teacher.

CHAPTER 3

Self-Discovery

In the fall of 1936, Charles returned home to his military style of life and roots and accepted a job with the Roosevelt Military Academy as its new athletic director, coach, librarian, and junior history teacher specializing in military subjects. The academy's cadets addressed him as Lieutenant Carpenter. His first season as a football coach had mixed reviews—two wins, three ties, and two losses. In basketball his team won four and lost three. But as a track coach, he excelled. During his first season, his cadets ruled the track, winning six meets and losing none. As a coach, he instilled hard running, hard tackling, and deception as to his mantra for the cadets. But it was the use of "deception" that would continue to be one of his tried and true methods of success, especially during World War II.

As a new teacher, Charles struggled with certain protocols and education rules:

> My few months as a teacher of athletics and academics has shown me that what needs most to be taught to our youth are proper attitudes rather than facts about science, and history, and language, and mathematics. In most cases, I believe that if a sacrifice must be made, it is better to sacrifice the subject for the boy rather than the boy for the subject. Our present system of grading in school is a weak, ineffective substitute for proper pupil motivation.

But as a history teacher, and a person who consumed both current and historic information ravenously, Charles Carpenter was very keen on what was going on in the world, especially in Europe:

Life's greatest danger is our civilization at this time lies in the existence of those hellish, manmade institutions of jealously, hatred, greed, and destruction known as nations. Peace will come only when nations go.

He read about the death and destruction occurring during the Spanish Civil War and the toll it took on civilian life in daily newspapers, while others around him were interested in baseball scores or record aviation triumphs, like Howard Hughes setting a new transcontinental speed record as he dashed across the country from Los Angeles to New York City, in his specially built blue-winged, polished metal, sleek H-1 Racer in less than seven and a half hours. The racer was faster than most military aircraft of the time, and its radical design and radial engine combination influenced later military aircraft, including two starlets from World War II—the Grumman F6F Hellcat and Republic P-47 Thunderbolt. And as to the latter, in a few short years, Charles would witness first-hand the awesome brute power and destructiveness of the Thunderbolt.

Charles consumed so much information that at times he admitted:

My head ached so much from what I was absorbing and my old desires to soak up knowledge of all kinds, and to grow in wisdom has taken hold of me again.

To alleviate the building pressure, Charles used pen and paper to secure his thoughts for his audience of one.

Sunday, March 14, 1937 (*diary excerpt*)

My mind was certainly dull when I attempted to begin my diary again last night. Everything is clearer now. I think I'll just skip most of last year and pick up with the present again. Life has been steady and serene for me this year but marked by no particular brilliance upon my part. I'm steadier and more confident than ever before. Perhaps it is because the last glimmer of adolescence is fading behind me.

I am twenty-four years old now, in good health, more or less intro-spective by nature, and resentful of any encroachments upon my mental and physical freedom. In this job, I am surrounded with a multitude of opportunities to gain a liberal and broad education, and I am taking advantage of many of them. I seem to be a little more stable and efficient than at any time before this year. However, I can see some of the sterner and rather unsocial traits of the Marston's hardening into my character.

I must be careful not to grow too old before I die. Because, after all, in my saner, thinking moods, I realize that it is better and more enjoyable not to take most things of this world too seriously. Most of my faults have not improved but some of my virtues have. I speak my mind more these days, still talk too much, am less hypo-critical, sterner and more easily irritated, and more selfish about many petty things.

One of my grandest abilities has always been to see most of the glory and fun that lies in the present. My life would indeed be a pleasant one if the next twenty-four years could bring me as much mental growth, improvement in character, and pleasant associations as the past twenty-four have. Perhaps a goodly share of my future lies in my own hands, but the biggest share is on the Wheel of Chance. At best life is such a gamble that it seems so very foolish to take the unnecessary gambles with health, friends, and fortune that most people take.

March 19 (*diary excerpt*)

Another week is done. I am tired and ready for solitude. I seem to love solitude. Maybe I am really an unsocial creature. Life is far crueler than Death. Death is one of the most beautiful features of our system to me, and I am glad that I am not forced to believe in the course of everlasting life. When I write this I am not unhappy or in pain. I am just melancholy and a bit thoughtful. Never before in my life have I noticed that time flies by so swiftly as it does for me these days.

My modern history and American government classes keep me pretty well abreast of current events and perhaps my mood indigo tonight is partly the reflections of a sick world. There is so much narrowness and prejudice in this talented world, so much hatred and suspicion, nations feverishly preparing to slaughter again, hundreds of strikes and riots taking place in our own country, the richest and most prosperous in the world. People starving in the midst of plenty, thousands wasting their lives in idleness with plenty of work to be done, marriages and homes breaking up everywhere around me, dull-eyed people in the prime of life seeking merely for some straw of security, a half a thousand school children dying in one blast, a million people dead already in a war-stricken Spain and nothing accomplished but destruction of a once beautiful, picturesque land. From now on we'll have to build our air castles somewhere other than Spain. Yes this is a sample of the blues that spring from little else than weariness and an aching loneliness for something that is not here.

March 21 (*diary excerpt*)

Here we go on another build-up program:

Better speaking English and less careless talk and gossip that might be harmful to someone and cannot help anyone. More generous with material things, more economical with the really precious things such as time, energy, and health.

Try to keep my mind free from base and trivial thoughts that are unworthy of it. To keep my mind clear and healthy. Always keep busy at something worthwhile. Always try to improve myself mentally and physically by the best standards that I know. Always walk and talk with the best company that I can find in books, or music, or people and spend all the time that I can with them.

Always tell the truth or tell nothing. Keep my honor clean, fear no one, develop poise and self-control, strive to be as independent of men and things as possible.

Live in the present with an eye to the future and an ear to the lessons of the past.

Even if my body and mind be shattered in the attempt, perhaps the world may be a little bit better for my having existed here for a brief time.

To always be a gentleman, and to live as though the finest person I can conceive of were watching me every moment of the 24 hours in a day. To seek the best and avoid the worst and do my part in increasing my heritage of the ages.

I shall slip and fall many times, but I shall always get up as long as I have the strength of today and keep pushing on toward my goal until I die.

April 3, **1937** (*diary excerpt*)

Perhaps our age will go down in history as the age of great events and little minds. One consolation is that Hitler and Mussolini, the "little boys of Europe," teasing the Great War God are sure to be destroyed too when his wrath finally breaks forth.

As a twenty-four-year-old, Charles Carpenter certainly had a firm grip on the developments around the world, its building war clouds, and his demands from himself for life and the path it would take him. But Charles was not alone. In 1938, his youngest brother Gene had graduated from Highlands University in Las Vegas, New Mexico, and decided to "reach for the sky" by enlisting in the US Army Air Force. As a child, Gene was a happy-go-lucky kind of kid. At times, according to Charles, he was "a rascal and carefree." But growing up under the shadow of an older brother, emulating his "never give up" persona, helped set the stage for the fledgling aviator and the atrocities he would soon face.

CHAPTER 4

Dance of Destiny

In the summer of 1939, Charles had applied for and was hired as one of the history teachers at Moline Public High School, a four-story maroon-colored brick building located along a lofty sweeping road on Sixteenth Street that overlooked the city of Moline and the wide dark muddy Mississippi River beyond. Situated on the banks of the Mississippi River, Moline was part of the "Tri-Cities" and later Quad Cities that consisted of Moline, Rock Island, and East Moline on the Illinois side of the Mississippi River, with Davenport and Bettendorf on the Iowa side. The first settlers arrived in the early 1800s, and that did not necessarily sit well with the Native Americans that called this land their home for centuries.

When the Black Hawk War of 1832 began, federal militia troops were called in to protect the local inhabitants from Native American attacks. A young twenty-three-year-old volunteer soldier, standing 6 feet, 4 inches tall and "who displayed physical strength and leadership," was promoted to the rank of captain. His name was Abraham Lincoln, who would later become the sixteenth president of the United States of America. A hundred and five years later, neighborhoods, automobiles, large factories, and retail stores stood where horses and men use to roam and battle. Moline and the surrounding cities were bustling with progress and prosperity. One of the well-known factories, especially for its aroma, was the National Licorice Factory. Inside, large brass vats simmered with hot sticky black licorice that when cooled was turned into licorice pipes, "nibs," and twisted strands. The factory itself employed mostly women to create and form the gooey substance. Before the workday was complete, the large vats had to be scraped of the sticky leftovers and cleaned for the next day's batch. It became almost a ritual of sorts when young children would gather outside, under the factory windows, while the workers inside hurled globs of warm licorice down to their waiting hands below.

One of these women was a petite, soft-spoken girl by the name of Elda Fritchel. Like Charles, Elda was also born in the later part of 1912 and grew up in Moline with a father who favored the bottle. John Fritchle was a butcher by trade and very handsome. Elda's mother, Esther, was a second-generation Swedish immigrant. Elda also had a brother named Brightman, who was four years older than her.

As a child, Elda was delighted with her family. She loved her brother, both her mother and father, and especially thought of her father as a good man. But when he drank, his personality changed. Even at an early age, Elda remembered her father coming home at Christmastime drunk and knocking over the Christmas tree. By the time Elda was nine years old, John was no longer part of the family picture, divorcing Esther and leaving the family high and dry. The three of them moved into a house described as no bigger than a garage and defined by Elda as a very simple, impoverished-looking home. With a mother struggling to make ends meet, working odd jobs and odd hours, Brightman took care of raising Elda and was very attentive to the needs of his sister. That Christmas, Elda's only Christmas gift was a pencil box.

Growing up, Elda had a lack of self-esteem, driven by many things in her young life, including a conversation she overheard her mother having with a neighbor: "I wish Elda had never been born." It was a devastating blow to her sense of being loved and confident. She felt that she came into the world as an unwanted child. At her core, Elda was a loving child but overwhelmed with life. As a student she struggled in school, the family doctor diagnosed her as having St. Vitus's dance, which is a nervous condition and anxiety disorder, most of it brought on from the trauma of an alcoholic father and broken family. Never developing a sense of self-esteem, she struggled with it her whole life, eventually dropping out of school in the ninth grade. Elda too joined the workforce, to help her struggling mother and worked in factories, including the National Licorice Factory, where she enjoyed seeing the smiles on children's faces at the end of the day as the hot black tacky goo she dropped from the windows landed in their waiting hands.

As a young woman, Elda looked for role models and escaped into the world of Hollywood starlets. She had aspirations to be like Joan Crawford or Betty Davis, who were part of the "who's who" in Hollywood, actresses who represented a new kind of woman. Elda was enamored with the sophisticated glamor and attention that came with it. As a young woman with very little means and one that grew up poor, those were the trappings of things that she longed for. With her closet practically bare, she had but one single dress. Bearing a lace collar, Elda would change collars to make the dress look different during her weekends out with girlfriends. Many of Elda's friends and colleagues remarked that she resembled Hollywood starlet Maureen O'Hara. By today's standards, Elda would have been described as a knockout.

Elda wore her wavy auburn brown hair just below her neck. She carried her 5-foot-4 figure with grace and was very feminine looking, with an intoxicating smile that showcased perfect teeth. But it was her mesmerizing deep-blue eyes that caught the attention of many that looked her way. One, in particular, was a tall drink of water named Charles Carpenter.

Like most eligible bachelors around the Moline area, Charles Carpenter and several of his Moline High school associates would attend big band swing dances at the local halls. One of the more well-known establishments was the Coliseum Ballroom, just across the river from Moline on the Iowa side in Davenport. Known locally as the "Col," the ballroom had been in business since 1914. By the late 1930s, many of the big bands that were touring the country made their stops along the Mississippi and played at the Col. This included the Kay Kaiser Orchestra and his glee club—Sully Mason, Virginia Sims, Richard Barrio, and Merwyn Bogue—also known as "Ish Kabibble." The cost of entry was .66 cents plus tax for gentlemen, or .40 cents and no tax for the ladies.

Two of the ladies that took advantage of these prices, both single and both hailing from Moline as well, were Elda Fritchle and her girlfriend Ethel Herbst. The rules of engagement were simple, similar to rules that carry on today. The men went with their male friends while the women attended with their girlfriends, and in most cases, both sides would look around for someone attractive to dance with. It was during one of these dances that Elda spotted a fellow in a dark suit that had what she could only describe as a "mesmerizing presence" about him. He was tall, just a hair under 6 feet. His neck was straight, thick, and muscular, which matched the rest of his toned body. He was "as straight as a rail" according to Elda. His hair was dark chocolate brown, and he had stunning grey eyes. The eyes were what caught Elda's attention as they had a twinkle in them which reflected a sense of openness and welcoming. After sizing him up, Elda turned to Ethel and said, "Now, that's my idea of a real man."

In utter amazement to Elda, the striking gentleman walked up to her and introduced himself as "Charles" and invited her to dance. Both would admit later that they were immediately attracted to one another. But in the midst of big band music, the blue haze of cigarette smoke, and dozens of other twirling bodies, the pair continued to lock onto one another's eyes for the next several dances. During their brief conversation, Elda listened more than she spoke as Charles talked about world politics, the brewing tensions in Europe and Asia, teaching history, and the latest book he read. By the time the last note was played and the dance was coming to a close at 1:00 a.m., Charles mustered up his courage and asked his dance partner if she would like to go out on a date next weekend.

As the words coming out of Charles's mouth sank in, Elda reverted to her lack of confidence and unsteady self-esteem and blurted out, "I have a commitment with my girlfriend next weekend."

Charles smiled, thanked her for the dance, and turned and walked away. His initial thoughts swirling in his head were, "Well she's not interested in me." And headed home with his friends in tow.

Elda was beside herself. All Ethel could do was shake her head in disbelief at her girlfriend. There were no points of contact exchanged, so even if she dug deep within herself and tried to find this mystery man with the first name of Charles, she knew it would be futile at best.

Elda held the memory of those dances with Charles in her heart for over a year. She continued to work in a factory, and in her mind, she considered herself an "old maid" at the age of twenty-eight years old. She convinced herself and confessed to her dog, "Ming Toy," a licorice black colored Pekinese, she would probably grow old alone. Elda continued to attend local dance halls, secretly hoping her "Prince Charming" would show up and whisk her away like a damsel in a fairy tale. But after a year, she convinced herself it was no more than a dream, and there would be no happy ending. That was until she received a tap on her shoulder.

Turning around, her crystal blue eyes grew wide. "Would you like to dance?" asked Charles.

Elda, older and wiser, was not about to make the same mistake as she held a death grip on that second chance that stood before her. She giggled and said, "I don't know if you remember me, but we danced together over a year ago." Charles smiled, drawn to her stunning beauty, and held out his hand as the two of them danced once again.

The courtship of Charles and Elda did not last long. By the time they had gone on their second date, Elda found new energy and a renewed self-confidence and said to Charles, "We have got to get married because neither of us can eat!" The two of them were lovestruck. Charles also had a pet name for her and began calling her "Bunny." On April 12, 1940, Charles proposed to Elda. As their love for one another intensified, they became husband and wife on July 5 of that same year.

Rev. Axel Pearson officiated the small ceremony at the parsonage of Bethel Methodist Church in Moline. Elda wore a pink satin wedding dress with an open back, a Christmas gift that had been given to her by her brother Brightman and his wife. Elda's dance cohort and best friend Ethel Herbst was the lone attendant, while a handful of invited guests including Charles's mother, Lois, witnessed the ceremony.

With tin cans adorning their '32 Ford, Mr. and Mrs. Charles Carpenter made a mad dash to get inside their old jalopy while several of Charles's friends showered them with rice. From there the newlyweds traveled to Chicago. Elda jotted a quick note in her memories section of her wedding book that stated:

Spent the weekend in Chicago and come home Sunday night. Our honeymoon is my most pleasant memory. We spent one afternoon along the lake. We also had a wonderful dinner at Eitel's Old Heidelberg Rathskeller restaurant.

Located at 14 W. Randolph near State St., in the heart of the Chicago Loop, patrons were seated at four-person, round dark wood tables with matching chairs, under golden-colored lighted chandeliers. Servers wore traditional German garb of blue satin knee-high pants, billowing white shirts with a shimmering red vest. The menu consisted of both traditional and old-world German fare. From frog legs to whitefish, steaks, chops, and chicken to Weiner schnitzel, the Carpenters were living large.

But it was back at home that Elda felt more than secure in the arms of Charles. He was a bright light for her, a man of integrity, light-hearted, uncomplicated, and a visionary. He was by all accounts her "knight in shining armor." Charles considered himself the "luckiest guy around" to have a beautiful woman like Elda as his bride. Elda's new life was like a dream come true for her. She was no longer the "poor family on the block" and instead occupied one half of a house, adorned with a front porch and respectable backyard. She had her own kitchen to make her husband meals. Her specialties were roast beef and fried chicken, as she followed her guidebook to overseeing a household. *The Settlement Cookbook* was not onlyh er go-to periodical for recipes and serving suggestions; it also provided a new bride with tips on cleanliness and logistics. Life was good for Elda, and family and friends remarked that she was absolutely "glowing" as a new bride. But what she probably didn't realize was that with a war raging in Europe and Asia, the United States could not remain neutral forever. Her last entry in her wedding book was a short note of happiness:

> We are at home at 724 ½-21 St. A. We have a three-room apartment. Very pleasant. We also have Ming Toy, with me. At this present minute, Charles is sitting in our only big chair, studying for his night class, at high school. He is a ground school (flight) instructor.

Elda or Charles had no idea how the carnages of a half a world away, with dark war clouds growing larger, foreshadowed a heavier human toll that was to come, and change their lives seventeen months later.

CHAPTER 5

Brothers in Arms

In 1940, Charles had already received specialized training in aviation ground school and was recommended to the Civil Aeronautics Authority (CAA) for this task of helping to enable young men between the ages of eighteen and twenty-six to take ground school training. He was doing his part in helping a nation learn how to fly. Besides being a ground instructor, Charles was also a fledgling pilot himself. He had applied for and after paying an initiation fee, was accepted as a member of the Rockets Inc. Flying Club of Moline, Illinois. In 1939, the club merged with other local flying clubs, the Rock River Flying Club and the Zephyr Flying Club, to make ownership and operations of airplanes less costly for both pilots and those learning how to fly.

Before he married Elda, Charles began his early flight training in a 1939 Taylorcraft, which claimed to be "America's Finest, Low-Cost Airplanes with enhanced, Safety, Comfort, Performance and Economy."

The airplane was easy to fly, with side-by-side seating in an over 39-inch-wide cabin. Instead of control sticks, the pilot and passenger flew with "automobile-like comfort" utilizing a large, rubberized spoked control wheel to aviate across the sky. Charles was hooked on flying, and it provided some bragging rights as well with his younger brother Gene on "who was the better stick in the air."

By September 9, 1940, Gene had completed primary, basic, and advanced, and had earned his silver wings. He later was assigned with the 20th Pursuit Group and eventually stationed in the Philippines during October 1940. Charles was extremely proud of Gene and had a tad bit of envy for the young flier.

Clark Field, P. I.
February 4, 1941 (*letter excerpt*)

Dear Charles and Elda,

When it comes to the point a fellow has to fiddle around for ten minutes before he get started on a letter to his own brother and sister-in-law, it seems to me that things have reached a pretty sad state. Well that's the way it was; but now that the ice is broken I believe I'll be able to carry on OK.

Perhaps the first thing in order would be a few "better late than never" congratulations and wishes for happiness. I am proud to tell you that it is an honor and pleasure to have you for a sister-in-law. (That will cost you both a quarter by return mail.)

Now just what is there about me and the Philippines that you want to know? There's not much to tell about either but it would be some sort of breach to step so soon. In general my day consists of aerial photography, aerial gunnery, ground gunnery, operation missions with the field, and coast artilleries. "Official trips" to Manila and the frequent "buzzes" on fishing boats. Incidentally, Chas, what's the straight dope on you "shinning your wings" over Reynolds?

Flying is still new enough to me that I am still walking on air, both figuratively and literarily, every time I go up. With my 330 some odd hours of flying time, I know just enough about it to know I've got a lot more to learn. The army has two control towers—one here and one at Nichols Field at Manila—and the navy has one for their flying boats and the Clippers.

Now I'm wondering if this proves that I can really write a letter once I get Satan behind me. If you think I'm not especially eager to hear from you, and it took only a Christmas card to arouse this eagerness, just try me and see.

Love, Gene

Charles was not the only one proud of his brother. Delighted with her son Gene's aerial achievements, Lois Carpenter proudly hung a Blue Star Service Flag in the window of her home, prominently displaying to her neighbors and the entire city of Reynolds that she had a son in the military service. But Gene's early flying career was not without danger, especially with some of the older equipment he was operating. His letter home was more than sugarcoated compared to the real dangers he faced, including flying over inhospitable terrain, fast-moving storms, and watching out for lurking head hunter tribes that lived in the dense jungles nearby:

Things are going on just as usual with nothing more exciting happening than an airplane nosing over now and then. I flew a plane this morning that was eleven years old, and in this day of modernism that is quite old for a car, let alone an airplane.

The fighter and bombers along with the observation aircraft that were based on the Philippines Islands in late 1941 consisted of a hodgepodge of old and new. Four-engine Boeing B-17 Flying Fortress made up the lion's share of heavy bombers, which were augmented with an assortment of older twin-engine Douglas B-18As and Martin B-10s. On the fighter side, the most modern were Curtiss P-40s and Seversky P-35s and several North American A-27s (the attack variant of the AT-6 Texan). The Observation squadrons scattered around the islands enlisted the Curtiss O-52 Owls, some long in the tooth Douglas O-46s and even some post–World War I single-bay biplane Thomas-Morse O-19s as the primary scouting force.

Clark Field, **Pampanga**, **Philippine Islands.**
December 2, **1941** (*letter excerpt*)

Dear Mother,
Leaving Honolulu, we spent an uneventful eight days getting to Shanghai. It could have been quite eventful, however, if we'd happened to connect with a mine in some of the Japanese waters we went thru.

Shanghai is a sight to behold. You never dreamed of so much poverty and strife, and I guess it is nothing to what it was several years back when the Japs were getting control of it. As far as buildings are concerned, it is fairly well rebuilt from the bombing and shell fire that it got when the war began but the people are hopelessly beaten down. And if it weren't for the American Marines stationed there, were be worse off still. We spent three days there and after another two day voyage we docked in Manila.

A working day over here consists of four and one half hours, from 7:00 a.m. to 11:30. For us of the air corps, the biggest part of that time is spent flying. We and Nichols Field fly half of the coast line every morning, to spot any Japanese activity that might be going on. By half the coast line, I mean the coast of the island of Luzon, which is THE island of the Philippines.

I'm stationed at Clark Field, county of Pampanga, island of Luzon, one of the 1,700 odd islands of the Philippines. Clark is about 60 miles north of Manila. How I came here I'll relate briefly. Before we even got off the ship at Manila, we were informed that five of us would have to go to Clark to help it along in the expansion program. I drew one of the slips out of the hat marked "X."

I am unlucky only from the fact that I am no longer in pursuit squadron. Clark has nothing but observation and bombardment, and I don't have enough hours to a fly a bomber so now I'm an observation pilot. As soon as things get squared around, I'm sure I can get back into pursuit. I'm going to like observation, but it's not nearly so thrilling and fascinating as pursuit.

As far as the war situation is concerned there is no more to worry about over here than where you are. As long as the Philippines are under US protection, they're being armed right in step with the US, and the more arms that come into being, the less likely the chance of anyone wanting to rub Uncle Sam's hair the wrong way. Give the season's greetings to everyone on my behalf.

Lt. E. H. Carpenter
2nd Ob. Squad
Clark Field, Pampanga
Philippines Islands.

Not only did Uncle Sam's hair get rubbed; his nose was bloodied and his eyes blackened. While Japanese bombers and torpedo planes struck the Islands of Hawaii and its naval and air bases in and around Pearl Harbor on December 7, 1941, they mimicked their success by attacking US airbases at Mindanao and Luzon in the Philippine Islands on December 8 (December 7 in Hawaii). A day later, Japanese soldiers assaulted Luzon as wave after wave of invaders came ashore while American and Filipino soldiers fought valiantly to suppress the attacks. Charles and Elda, like millions across the nation, sat glued to their Philcos or Zenith radios waiting for any word or hope from the radio announcers who would cut in with updates and presidential speeches. The nation listened in horror as President Roosevelt stated,

"This morning the forces of Imperial Japan attacked Americans at Pearl Harbor, Hawaii." Those lines sent a shock wave through the Carpenter household.

Things only got worse from there for the Allies and General Douglas MacArthur, Supreme Allied commander of the United States Army Forces in the Far East (USAFFE). With most of their airpower destroyed by earlier Japanese surprise bombing attacks, including the observation airplanes that Gene would have used to spot the growing enemy fleet that was just offshore, there was not much that could halt the onslaught. On December 22, more than 100,000 Japanese troops landed in force at Lingayen, Luzon, as more than 15,000 Americans and 65,000 Filipinos stood their ground on Bataan, hoping against hope that the ships and transport aircraft promised by President Roosevelt would arrive to deliver them from hell. That hopeful day would never arrive.

By January 2, 1942, the Japanese conquerors were occupying Manila and Cavite naval base, and for the next four days, Corregidor was in the Japanese crosshairs as the defenders endured what seemed like an endless round of bombing attacks by Japanese bombers who flew relatively unmolested from the lack of American airpower. With rations running low and becoming nonexistent, the famished and diseased soldiers on the ground resorted to eating snakes, monkeys, dogs, and iguanas. Gene's latest letter home showed a stiff upper lip and the grit of a true Carpenter. Charles and Elda held out hope for Gene, wondering if any of the letters and cards they sent him had made it through. As the declaration of war sunk in, they knew their lives would never be the same again. But there was something else going on in their lives that brought bittersweet joy; by the time they sent their Christmas card to Gene, Elda was pregnant with their first child.

In the Field
Bataan, P.IP.
February 19, 1942

Dear Mother,
Won't be able to say much about what I've done, what I'm doing or what I will do, but if you get this you will at least know that as of this date I'm still hitting on all sixteen cylinders. Have had my hair stood on end a couple or three times, but if Providence doesn't decide to change sides at this stage of the game I'll be home by November—maybe this year, surely next.

If the Finance Co. gets excited about the remaining four or five payments still due on the car, tell them as soon as we set the Rising Sun they will be taken care of.

Seeing as how I haven't been living on peaches and cream, fried chicken, etc., I'm putting in my order for some of the same when I hit the old homestead.

Am enjoying exceptionally good health, my morale is high; in fact the only things I lack are the few small conveniences a soldier must give up in times like these.

I trust that you are not spending sleepless nights and the like—there is absolutely no need for it. If I was better off I would think I was on maneuvers instead of playing for keeps.

I didn't receive my Christmas present and I'm still gunning for the Nip that did. It may be waiting for me when it's all over, but I have my doubts.

For you to try and write me would be almost useless at present, but I'll give you the high sign when the way is clear. I've even attached a prayer to this asking the Great One to not let it get short-stopped.

Keep your fingers crossed and your mind at ease and it will be all over before you know it, and again let me handle the worrying.

Best of health to you and all,
Love Gene

Attached Prayer

The War This Far

'Twas on December eight, just back in forty-one; Japan set out to concur, the battle had begun.

She hit at Pearl Harbor, she dealt a thunderous blow; Alas, Alack, Oh God! From there where would she go?

She aimed across the ocean, stopped off at Guam and Wake; Tojo says, "Now I've got." Unc' Sam says, "No, we take."

Then onward to the West, to these familiar scenes; O Lord! She couldn't do it, but she hit the Philippines

She smacked the mountain province, she raged in Mindanao. She struck at Clark and Nichols she bombed them, boy and how!

Then onward south she swept on wings so high. But there she hit a wall, to wit, Old N.E.I.

She's found things not so easy, getting tougher every day; her doom is swiftly coming, it isn't far away.

But lets not rush the story, we've done that, so it seems; cause she will never win "till she takes the Philippines.

She started at Lingayen, worked downward towards the bay. We didn't let her whip us, but slowly we gave 'way.

USAFFE in Miami, our forces being spent; nothing but to leave, Pearl of the Orient.

The brass-hats got together and decided to a man, to move the whole USAFFE to peninsular Bataan.

It isn't wide in width; it isn't long in length; but take it easy, Tojo, she's jammed with fighting strength.

We landed here on Christmas; have been here since that day; still sweating out a convoy so we can get away.

At first things were quite easy, I'm speaking of the chow but all good things must cease, and man look at us now!

We're growing thin from hunger, slowly wasting away; but is it any wonder, living on two a day.

But that is not the worst! It might be cut to one. If such should be the case you win, Tojo; I'm done.

In the morn it's rice and fish. Filling, but now too nice. In the eve, great God almighty they've changed to fish and rice!

When this war is over, Oh, these wrinkles on my brow; I'll tell my ma I got them from sweating on the chow.

Some days I just don't feel well, my guts I fear I'll lose; Lord, spare me from my plight. I've got those mess kit blues.

They come in many forms, but most common seem to be Amoebic dysentery and plain old diarrhea.

Water from a canteen, bathing in a creek; from these come all the ills that make the strong so weak.

Now we come to foxholes; many of them I've dug; a helluva lot of work, but they'll save you from a slug.

"Dig in, sorry soldiers, but dig it small and deep. Save yourself from Tojo so folks back home wont weep."

To a steady shooting eye Tojo cannot lay claim. He keeps us in our foxholes 'cause we cannot trust his aim.

Run for the foxhole, soldiers. Here comes a one-five-five. Keep you head down low or you won't come out alive.

Foxhole, patrols, and guard, may I never see any more. Come back from a long patrol then ouch, "off two, on four!"

And curses on the sniper that sneaking, sniping brat. One lowered to the type of war is nothing but a rat.

He'll clip you from a treetop. He'll snip you from behind. Whoever thought of sniping had not fair play in mind.

But now we've got his number, he's getting it the worst. Before he gets a bead, we up and clip him first.

The "skeeters" are big on Bataan, the biggest I've ever seen; last night I saw one the size of a B-19.

As I said before, they're really big, you never see more than four; 'cause Bataan is just to small to allow anymore.

There are flies, too, by the millions, God, it just ain't right flies biting in the daytime and "skeets" drilling in the night.

There was one big mistake. We made than, it's true. But the Air Corps on the front line that strictly is "Snafu."

Oh, God, please get us off; lets to the air again. We'd give our seats in Hell just to get up in a plane.

We don't mind being dodoes, we mind it not the least; but in airplanes we'd show just who's who in the east.

I have just one more gripe, and not without a reason. Right now I'm spending time sweating out the rainy season.

I've said nothing of the heat. It's hot, that's understood. But to have it hot and rainy, God, but that's not good!

And when the fighting's over and the victory is ours, freedom; it will still prevail in the land of stripes and stars.

The brains are on the "Rock" the soldiers in the field. MacArthur's Miracle Men are not about to yield.

One last request I have, 'though I'm not afraid to die; Pray God that death don't find me still on Bataan P.I.

E. H. Carpenter
1st Lt., A.C. (Air Corps)

By February 22, General MacArthur was given specific orders to leave the battle-ravaged Luzon area and make his way to Australia. He reluctantly left a month later, leaving behind thousands of brave men, with whom he had fought side by side, making their last stand. Although he vowed he would return, it would be two long bloody years before he waded ashore and set foot on the Philippines once again.

Gene's words and poem were like a 2-ton weight wrapped around the hearts of the Carpenter family. That was the last correspondence they would ever receive from him. On March 24, 1942, Lois Carpenter added another Blue Star to her service flag as US Army reserve officer, 2Lt. Charles M. Carpenter answered his nation's call and headed off to war to join his brother Gene in the battle for freedom.

CHAPTER 6

Roughing It in Miami

With orders to report for duty, Charles packed his bags, loaded up his car, and headed to Rantoul, Illinois, 190 miles away. Charles was a second lieutenant in the US Army assigned to the infantry. As a teacher, he thought he could assist the war effort by retaining that title and help prepare a nation for war. But as a military man, one that was considerably older at twenty-nine years old, and wiser than many of the boys that were called up, Charles knew there were never any guarantees in the military. The only thing he had to concern himself with was to follow orders, however, fouled up they might be.

Indianapolis YMCA
Sunday (March 29, 1942) morning, 6:30 a.m.

Dearest Elda, (*letter excerpt*)
Grab hold of your chair and hang on because some changes have been made. I came clipping into Rantoul (Illinois) about 1:00 p.m. yesterday. I finally got to the adjunct, and he sent me off to the hospital for another checkup.

I came back for the hospital with a slip from a doctor there saying I was still all right physically. The adjunct took the slip, looked at it, and said, "Well, your temporary duty is ended here; you can get going."

Of course, I was set back a bit but I recovered enough to ask what I should do with my car. He said I could go get a railroad ticket good only from Rantoul, or I could drive to Miami Beach and collect eight cents a mile on my arrival there. I had to decide quickly, so I decided to start driving; and here I am. I have about $85. If anything goes wrong, I will get rid of the car for what I can and grab the nearest train. However, by driving carefully, I expect to make it without trouble. I haven't had a chance to look at a US map yet, but I believe the distance is over a thousand miles. Therefore I should be able to collect over $80 on arrival to help me get started off there. I figure roughly that it will cost no more than $30 to make the trip with average good fortune. One fellow told me that even old cars were worth considerably more in Florida than here.

According to government rules I must proceed by the most practicable route at a rate of not less than 250 miles per day. I expect to drive between 400 and 500 miles a day.

From rumors I picked up in my several hours at Chanute Field, I am going to a school which trains officers for the administrative work of the air corps. So I may not be a teacher after all. I feel that things are turning out for the best, and I hope you feel that way too. Getting such an early start in Florida may enable me to get a furlough home before the baby is born.

As a high school teacher, Charles was not a wealthy man. Newly married, he was now feeding two mouths with another one on the way. In fact, in one of the letters he wrote to his students back home in Moline describing his route and what he observed while traveling from Illinois to Florida, he pointed out what true wealth was:

I only wish you could know how my heart warmed with the interest and concern shown by some of you on my last day at school. No man, I believe, ever engaged in school teaching who expected to gain financial success that way; but the real rewards are great for those who can linger close to the throbbing, adventurous world of youth; and such was my privilege in my five years of high school teaching.

Setting out in his well-worn '32 Ford was an adventure in and of itself. With a world war raging, rationing across the nation was self-evident. Rubber, metal, sugar, gas, aluminum, and animal fat, among many other daily necessities now deemed luxuries, were needed to help ensure victory. Because of that, Charles crossed his fingers and set out, hoping he could make it with a bald set of tires. His route took him through Indiana and a late spring snowstorm before he stopped for the night.

Passing through Kentucky, familiar territory from his Centre College days, took him right by Fort Knox. Charles had waited tables there in the officer's mess one summer while he attended summer camp and drills:

Driving by I saw the building where a good part of the worlds gold lies closely guarded. Fort Knox has grown the mechanized part of the army. There they have thousands of acres of wooded hills and ravines where our growing mechanized army maneuvers its armored sham battles, getting ready for the real thing that lies not far ahead.

Traveling farther south, he encountered twisting and winding black top roads that were sometimes so tortuous he almost met himself coming around the corners. Charles described the south as contrasting land of sentimental beauty and shabbiness. He passed shacks and people that he thought only existed in comic books. Pulling into Albany, Georgia, for the night, Charles checked into the Hotel Lee and wrote Elda a letter the following day about his experience in seeing an old friend and coworker, Sam Drake, from Moline High School, who was already experiencing army life and preparing for war:

Tuesday morning
March 31, 1942

Dearest Elda,
Good morning! It's your "old man" speaking to you again, from deep in the heart of Georgia this time. Yesterday was a day that I will live long in my memory. I left Murfreesboro early and drove over some corkscrew road to Alabama. I passed Guntersville Lake, the biggest lake in Alabama, and finally came to Fort McClellan. I had a wonderful visit there with Sam (Drake). He was just returning from drill when I arrived about four o'clock. He was strutting into camp at the lead of about two hundred men, and marched right by me without looking to the left or to the right.

He almost fell out of his uniform when I shouted to him a little later. He sure looks swell, all brown and tough looking. I know his men like him by the way they look at him and talk to him.

We had quite a nice visit for the next several hours. I asked him a lot of questions about army life and learned a lot. He is very busy but is just the man for his job. He is getting a company of men, mostly boys I would say, ready for active service against the enemy. I saw his little cubby-hole tent where he sleeps. It had just room for bunks and stove and clothes and Sam. I left after supper and drove until I had to stop because I had no more gas and all the stations were closed.

Outside this morning it is bright and cool. Army planes are roaring overhead continually from nearby airfields. That's the only reminder of the great war in an otherwise peaceful and beautiful world.

There were many scenes I never want to forget. Haze-topped mountains and small valleys; the darkie and his mule patiently preparing the red, thin soil for another profitless crop, neither hurrying, nor worrying, nor even wondering the reason for it at all; the tired mansion with the tourist sign out, the silvered music of the southern landscape by moonlight, the moss-veiled trees on the Florida swampland—all these and many more.

Even though I hate war for the evil and the misery that it breeds, it is not without some compensations. To some soldiers, going to war, life takes on a new deepness and beauty, a new poignancy that was not there before. So it has been with me. It is not so much the thought of death as the feeling "I may not pass this way again; therefore I must experience everything, see all."

During one of his driving legs, Charles picked up a hitchhiker, a young sailor on his way home to see his folks in Tampa. He shared with Charles his near-death experience. While on his ship, with the shore of Iceland insight, he watched in horror as the slick streak of a German U-boat torpedo found its mark. Most of the men were rescued, but not all. His parents had no idea if he had survived. Charles was delighted to help reunite them as the realities of war sunk in.

Pulling into his final destination of Miami, Charles was awestruck and felt as though he was in some exotic land, not one at war, surrounded by luxurious shopping districts, five-star hotels and restaurants, and warm, sandy beaches with inviting ocean waves.

Greenview Hotel
April 1, 1942 (*letter excerpt*)

Dearest Elda,

Will wonders never cease for Charlie Carpenter? First of all, I'm well and feeling swell, any moment though I expect to wake up out of a dream. All this place needs to make it paradise is "Bunnie" Mae Carpenter. Gee! But I love you and the world tonight! I can't even hate the Germans and the Japs. Even the holy cannot say that the Devil's life is without enjoyment.

I'm paying a dollar a day for a beautiful room in this hotel. It seems at present I'm going to be an instructor of some sort in Officers School here and I'm starting out a regular second lieutenant in the army.

My car is broken down, but I can still drive it if I do so carefully. The front spring is broken and the car leans to one side all the time. I have nothing but warmth in my heart for the old bus, though. She certainly bought me through in fine style. One of my tires wore down until the fabric showed through. I paid $24 for the three used tires on the way down and felt mighty glad to get them. Only parking lights are allowed on here at night to drive by and no honking of horns allowed.

In spite of all the excitement and wonders, I really miss you dear. All windows toward the ocean must have curtains drawn at night and all neon signs shut off. It's called a "screen out." The purpose is to prevent the glow of the sky above the city from showing up ships at sea to make it easier to torpedo them by the enemy.

April 5, 1942 (*letter excerpt*)
Officer Candidate School, Miami Beach

Dearest Elda,

Personnel work, in case you are puzzled, consists of interviewing, examination, and classification of men so as to get the round pegs in the round holes and the square pegs in the square holes. Beginning tomorrow, our job for the next two weeks is to interview and classify the five hundred upperclassmen of this school who will graduate as commissioned officers in the next six weeks. There are many highly specialized jobs in a modern army, and the personal department has the highly important job of getting the right men into the right jobs.

When I came down I was hoping I wouldn't get a desk job, but I have changed my mind somewhat. Other fellows tell me the personnel department is one of the finest places to be in the whole army set up. The work is pleasant, and there is more freedom and opportunity for individuality.

Just got back from my first swim in the ocean. The air and water are nearly always the same temperature. The waves come rolling in and knock you down, but you just laugh and get up in time to get knocked down by the next one.

The view at the beach is as beautiful as one could ever hope to see. There are waving palm trees not far back from the water. The water is deep green out to where it gets deep. Then it is bluer than the sky. The whole atmosphere is a cosmopolitan one. Beauty and brilliance, rather than sincerity and warmth, are the most redeeming features, however.

From what I read in tonight's headlines, it looks bad for Gene if he is still alive in the Philippines. Somehow or other, I'm beginning to feel a little warlike myself. It bothers me when I feel that I am not doing a good job at something that I feel is so important.

The frustrations Charles and most of the rest of the nation felt also resonated with its military superiors and commander in chief. By the time Charles's latest letter had reached Elda, the USS *Hornet*, on its maiden voyage and mission, had made its way from the naval yard near San Francisco with sixteen brand-new Army Air Force twin engine B-25 Mitchell bombers lashed to its deck—destination top secret. But across the Pacific, especially in the Philippines, the battered American stronghold on Bataan had given up its last breath and fought its final battle. On April 9, Bataan surrendered. Three weeks later, after enduring two dozen Japanese bombing raids in a forty-eight-hour span, the last remaining American soldiers on Corregidor raised blood-soaked white flags and surrendered.

The remaining survivors, many of whom would have rather welcomed death like an old friend, including Gene Carpenter, instead began a long and torturous journey known as the Bataan Death March.

April 18, 1942 (*letter excerpt*)

Dearest Bunny,

Right at present, I have nothing officially to do. With a war going on, and a brother who is probably dead or a prisoner, I feel restless and useless. I probably could go down to the beach or play tennis, but then my conscience would bother me still more.

Personally I do not care much to spend my part of the war here. It is an interesting place and I live in the lap of luxury almost, but I would prefer training troops, or in the field with troops. At present, I realize that I am not prepared for such duty as that. I hope that if I stay here for a few months, I will be able to pick up enough army background and knowledge to perhaps ask for a transfer.

I am not unhappy at all here, but it is not my idea of wartime army life. Really, Bunny, I want to get the war over with and get home.

On April 18, half a world away from the relative haven of Miami Beach, sixteen B-25 Mitchell bombers collectively started their Wright R-2600 Twin Cyclone radial engines. With USS *Hornet*'s nose pointed into the raw Pacific wind, with its engine room given orders of "full speed," the *Hornet* plowed through immense waves as the first B-25 held its brakes, revved its engines, and began a tail low takeoff roll.

The olive drab bombers had been stripped of all excessive weight that wasn't necessary, including most of its machine guns—those in the tail were replaced with wooden broom handles painted black. The lead bomber was piloted by a former daredevil, former record-setting race pilot named Jimmy Doolittle. Now a newly minted colonel, Doolittle held his control column aft as he nursed his bomber skyward and led the other B-25s off the deck of *Hornet*, setting a low-level course 620 miles away to one of its main targets—Tokyo, Japan. The battered "Sleeping Giant" was about to strike back.

Closer to home, less than 5 miles off the shores of Miami Beach, the certainties of war were now a reality for Charles. Under the same waves that Charles use to frolic in lurked German U-boats that stalked heavy laden freighters containing much-needed war supplies and the escorting warships that protected them. Between February and May 1942, the stealthy U-boats sank more than twenty-four ships off the Florida coast.

April 28, **1942** (*letter excerpt*)

Dearest Elda,

For once in my life I don't seem to be able to keep up on the news of the day. Last night an American destroyer was sunk not far from here off the Florida Coast. One Lieutenant told me this evening that he saw American ships dropping depth bombs right within sight of shore here. Big planes roar overhead hourly all day and all night long. They are patrolling the coast and sea lanes just off shore on the lookout for enemy submarines. War is closer here than I can realize, perhaps. In regards to my statement in the letter to my High School about returning to the Infantry, I can only say that no one here knows anything definite yet.

I told Ed Erikson to sell my share in Rockets Inc. and give the money to you instead of spending it here. There is a flying club here already among the young officers. I have no intentions of joining unless I see first the time and opportunity to get my private license. I still believe that aviation will be the boom industry in the postwar era.

Charles's comments were spot on. In fact, right before the war broke out the United States had roughly 2,500 airplanes in military service. By the time the war ended in late 1945, more than 300,000 aircraft had been produced to defend our nation's freedoms. As a nation, the ramp-up for war production was evident in all corners of the country as an aerial armada was hastily built up. From trainers to gliders to fighters and bombers, multiple factories including Ford and General Motors halted car production and began producing aircraft. Even after the final shots of the war were fired, aircraft manufacturers believed that returning American servicemen would reach for the sky and learn how to fly. Civilian manufacturers like Piper, Aeronca, Cessna, and Beech, along with others, built thousands of both two and four-place aircraft to meet the anticipated needs. Unfortunately, that marketing dream burst before it left the ground. One reason was the fact that there was a glut of ex-military airplanes that could be bought for a song, and secondly, most of the returning soldiers focused on families and careers and those that flew during the war wanted nothing to do with the horrors many had witnessed while at the controls of an airplane over hostile enemy territory.

May 31, **1942** (*letter excerpt*)

Dearest Bunny,
The more I see life and people here, the more I love my life with you. You can rest assured of that. Today I am about as "blue" as I ever get. That is a very light shade of pale blue. Gradually our teaching is getting cut and dried and tied up with red tape here. You know, of course, how I fret and chafe at restriction. This leadership course of mine is still left largely to me. I draw more compliments from it than anything else I do here. In fact, I now go around teaching it to officers all over the place. There is no overtime in the army. Do a good job for eight hours a day and you get complimented and a chance to do the same thing sixteen hours a day.

Charles would continue to "give it his all" throughout his military career. Others as well were working overtime to produce weapons that would not only destroy an enemy but also help shorten the war. On June 14, 1942, inside one of the sprawling buildings of the General Electric Company (GE), located in Bridgeport, Connecticut, directly across the sound from Long Island, New York, and 1,337 miles away from Miami, the assembled GE engineers and the newly formed US Army's rocket research officers put the final touches on their latest development. Christened with the name "Launcher, Rocket AT, M-1," it simply became known as the bazooka. Consisting of a 50-inch steel tube with an opening at either end, the shoulder-fired weapon employed rudimentary instructions. The basic principle was to insert a 2-foot rocket in one end that was ignited by an electric charge when the operator squeezed a trigger. According to early reports, the rocket had a range of 300 yards and was capable of disabling a tank. But it would be another two years before Charles Carpenter would utilize its destructiveness.

June 18, **1942** (*letter excerpt*)

Dearest Bunny
Yesterday an envelope came from Margaret with a clipping in it. The clipping was about Bataan. Near the end it had a verse of poetry written by Lt. Eugene Carpenter, who was now missing according to the article:

"O, God please get us off;
Let's to the air again
We'd give our seats in hell
Just to get up in a plane."

June 25, **1942** (*letter excerpt*)

Dearest Bunny,

I don't feel that I am doing anywhere near my best work. Such must be the case with many other Americans, however, or we would be making more progress toward victory than seems to be the case at present.

There is some possibility that I may get transferred. I have asked for a transfer, and the major said he would consider it. I took a physical exam for glider pilot training. Now there is much uncertainty as to whether I shall stay here or leave, and when I shall leave if I do. I believe that any move represents a greater opportunity. I want you to look at it that way too. We are told that promotions in the glider command will be more rapid, and of course, we will be on flying pay which is half again as much as I get now.

Many other Americans like Charles felt they needed to do more for victory. War was on the minds of everyone, so much so that even though Charles's much adorned '32 Ford had been stolen or taken for a "joyride," he didn't give it much passing thought and knew he could make do with his own two feet for a while. Charles was not alone with his frustrations; he had always felt compelled to give it his best as well as many others. In the early summer of 1942, a new officer candidate presented himself for classification in Miami Beach at the Air Force Officer Candidate School. He was a handsome devil, with a well-worn California tan, and his trademark mustache was hastily removed. Upon his arrival, he announced, "I just want to carry my share." At forty years old, Clark Gable was treated like all others, including his salary of $66.00 per month. Gable eventually flew as a gunner on a handful of combat missions in B-17 Flying Fortresses with the Eighth Air Force in England, a country and its people that Charles Carpenter would become very familiar in due time.

June 28, **1942** (*letter excerpt*)

Dearest Bunny,

Today I have thought a lot about you and life back in Moline. War has certainly begun to have its effects upon us too now. My conscience hurts me more than a little. I have done quite well here in general, but not half so well as I could if I had done my best.

My personal finances are not in very good shape either. Part of it comes from being, perhaps, too much of a "good fellow." As always, I buy things and incur obligations that are often difficult to pay for. I have not, since arriving, succeeded in paying off my original debt here.

I am still confident that I can get even with the world soon. Especially if I get away from here where dollars go like half-dollars anywhere else.

My life is not at all hard here. I have just been careless and lived too much for the present instead of the future. War seems to make the future all so uncertain. You have been very brave and sweet. I'll be so glad when the baby is born. I'll have another stake in life and you'll have something else to love and live for. We will always have so much to be happy for.

I'll come out of this war yet, though, a real man and a real soldier. I promised myself that.

One of my greatest faults is a certain easygoing adaptability that lets me drop into almost any routine of life without much struggle. Life is oft and easy here. Any discipline and hardship almost have to be devised and imposed on oneself by oneself. That is why I welcome any transfer to the harder life. I do my best under pressure, and the pressure is not much here.

But back at home in Moline, Elda was receiving the inside details from her mother-in-law, Lois, about more of the true heartfelt feelings of Charles. As a new wife and expecting mother, she wanted her husband to be safe and secure. But she also knew the patriotic motivation her husband had, along with his voracious appetite to always strive to do his best. Charles Carpenter was about to embark on what probably would become the greatest adventure in his lifetime:

(Excerpt from a letter written by Lois Carpenter, June 1942)

Dear Elda,

Your letter came this morning. Chas had written some time ago and said he had asked for a transfer to join the gliders, but not to tell you as he didn't want you worried. I was a little upset with him and didn't hesitate to tell him so. I didn't see why he couldn't be satisfied with what he was doing, on the ground and his neck reasonably safe. But of course I didn't know it—till it was too late—but I had the satisfaction of telling him what I thought about it.

I also heard about the car, but just last week. So he got a second bawling out about being so careless or forgetful or whichever it was as to leave his keys in it so someone could go off with it. But that is him and he doesn't worry, so I don't know why I should.

Lois

July 12, 1942 *(letter excerpt)*

Dearest Bunny,

Just a flash of the latest news of the day. This morning I was notified to head for Randolph Field, Texas, from where I would be sent to some glider school. I am leaving tonight or early in the morning for San Antonio, Texas, with a Lieutenant Weaver. He is one of my fellow officers here and is quite wealthy. I and another officer will accompany him in his Cadillac.

You still have the biggest job, Bunny dear. You have not much energy to waste in worrying about me. I'm still, as always, the luckiest devil I know of, especially lucky in love.

CHAPTER 7

Reach for the Sky

In 1929, one former Luftwaffe pilot, Gunter Voltz,[1] who in September 1941 began flying reconnaissance missions over the Russian front in a Fiesler Storch, stated, "Even though World War I had ended eleven years earlier for Germany, and we only had gliders to fly, we did have a 'secret weapon' at our disposal that the Allies had overlooked. The stick and fabric powerless sailplanes we flew seemed harmless to the Allied observers, but the former World War I combat veteran pilots who were our mentors taught us the basics of flight as we became the foundation of the mighty Luftwaffe."

In 1935, the Luftwaffe was formed in Germany and there had been a decree from the air ministry stating that pilots who were trained by the Luftwaffe and wanted to continue flying had to sign up for twelve years of service. By 1939, that order was rescinded as the Germans were rapidly building up their airborne assault group as they had already proven themselves and the success of airborne glider troops by capturing and annihilating the Belgium defenders of Fort Eben-Emael. This Belgium stronghold was reported to be the most impenetrable fort in the world—until the German glider forces proved them wrong. The success of German gliderborne forces early in World War II caught the US Army Air Forces (AAF) off guard and propelled them into a glider program in February 1941.

In December 1941, military planners called for training 1,000 AAF glider pilots. By war's end, more than 5,500 received their glider wings. Most of the newly minted glider pilots came from the enlisted ranks and all were volunteers, eager to get into the air, even if it meant only a one-way trip into combat.

Glider pilot training was divided into two stages. The first was for those cadets that had little to no prior flight training. To ensure they were cutout to become a pilot in the army air forces, they needed to pass primary training in a PT series aircraft like the Stearman PT-17 biplane or the Fairchild PT-19 monoplane.

July 17, 1942 (*letter excerpt*)

Dearest Bunny,
I'm still fooling around here more or less waiting for an assignment to glider school. Today I visited the historic Alamo. If ever I get to teaching American history again, I'll be able to bore my students with firsthand accounts of my travels and the historic spots I have visited.

Tonight Dempsey Weaver treated me to a fine dinner in the Amacacho Room here at the St. Anthony. I know it took the biggest part of a ten-dollar bill for him, but the music and food were wonderful and I am sure he could well afford it. He told me tonight that his mother alone was worth about a million and a half without saying what he himself had been left by his father.

Weaver is a restless, bored sort of fellow who is probably characteristic of a good many of his class—that class that has been too many places, done too many things, and spent too much money. He doesn't like to be alone much. Since I am always more or less available, he prevails upon me to go out for supper with him or wherever he decides to go. He has a tendency to not always hold his liquor well, and he loves to drink. He has many fine qualities in spite of the fact he is somewhat of a spoiled rich boy, but he has good stuff in him and he thinks quite a lot of me. He has never had anything but rich friends, and now he tells me that he never knew such good fellows as he has met in the army. He is in the glider command because he seemingly wants to prove to some people that he can take it and is not looking for a soft spot.

Dempsey Weaver Jr. was the son of Mr. and Mrs. Dempsey Weaver of Nashville, Tennessee. At twenty-seven years old, he had been a vice president at his father's company, McWhorter, Weaver, and Company, before the war and was commissioned a second lieutenant in the US Army Air Corps. Before World War II broke out, he had attended Vanderbilt University before transferring to the school of law at the University of Virginia. Charles was correct in his assessment of Dempsey; he had been born with a silver spoon in his mouth but, like Charles, knew there was something greater than himself ahead that he needed to overcome. Dempsey Weaver's date with destiny would eventually occur in the early morning hours of June 6, 1944.

July 24, 1942 (*letter excerpt*)

Hello! Sweetheart:
How are you this fine evening? I wanted to say "Hello, Mother" but that sounded too dignified. I still like the sound of "Sweetheart" though, and I always shall where you are concerned. I can only say I was thrilled when I tore open the telegram this morning and found that a dream had come true and that both you and the baby were doing fine. I still don't feel like a father because I didn't get a chance to pace the floor in the waiting room. It's too bad in a way that ours had to be a war baby, but I feel so much better now that I know you are not alone.

Tell me if our name (Carol Ann?) has been tacked on yet. I bet your mother is thrilled, and I know mine is. Although don't expect her to show it. It is the first granddaughter in either family.

I have been taking a very comprehensive physical exam that lasts two days. This afternoon I was interviewed for about two hours by a doctor. It was a psychological exam for mental stability and bearing. He asked many very personal questions about my sex life, religion, philosophy of life, and everything else. It seems as though I shall pass the examination.

The old Carpenter luck is still with me. I have always been the luckiest person I ever knew, and I believe that luck is going to stay with me until the end.

August 3, 1942 (*letter excerpt*)

Dearest Bunny,
Brightman has been doing a fine job of keeping me posted on all the developments concerning you and the baby. He writes very well and naturally.

Last night I went up for a two hour and fifteen minute plane ride here with one of the flying officers I met at the swimming pool. It was my first night flight, and you may be sure that it was an experience for me. Barrel rolls, loops, and chandelles and I didn't get sick. I even had earphones on and talked with him over the radio.

Because discipline was getting rather lax among our recruits for glider school, some of us officers were assigned to groups of men or flights, as they are called here. I have about one hundred men in my flight, although a good many of them are being returned soon to their old units. It seemed that more glider pilot students were called in that there are places for at present.

Tonight I sat down in the elegant lobby of the St. Anthony again and listened to the ensemble play beautiful dinner music—Tales of the Vienna Woods, Ave Maria, La Paloma, Cavalleria Rusticana, and many others that I have grown to love.

August 9, 1942 (*letter excerpt*)

Dearest Bunny,

I'm writing to you from the room of another officer. I just met him today but I know already that he is a fine fellow. We just came upstairs from a big steak dinner. It's the only meal I expect to eat today. This fellow, a 1st Lt. Charles Parmele, just flew a big four-motored bomber into San Antonio yesterday from some secret island base in the ocean off South America. It is the first time he has been in the US for fourteen months. He has been telling me about his life as a bomber pilot doing patrol duty day after day out over the ocean in a huge bomber with a crew of eleven. He described the dreary monotonous life he has been leading on the island where the bombers are based. He said until yesterday, he hadn't seen a woman of any kind or color for more than three months. I guess goats are about the only companions they have.

Tomorrow he is scheduled to take off again in a big bomber for the return trip to take up his patrol duties again. He is a quite likable young fellow and is only twenty-two years old right now. He, of course, appreciates even a short visit back to civilization. He told me that at the island base he gets 3 qts of water a day for drinking, bathing, and laundry purposes. He flies about nine hours every day without ever seeing shore. Several of his buddies have flown out over the ocean and disappeared. Already I have met several fellows like him who lead strange, adventurous lives, and they always speak of it just as though they were delivering groceries or driving a bus. One of the boys in our group was telling me about his talk with a pilot who just returned to Randolph from General Chennault's Flying Tigers in China. He had a record of twenty-two Jap planes already to his credit.

I'm getting more than a little impatient to be away from here. I feel as though I am wasting my time. Once we do begin to move, though, things will probably move fast from then on. All the news I get from you and home seems to be pretty good. I certainly enjoyed the snapshots of you and the baby. You're looking mighty pretty yourself. I believe motherhood has taken nothing from your good looks and has instead added to your charm.

There were many red-blooded Americans who chose to join the ranks of foreign air forces before America entered into the war. Many returned home to sign up for army or navy pilot slots to continue the fight. While many fought with groups like the American Volunteer Group (AVG) Flying Tigers in China, or with the Eagle Squadron during the Battle of Britain in England, some of their war stories on their return back home may have been somewhat exaggerated. A case in point was the pilot Charles wrote home about with the claim of twenty-two victories. While there were many legendary aces with the AVG Flying Tigers, there were only a handful of double aces like George Burgard, David Lee "Tex" Hill, Ken Jernstedt, Robert Little, William McGarry, Robert Neale, Jack Newkirk, Chuck Older, and Bill Reed, and none of them claimed more than eleven kills. Such was the demeanor of several frustrated hotshot fighter pilots who may have blurred the lines between fact and fiction.

August 12, 1942 (*letter excerpt from Elda Carpenter*)

Dear Gene,
I better let you know who is writing you. This is your sister-in-law Elda Carpenter, Charlie's wife. This letter is to inform you that you have a new niece. She was born July 23, 1942. Her name is Carol Ann. She weighed 6 lb 7 oz when she was born. Every feature she has reminds me of her father.

Charles wasn't able to be here, as he has been gone for four months now. He is serving his country too. He hopes to come home soon. He is going to attend Glider school. This is going to be a short letter as I don't know what I can say, or cannot say.

I am still in my home; we have an apartment upstairs that we rent out. I say we, but it is only I and the baby here, downstairs.

Well Gene, I have little hope that this reaches you but it was a try anyway. God bless you and may I see you and Charles together someday safe and sound.

Lovingly, Elda

Elda's letter and the news about Carol Ann being born would never reach Gene. Elda knew the news was not good when she received her letter back with the big bold black capital letters across the front that said, "RETURNED TO SENDER BY CENSOR."

Inside she found a blue-ink-typed 3-by-5 card taped to the letter that stated:

This communication is returned to sender because the addressee has not been officially listed as a Prisoner of War. Immediately upon receipt of official information from the enemy power holding prisoners, the Information Branch Alien Division, Provost Marshal General's Office, Washington, D.C., inform the next of kin of the correct mailing address. No attempt should be made to correspond with anyone through a prisoner of war correspondence channels until that person has been officially designated as a Prisoner of War by the appropriate Military or Naval authority.

Without Charles there to wrap his strong arms around her and shelter her from the horrors of the world, Elda was forced to cry alone.

August 17, 1942 (*letter excerpt*)

Dearest Bunny,
Yesterday I got a letter from the post office that stated 2nd Lt. Charles M. Carpenter would now be known as 1st Lt. Charles M. Carpenter. It doesn't mean a great deal. I'm still the same good-natured, blundering

fellow, but I will get a few dollars more each month, about twenty-five I think. I still have the job to do that will make you proud of me, but I hope to be ready when the time comes. Now I suppose I'll have to act just a little bit more dignified and try to look just a little more serious. So far I have not done much to earn my pay, but perhaps I may have to work overtime later. Here's some definite news. I'm leaving San Antonio sometime Monday for Glider School at Okmulgee, Oklahoma. I'll go with Weaver. I'm very anxious to make good at Glider School, and I intend to work hard.

A 1942 travel brochure proclaimed that Okmulgee was "Oklahoma's unusual city." Located 107 miles east of Oklahoma City, 50 miles south of Tulsa, it housed a population of over 17,000. Home to Phillips 66 and Ball fruit jars, the citizens proudly proclaimed their town as "Where oil flows, glass flows, and glass glows." They could have also added "Where glider pilots earn their wings."

August 28, 1942 (*letter excerpt*)

Dearest Bunny,
This morning at 8:30 I started my flight training. Weaver and I are assigned to the same instructor. He is a rather quiet young civilian who let me do just about as I pleased for the fifty-five minutes that I flew this morning. The planes are small ones, just about like the one I flew in Moline. They are built a little more rugged, however, and they certainty do take a beating here

There are four airports at distances of from 6 to 10 miles from Okmulgee that are being used. We have been assigned to North Field. It is nothing but a cow pasture, and not a particularly smooth one at that. From what I hear, it is the best of the four fields.

I did fairly well on my first flight this morning, although I did get slightly nauseated doing spins and stalls. Any time after two hours our instructors can solo us if they think we are ready. The flying promises to get very interesting before it is all over. We even have night flying and landings by smudge pots.

After completion of primary flying maneuvers, the cadets quickly moved into a new training syllabus. This consisted of both dual and solo training in light aircraft, like Piper L-4 Cubs, Aeronca L-3s, or Taylorcraft L-2 types. This course was designed to encompass thirty hours in a four-week training block where cadets needed to master engine out "dead-stick" landings, steep gliding turns, and precision approaches and landings in a confined area.

August 30, 1942 (*letter excerpt*)

Dearest Bunny,

My birthday has come and gone, and now I'm thirty. The years seem to come faster now, and I seem to grow more slowly with their passing. Thirty isn't so old, yet my life and character are probably already well set in their respective molds.

When I speak of "washing out" I mean failing in the flight course. Each day we are graded by our instructors on everything we do. The only real mark against me is a tendency toward nausea. Weaver got a pink slip today and he is quite worried. Three pink slips and a bad performance on the check ride and out you go, back to the classroom or desk.

I soloed today. Flew by myself for an hour and five minutes. I enjoy the flying very much except when I get slightly nauseated in some of the more violent maneuvers like spins and steep turns. The possibility of being eliminated is always hanging over your head to keep you from getting too gay and lightheaded.

September 9, 1942 (*letter excerpt*)

Hello! Bunny:

Every day is pretty much the same now, but all of them are pleasant days. I get to be here earlier than I ever have, I believe, since my farmer boy days. Six o'clock is not early but Weaver and myself still roll out quite reluctantly.

I made a couple of bad landings today, but Weaver got lost and had to land and ask a farmer the way back to Okmulgee. Weaver said he rolled almost up to the front porch of the farmhouse, and the farmer and his wife never got out of their rocking chairs.

Today we had fun "shooting dead stick landings." On these we shut the motor off entirely about a half mile from the field and glide and try to roll to a stop at a spot marked out on the field. We always make sure at least to clear the fence at the edge of the field. I got stuck in the mud once and had to be pushed out.

I flew above the clouds today too. From up above they looked like the biggest flock of wooly white sheep you ever saw.

September 20, 1942 (*letter excerpt*)

Hiya, Bunny:

I soloed in my night flying Friday night. I felt very good about it as I hadn't done so well in the previous night flying. It is quite exciting. Friday the weather was almost storm and the air was very rough. Our techniques for night landing is to head the plane down a row of smudge pots in the pitch dark in at about 55 miles per hour until we hit the ground and bounce. Of course, the proper thing then to do is to level off gradually from the big bounce and land, getting out of the way before the next plane, always on your heels, lands on top of you. We have a lot of fun and so far there has not even been a minor mishap. Weaver has not soloed yet at night and he is quite worried about being eliminated. There is just one more week in the regular course here for us. We will get check rides or final exams in flying this week. All of us our quite serious because everyone like it and wants to make it to the next grade.

Charles ultimately passed his check ride and was well on his way to earning his silver wings. Ordered to return to Randolph Field to await further orders, Charles and Weaver set off again on their cross-country road trip. No sooner had they arrived when they were told to report to Smyrna Army Flying School in Smyrna, Tennessee. Located 30 miles southeast of Nashville, Dempsey Weaver invited Charles to spend the night at his mother's home in Nashville.

November 1, 1942 (*letter excerpt*)

Bunny Dear,

Everything is fine here, although we glider pilot students are still doing little of a productive nature. I went in to Nashville and spent Saturday night and Sunday evening with the Weavers. Mrs. Weaver thinks I am good for Dempsey and places far too much confidence in me. Our stay was very enjoyable.

Mrs. Weaver gave me a sterling silver baby spoon that she had picked out while I was gone. The pattern is quite lavish, but it is the same pattern as her table sterling.

Rumor has it we glider pilots will move again shortly, perhaps, not even to glider school but to a new glider pool at Stuttgart, Arkansas.

November 6, 1942 (*letter excerpt*)

Dearest Bunny,

It's raining outside now and it has rained almost every day that I have been at Smyrna. The big bombers seem to fly anyway though, rain or shine, day or night.

The war news this morning is the most cheering I have read in a long time. The German army in Egypt seems to be routed, the Japs are being forced back a bit in the Solomons, and the Russians are still holding. It may well be that the turning point of this war has arrived. Of course it is much too early for unfounded optimism, but there seem to be a ray of light now where all was dark before.

The only ray of light for Charles Carpenter was the continual uncertainty of what his future held. Shortly after his latest letter, he was ordered to move again, this time to Greenville, South Carolina, for advanced glider training. Like a "rolling stone that gathered no moss," Charles and his sidekick Weaver hit the road once again. While they were in Greenville, both lieutenants learned the finer points of glider flying. It was here where they strapped true, engineless gliders on and soared like a bird:

Have had two flights in a glider now. It is somewhat different-more like a bird, I guess, than flying behind an engine. An army tow plane tows two gliders to a height of 4,000 or 5,000 feet where we cut loose. On the way down, which takes a remarkably long time it seems, we turn and swoop, do stall and spins and banks, and then, when there is just enough height to safely reach the field, our instructor tells us to head back and we sail into a landing.

November 24, **1942** (*letter excerpt*)

Dearest Bunny,

Well I have a piece of paper now that says I can glide—at least a little bit.

Finished the course here this afternoon with a couple of last rides. I received the diploma I'm sending along to you. I surely wish it were a pair of silver wings instead, but, perhaps, that day will come soon.

Weaver and I are leaving tomorrow for Stuttgart, Arkansas.

By 1942, government contractors had descended on Stuttgart and had dug up and displaced over 2,600 acres of Arkansas soil to build four, 5,000-foot runways. It was here that Charles and his fellow glider pilots were scheduled to be introduced to gliders that would in due course be used in combat. The Waco CG-4 Hadrian was like a flying boxcar. When fully loaded it carried a crew of two pilots, thirteen troops, or a quarter-ton Jeep that would exit through an upward-hinged nose section. With a plywood-covered wingspan of over 83 feet and a length of 48 feet, the fabric-covered Waco weighed in at over 3,900 pounds and could almost carry its own weight. With a maximum takeoff weight of 7,500 pounds, twin-engine Douglas C-47 Skytrains were used to pull the massive glider skyward. Built specifically to assault an enemy's stronghold, most of the men in training understood that Europe would probably be their intended destination and the one-way trip that would follow while at the controls of the Waco.

December 11, **1942** (*letter excerpt*)

Dearest Bunny,

Living conditions here are somewhat rougher than what we have been used to. At the present rate of progress here I will not fly until June, as there are eleven classes ahead of me and each class takes two weeks. The whole thing is pretty much of a mess here, but something different may be worked out before June. The barracks are rough-tar paper and wall board, heated with coal stoves that roast me in front while my back freezes. We walk in mud and dust. It's so cold in the morning that it takes all my will power to get out of bed, the food is the poorest we have had yet, I sleep on canvas cot without a pillow case, I can't keep anything clean. Almost everyone in my group moans and grumbles, and yet—here's the amazing part I like it better than any part of my army career. I'm beginning to feel like a soldier. I only hope I can continue to work with men and planes for a while, instead of papers and figures. Then Stuttgart might become a prison to me.

Many of the officers have been trying to change the appearance of things here by looking at this place through a whiskey bottle. So far, it hasn't affected me in that way in the least. It's like camping to me.

Halfway around the world, it was no "camping trip" for those survivors of the Bataan Death March. Living in squalor, many who had survived this long were disease-ridden and starving. Those too weak to walk were beaten or bayoneted to death. The Carpenter family held out hope for Gene and knew he would rely on his disciplined upbringing and being part of the "Carpenter Clan" to see him through any hardships that came his way. At least that was their hope.

December 16, 1942 (*excerpt from a letter written by Lois Carpenter*)

Dear Elda,
I had a card last week from Chas that he was leaving for Stuttgart, but have had no word from him since. Also had a card earlier, and he said that the car had been found and he had given it to somebody but no other details.

A telegram from the government arrived last night, says Eugene is reported a Prisoner of War, of the Jap. Govt. in the Philippines, which only verifies what we thought.

Lois

CHAPTER 8

A Sheep in Wolf's Clothing

Sunday, **January 3**, **1943** (*letter excerpt*)

Dearest Bunny,

Things have happened rapidly today: a wire came to the air base last night asking for eleven officers to report for liaison training with the Field Artillery. In view of recent developments in the glider program, I thought maybe I should "change horses," even in the middle of the stream. My name is on the list and it appears that I shall be leaving tomorrow for Waco, Texas, for some new type of training.

A liaison pilot is a fellow who observes artillery fire, generally from small, low-flying plane and radio back to the gunners the information he finds out as to range, effect of the shells, etc. Beyond that I know very little about it. Weaver will probably never forgive me for pulling out like this while he is home on leave. One of the boys told me about it one minute, and the next minute I was on my way down to head-quarters to sign up.

Aerial observation was not new to the US Army. It traced its roots back to the Civil War, when the Union army used gas-filled balloons as aerial observation posts.[1] Early aerial observation made at least one unqualified contribution to the Union victory, but it was ignored at the time. A lone balloonist assigned to the Department of Missouri succeeded during the battle of Island Number 10 in directing the fire of motorboats onto the Confederate water battery.

But it wasn't until 1909 when the War Department purchased their first airplane from a pair of former bicycle-building brothers, Orville and Wilber

Wright, that the US military began to investigate the use of aerial reconnaissance.

By the time Charles Carpenter was five years old, the United States entered the fray in Europe, known as the "war to end all wars," in 1917. While the soldiers on the ground during World War I had endured the horrors of trench warfare—poison gas, bayonet charges, machine-gun nests, and flame throwers—the pilots from both sides who flew observation airplanes overhead were much more civil to one another. Shortly before fixed weaponry was bolted to these fabric-covered aircraft, the observation airplane was the only game in town. These early warriors of the sky were more like modern-day traffic reporters as they flew over battlefields and enemy front lines documenting troop movements, buildups, and potential weaknesses. When two opposing observation airplanes encountered one another over the skies of Europe, these "great men of honor" smiled and exchanged pleasantries to one another as they flew by. Chivalry, at least in the air, was far from dead; that was until someone threw a brick at their opponent.

Soon, new, more aerodynamic weapons such as grenades, rocks, and pieces of rope with grappling hooks attached were brought aloft and hurled at one another in an attempt to bring down a passing foe. But the one true facet that forever changed how the airplane would be used in combat was the first time an observation pilot brought a pistol to a rock fight. As the first shots of aerial combat rang out high above the trenches, the killing machine of the air was born.

By the time the first shots were fired, the technological advances of aircraft design grew by leaps and bounds compared to the earlier powered kite-like Wright Flyer models purchased eight years earlier. Now the newly formed US Army Air Service utilized metal tube, cotton-fabric-covered, externally braced biplanes with fixed landing gear and armed with machine guns.

Even the communication from the air to the ground problem was addressed with the use of spark-gap transmitters that sent bursts of static Morse code over a wide-ranging set of frequencies to the field artillery units below. That was of course if the static produced by the aircraft's engine did not interfere with the code being sent. There were several successful uses of the "eyes in the sky" during World War I, including the use of message drops to US cavalry and infantry units informing the troops on the ground where the German positions near the front lines were located. But when the war ended in late 1918, the fast-developing use of aerial observation died as quickly as it came into being. A visionless military believed battleships and infantry were the only future needs in warfare.

In 1919, Brig. Gen. William "Billy" Mitchell indicated that the use of aerial observation in the US military was the least important facet of the Air Service mission.[2] Regrettably, Mitchell's words carried weight, a weight that soon dragged down any advancements in aerial reconnaissance for many years to come.

In 1926, the US Air Service changed its title again and became known as the US Air Corps with the lofty goal of producing over 1,800 aircraft during the next five year period. But that goal came to a crash landing three years later with the advent of the Great Depression. During the early 1930s, the priorities of the military began to shift as greater financial support was allocated to the air corps; most of that, however, was for the development of strategic bombardment, which in essence created a design revolution in this country for aircraft design and manufacturing.

By the late 1930s, bombers and pursuit (fighters) were inching over 300 mph and reaching altitudes where only "the angels played" of 30,000 feet or more. Unfortunately, the same advancements did not hold true for the observation types. Many of these earlier types, like the ones Gene Carpenter flew in the Philippines, were large, heavy, and required hard surface runways of almost 1,500 feet to operate from. Many like the North American Aviation O-47 or Curtiss O-52 Owl, which weighed in at over 5,300 pounds, were both ill-suited for frontline cow pastures, fields, or dry creek beds.

Many aircraft designs, especially the single-engine types from the late 1920s into the 1930s, were designed for speed and long range. Many used powerful radial engines to push the airspeed needle higher. Others had an assortment of fuel tanks for long-range flying—proving that crossing the Atlantic and Pacific Oceans could be conquered as long as you had fuel to spare. Most of this era became known as "the Golden Age" of aviation, where it certainly evolved and romanticized the daring men and women of the sky as the flying feats of these record setters and daredevils made headlines weekly across the globe.

But it was not all fun and barnstorming around the globe like it was for the sleeping giant here in the United States. Germany, Italy, Japan, and Great Britain all began to focus on high-performance fighters and bombers. Germany, still reeling from the First World War, disguised their designs as transports, airlines, and aerobatic competitors, before employing their future military might for the whole world to witness during the Spanish Civil War. When the Luftwaffe's Condor Legion was unleashed in the summer of 1936 and began their reign of terror over Spain, the world took notice but did little to stop their blatant disregard of the earlier armistice restrictions placed upon them.

In the United States, some military officers began to take notice of other German innovations and technologies, especially those suited for observation. During the Cleveland Air Races of 1938, many astonished officers were extremely impressed with an aerial ballet of grace and finesse performed by a new revolutionary German airplane called the Fi 156 Fieseler Storch. Its slender, tandem two-seat design, with an inverted inline Argus 240 hp engine, supported an equally long set of 46-foot, 9-inch wings with large flaps and slats that gave it snaillike slow speed ability. The Storch could practically hover.

On the ground the Storch, supported by the straight stilt-like landing gear, resembled part praying mantis, part stork. During one contest of aerial achievement, it not only outperformed a state-of-the-art American auto-gyro (part airplane, part helicopter) in the shortest length of takeoff; the Storch used a miserly 92-foot takeoff roll before becoming airborne, and knocked the socks off a bewildered Army Air Corps. The military wanted an equivalent for themselves.

Calling on the top US aircraft manufacturers to produce a copycat design, the manufactures answered with an overbuilt, overengineered, overcrafted, rugged model known later as the Stinson O-49/L-1. As an observer, it was gigantic. Standing over 10 feet tall with a 50-foot wingspan and powered by a 295 hp Lycoming, nine-cylinder radial engine, the interior was as large as a one-bedroom utility apartment in New York City. Models were soon sent to Observation and National Guard squadrons across the United States. The air corps seemed satisfied with their new mount, but the field artillery and ground elements of the army thought otherwise. What the army needed had already been designed, inexpensively built, and flown, and was already busy teaching a nation how to fly. What the ground Army needed was a "light plane" called the Piper J-3 Cub.

In 1937, the Piper Aircraft Company of Lock Haven, Pennsylvania, came out with their newest model, called the "Cub Sport." It was the third iteration of the model and it was further known as the J-3. The Cub's innards were made of metal tube, aluminum, and spruce wood products, which were all primarily covered in Grade A cotton. The narrow fuselage supported a high wing that resembled a "Hershey bar," and the entire aircraft was painted a bright-yellow color with a black lightning bolt running down the fuselage. The tandem-seat cockpit arrangement allowed for the pilot to fly it from the rear upholstered bench seat solo, or could be flown from the front seat with two onboard. Instrumentation was minimal and rudimentary. The standard equipment included an airspeed indicator, tachometer, oil temperature, and pressure gauge, altimeter, and compass. But rarely did a well-seasoned Cub pilot take more than a glance or two at them from time to time. The Cub required more "seat of the pants" flying using the senses of feel and sound while the pilot controlled the forces of flight with a floor-mounted control stick and a set of metal T-shaped rudder pedals. By 1940, most Cubs were powered by four-cylinder 65 hp engines that swung a two-bladed wooden propeller, a propeller that had to be swung by hand on the ground to engage the engine. Because the wing struts were recessed along the backside of the landing gear, an experienced Cub pilot could stand on the backside of the propeller and flick the blade with one hand to get it started. By far the greatest attributes of the Cub were that it was easy to fly, inexpensive to operate as it sipped fuel at the rate of about 3 to 4 gallons per hour. Some would refer to it as the "Model T of the sky."

The Cub could cruise at 85 miles per hour and had a ceiling of over 9,000 feet and a range with full fuel of 190 miles. What impressed the ground forces the most, however, was the fact that it could take off from sod or unimproved field in under 300 feet and return to land with a final touchdown speed of 35 miles per hour. Weighing in at 730 pounds, it could be easily moved on the ground by a single soldier if needed and quickly placed under trees to camouflage it from any prying eyes of enemy aircraft flying overhead. The army ground forces knew what they wanted and requested the ability to acquire Cubs. But their requests fell on deaf ears.

The Army Air Force was in charge of aviation and they would determine—not the ground force—what if any airplane they would receive. To the high brass, the all-metal, midwing O-47 was already a proven commodity for aerial observation, aerial photography, and reconnaissance. But that thought process changed dramatically during the collapse of the Western Front in May and June 1940, when British and French air forces flew similar aircraft near frontline battles that proved the US Army Air Force planners wrong. The slow speed and vulnerability of the large lumbering observation planes were easy prey for Luftwaffe fighters, with many Allied aircrews paying the ultimate sacrifice. The army air force abandoned any further plans to send the O-47 into harm's way. The new idea floating around with Army Air Force planners was to provide twin-engine light bombers to fill the void. The army ground forces shook their heads in collective disgust.

But that quandary soon changed when some forward-thinking army officers investigated the use of light aircraft as an alternative better suited for their organic needs during several of the war maneuvers that were taking place in the United States during the summer of 1940 and continuing into 1941. With President Roosevelt's announcement in May 1940 that "I should like to see this nation geared up to the ability to turn out at least 50,000 military planes a year," the Piper Cub would soon become a "citizen soldier" as it was drafted into service.

Civilian Piper employees were called upon to fly J-3 Cubs in conjunction with military exercises at Fort Knox, Kentucky.[3] The Armored Force Board inspected the aircraft and decided that it had "very definite possibilities for use on the command, liaison and courier missions." The stone had been cast as the board further recommended the purchase of two Piper Cubs. Given the military designation of O-59, the Air Corps decided to hold a service test in May 1941 between the behemoth Stinson O-49 and the pipsqueak Piper O-59. Although the O-49 possessed the best speed, climb, range, and service ceiling, the air corps did reluctantly report that the Cub was an acceptable substitute. They also stated that because of its greater maneuverability and smaller size, the Cub was more likely to survive if attacked from the air by opposing pursuits. Another more economic advantage was the fact that a brand new Stinson O-49 cost the US government more than $28,000 ($455,000 in today's dollars). The lowly Cub was a mere pittance compared to that with an off-the-shelf price of just under $2,200 ($35,000 in today's dollars). But it was in the summer of 1941 that the Piper Cub proved its weight and might to army ground forces. The gentle sheep with the eye-appealing coat of sunflower-colored yellow paint was a war wolf in disguise.

Flying in both the US Army's Tennessee and Louisiana maneuvers, officers began directing artillery fire and reconnaissance from their aerial mobile command posts, much to the disdain of opposing ground forces. Their mere presence caused much consternation with military umpires; they ultimately ruled that those with the Cubs "had an unfair advantage." But it was during one of those maneuvers in the dust fields of Texas later that summer that the Cub finally earned its military nickname.

When the commander of the 1st Cavalry Division, Maj. Gen. Innis P. Swift, observed an O-59 bounding and bouncing to a halt after landing on the unimproved desert terrain, General Swift turned to his aide and remarked, "That airplane looks like a damn Grasshopper."[4] From that point on, the light planes assigned to the ground forces became known as the "Grasshopper

Squadron." Some were later adorned with hand-painted grasshopper caricatures garnishing the fabric sides of their airplanes. The name stuck and became synonymous with all light planes during World War II.

In mid-1941, Piper began to modify its civilian J-3 model and turned the O-59 into a military aircraft with a new designation of L-4, the L standing for liaison. Painted olive drab, the Cub matched the other military vehicles on the ground and began to build a persona of its own. To assist with greater observation capabilities and the added ability for the back-seat observer to scan for approaching enemy fighters, Piper installed plexiglas windows from the wing root back along the spine of the aircraft. Additional glass was added to the sides as well. Piper called it a "greenhouse." A small table was located behind the rear seat, where the observer could sit facing rearward after removing the rear control stick. With his area map spread out, the observer could easily radio reports or enemy coordinates to artillery units below. With a suitable aircraft that could operate from rough terrain, near the front lines now in place, the last item the ground army and more specifically the field artillery needed to prove its concept was to train pilots in this new form of low-level flying.

Fort Sill, Oklahoma, was selected as the post used for operational training of pilots, mechanics, and observers in "the tactical employment of organic air observation in field artillery units." By June 1942, pilot courses were designated to be five to seven weeks long, depending on student experience levels. Its primary focus was to train the students in the extremes of the limits of the airplane and flight envelopes they would face. The course was developed in stages, with Stage A comprising refamiliarization with flying techniques. Stall and spin recovery along with rapid descents were given top billing before students were allowed to proceed to Stage B. During this stage, a minimum of twenty to thirty-five hours—emphasizing techniques and accuracy for short-field landings and takeoffs over 20-foot barriers, minimum landing rolls, crosswind landings, learning to operate from tactical airstrips that were as close as possible to supporting artillery units and battalions, and evasive maneuvers—gave the student a glimpse of what was to be encountered in actual combat. Stage C brought all the previous stages together and focused on a minimum of ten hours where students participated in live-fire exercises with observers, along with focusing on aerial resupply, aerial evacuation of sick and wounded soldiers, aerial photography and message relay, motor convoy, and camouflage inspection and control and rapid transportation of unit commanders.

The tactical artillery phase brought all earlier learned components together that included reconnaissance, selection, and occupation of tactical airstrips, camouflage, tactical location, and the actual conduct of artillery fire as an artillery observer. The ability to read and interpret tactical maps was stressed with no room for error. The motto became "five days of learning by doing" was instilled in all of the pilots.

When the students weren't flying, they were taught how to maintain the aircraft in the field with a small assortment of tools and perform simple repairs, such as fabric patching and wing rib mending. There were also a dozen half days of navigation and meteorology.

In late 1942, the normal pilot-training class size at Fort Sill was thirty-one. By March 1943, beginning with Pilot Class 25 (P25), that number increased to sixty students as the need for aerial artillery pilots began to double. As a member of Pilot Class 17 (P17), Charles Carpenter was about to embark on one of the greatest challenges in his life, one that would not only define him and the untested abilities of his Piper L-4 Cub that would become folklore later in World War II, but more importantly, unleash a fearless warrior spirit in combat as well.

CHAPTER 9

Leap of Faith

January 6, **1943** (*letter excerpt*)

Dear Bunny,

I'm writing to you from the Waco Army Flying School. It appears we shall be here only one or two days before being sent to the Field Artillery at Fort Sill, Oklahoma. What will be done with us at Fort Sill is still a very much an unanswered question.

In order to stay in this liaison business I have to be under 170 pounds; at present I weigh about 178. I'll be living on a little leaner diet from now on or else be eliminated.

From all that I hear there will be a pretty rough training course ahead of us at Fort Sill. My only hope is that I can qualify for it and eventually, perhaps, be of some service to some part of the army in this war.

At Fort Sill, Charles was about to receive both formal and "informal" training on what it took to be a liaison pilot. One of the training documents he received, titled "Liaison Flying: Getting Down to Earth … but Gently!… in Liaison Aircraft," stated the following:

You have to be more than a pilot…. A capable liaison pilot must possess the knowledge and ability of both crew chief and pilot. He is expected to know what makes his ship fly, to know what his ship can do and what it cannot do. Because liaison planes are comparatively small ships there is a tendency for pilots to take them for granted, to believe their ability to fly without first making a comprehensive preflight check to make certain they are in first class flying condition.

The primary function of liaison planes is to support ground troops in training and combat. Frequently, a group of liaison planes will leave their base and proceed to a field on or near an encampment of ground troops. They may remain there for an extended period. Spare plugs, gaskets, etc. are carried in the ships but ground crews are seldom taken along on such missions. All inspections, repairs, and replacements, except for major overhauls, must be accomplished by the pilots.

It has been observed that liaison pilots will gas and oil their ships and let them go at that. This is not sufficient. Many seemingly trivial things cause accidents that are not so trivial. A loose-fitting may cause the fuel line to break loose, spraying the hot engine with raw gasoline and setting the ship afire. A pilot should be alert and confident. He should have a thorough knowledge of his plane. He should make sure that his plane is properly prepared for flight before taking off. He should not be careless either in action or in thinking.

There is a purpose behind the training of all pilotsb...t o win the war. Our country needs pilots and it needs planes. To deprive it of either through carelessness or shoddy thinking is to hinder the war effort.

It takes time, it takes money, it takes manpower and it takes materials to make a pilot or a plane. It just isn't patriotic to <u>waste</u> any of them now!

January 10, **1943** (*letter excerpt*)

Hello Bunny!
The situation here at Fort Sill is really better than I had expected. The accommodations are not all luxurious. We all sleep together (about fifteen officers) in one big barracks room.

Our new course promises to be lots of fun. We are supposed to learn to do about everything with a small plane that can be done. Among the maneuvers are one-wheel landings and takeoffs, flying for miles about 5 feet above the ground following the contour of the earth's surface, landing and taking off of highways, and many others that sound spectacular but are really not dangerous. We also have to learn to take care of our planes and make all checks and repairs except, of course the major overhauls.

January 13, **1943** (*letter excerpt*)

Dearest Bunny,

Our whole day is taken up in the classroom and out on the range where we observe artillery fire and learn how to direct the aiming of the guns so the shells land on or near the target, which is usually several miles away. We are learning how to pick landing fields, prepare them for the small planes, and also how to hide or camouflage the planes once that have landed.

It is all very interesting, and I have seen some amazing examples of flying skill already. The students go up in the planes to observe where the shell bursts land. Then they radio to the gun batteries how much to change their aim. Each day about $3,000 ($45,000 in today's dollars) worth of ammunition is shot away to train fifteen or twenty students in this procedure.

Once this mission has been accomplished, the planes dive for the ground and streak along through the trees for the landing fields, which generally looks like anything but a landing field.

Much of Fort Sill is rugged, rather mountainous country. We travel by truck to all corners of the reservation and bounce and jolt most of the way. Our school is just a small corner of the whole post, which itself is nothing but an enormous school training thousands of officers and soldiers for the artillery.

By 1943, Fort Sill had served the United States in three major wars, along with many frontier Indian campaigns. Located in what is now known as southern Oklahoma, Fort Sill was founded in 1869 as a base and fort for operations against warlike Indian tribes that resided in the southwestern plains. Fort Sill was named after Brig. Gen. Joshua Sill, a West Point graduate who had been killed during the Civil War at the battle of Stone River, Tennessee, on December 31, 1862.

As more and more settlers were moving westward, the 7th Cavalry established its presence in the Fort Sill area in January and February 1869. Led by a flamboyant lieutenant colonel with flowing golden locks of hair, George Custer was one of the notable soldiers who called Fort Sill home. Seven years later, however, he met his demise during the Sioux Indian massacre on the Little Big Horn.

Another historic presence in the area was Apache Indian chief Geronimo, who after years of battles with the cavalry soldiers eventually surrendered and was housed as a prisoner at Fort Sill in 1894. Geronimo died at the age of seventy-nine in 1909 and was buried with other Apache Indians at the Fort Sill Indian Agency Cemetery. By the early 1900s, Fort Sill was the founding location for the field artillery school of the US Army. With the outbreak of World War I, a large expansion took place, which included an Infantry training center as well. That was later moved to Fort Benning, Georgia, in 1918. The signal corps, which later became the air corps, also operated an aerial arm at Fort Sill. These early aviators were taught to fly in Curtiss JN-3 Jenny biplanes as early as 1915, and when World War II broke out, a specialized class was developed to train not only the aerial observing and correcting of artillery spotting, but more importantly the rapid development of specially trained liaison pilots to work in concert with field artillery units.

January 21, 1943 (*letter excerpt*)

Dear Bunny,
Had my first flying here this morning. It was called an orientation flight. My instructor "sort of wrung me out," and I had a fair case of airsickness before I got down. That isn't so good and it is often sufficient cause for washing a student out. In addition, my flying was terrible. I'm hoping for a better day tomorrow. I really do want to get through this course here, but if I am not made for this sort of thing I'll try to fit in somewhere else. There are several majors and three captains who are students in my class. Consequently, you can see that first lieutenants count for little here.

January 25, 1943 (*letter excerpt*)

Dearest Bunny,
It makes me a bit homesick to hear of your evenings at home, the music and the peaceful quietness of it all. For myself, I live in such a constant hubbub and rush that I'll probably have some difficulty in sitting still again after it's all over.
    Carol Ann's first half year of existence seems to have been a happy one for her. I believe that if a person can get a happy, well-adjusted

start in life, that battle is more than half won. I believe too that the first five or six years of life have more effect on a person's disposition and personality than any other period.

The war news does not look much better lately. The whole thing cannot last much longer, but there will be a terrible lot of destruction of life and property before the echo of the last gun dies.

The weather is so changeable here of late that we fly only about one day out of three. The wind velocities rise so rapidly that often ground crews have to catch the planes as they roll to a stop to keep them from being blown over. That has happened in several instances here.

I have a very fine instructor. He shows me how to do certain maneuvers the first hour of flight, and then I go up alone and practice the next hour. The country here is very flat, except for a small range of mountains in the Fort Sill reservation. The practice field I fly from is called Rattlesnake Field. I generally have a heck of a time finding it once I get out of sight of it.

I started my maintenance course this morning. I bought a pair of coveralls and was issued a kit of tools. When I finish this course, I'll be rated a mechanic for small planes.

January 30, 1943 (*letter excerpt*)

Dearest Bunny,

Took a mechanic's test this afternoon and made only 60. Guess that I'll have to spend little more time on my textbooks from now on. I finished the first 1/5 of the course today. My flying is better, but my instructor said I had a bad day today. I am nauseated somewhat many times due to the series of acrobatics maneuvers I must go through. However, I believe that I am getting less affected as the course progresses.

There are about twenty-five fellows in the same room that I live in. It's a lot like camping and hard to study or concentrate, but we do have lots of fun. The army is a great mixer of peoples and personalities. We have all sections of the country represented, varying professions running from radio announcers to high school history teachers, and nearly all branches of the service.

February 2, **1943** (*letter excerpt*)

Dearest Bunny,

This week I have a new instructor, a sergeant this time. Each of us have practice areas of two square miles. We are not supposed to fly in anyone else's area during our solo period. We have a sequence of maneuvers to run through. The flying is fun, but I'll be fidgeting until I get safely through "A" stage.

I was flying for a short while in the highest wind I have encountered in an airplane. The wind was slightly over 30 mph, and a Cub plane takes off at about 40 mph. When my check ride turn came, flying was called off for the day because of the wind.

February 7, **1943** (*letter excerpt*)

Dear Bunny,

Passed my Stage A flight check yesterday morning. I don't believe I had much to spare in squeezing by, as I had a rather bad case of "Buck Fever" and pulled several boners that I can ordinarily avoid. Tomorrow the most interesting part of our flying course here begins. It consists of one-wheel landings and takeoffs, road landings, barrier approaches, contour flying, etc.

We are constantly being crowded together more and more here as new officers arrive. Now there are forty-five of us living in a space not much larger than several good-sized living rooms.

Earning your silver wings in the US Army Air Force was a well-orchestrated, zero-tolerance-for-mistakes process. The nation needed the best, most qualified candidates to operate bombers, fighters, transports, and "grasshoppers." To accomplish that mission, flight training was broken down into three three-month training syllabuses. The first was called primary, which allowed for roughly sixty-five hours of training. This is where the "washout" rate was the highest, as some cadets just didn't have what it took to be a pilot. For every hundred men who entered US Army Air Force training as aviation cadets, sixty-one would receive their wings and thirty-nine would "wash out." Twenty-four of those washouts would occur in primary flight training—most of them in the first eight hours of dual instruction.

From there the cadet moved onto basic for an additional seventy-five hours. Nine more would wash out in basic training, and if he survived the rigors of that training, he moved on to advanced for the final seventy-five hours, where another three would fall victim to washing out before making the final cut. The main reason for washouts was lack of coordination, poor judgment, and general lack of ability. Qualified washouts were usually sent to bombardier or navigator schools, which, although somewhat less prestigious, required a challenging set of mental skills.

By the end of World War II, the US Army Air Forces training command successfully graduated approximately 250,000 pilots from its schools. Sadly, over 15,000 young men perished while in aircrew training as the nation ramped up its air force to meet the growing demands of fighting a global war. But by and large, the most unique advanced flying school was the one at Fort Sill, which had been established for liaison pilots. Most were informed to disregard "proper flying techniques" and focus more on seat of the pants and edge of the envelope flying—similar types they would encounter in actual combat. Although callously hard on himself, Charles Carpenter did have one advantage over several of his classmates—he had trained in gliders. Because of this experience, Charles quickly understood the meaning of energy management while operating his Grasshopper.

February 9, 1943 (*letter excerpt*)

Dearest Bunny,

Had a rather bad day flying today. Stage B is going to be plenty tough for me, I can see already. Made a couple of landings on a wide road this afternoon and didn't have much to spare with the crosswind that was blowing. My instructor seems pretty patient, though. Knowing me, you will know that I am already wondering if I can pass the Stage B checks that will be coming along in about three weeks.

About ¼ of our class "washed out" or "washed back" to a newer class. I'm really not concerned about my flying here for nothing. I'm pretty tired tonight. Wish I could snuggle up beside you and sleep for a long time. I doubt if I'd even be sleeping then, though.

During Stage "B" training, Charles had to perform a variety of maneuvers, which included precision ground handling, barrier takeoffs, crosswind landings, one-wheel takeoffs and landings on curved roads, contour flying (most of it well below 200 feet), fishtails, and actual road landings. While at Fort Sill, Charles operated off of postage-stamp-sized landing areas with clever names like Rabbit Hill, Rattlesnake Field, and Buzzards Acre, which was a short 300–400-foot landing strip that ran uphill with tall trees at the far end. Many of his classmates either earned their wings or washed out at these strips, as they used every ounce of energy and performance from their Grasshoppers. The pilots learned early on to forget many of the "proper rules of flying" and to instinctively learn instead to fly on the ragged edge. The army needed the "best of the best" because, in combat, it all boiled down to life or death for a liaison pilot.

February 16, 1943 (*letter excerpt*)

Dear Bunny,

I'm entitled to wear wings now. A rating came through for me the other day based on the check ride I took at Waco, Texas. I'm not buying any wings or wearing any, however, until I get through this course. I really don't know what would become of me if I didn't successfully complete the course here. According to the rating I'm still air corps assigned for duty with the field artillery.

February 26, 1943 (*letter excerpt*)

Dearest Bunny,

Yesterday was a beautiful day, and I passed my check ride with flying colors. Everything went perfectly on my ride, and the Captains complimented me at the end of it. We flew over a beautiful section of the Wichita Mts. National Park near here. Sometimes I could look down on the left and the ground was a thousand feet away while I would have to look up to see the mountain top on my right. I made landings on roads and cleared patches in the woods and flew to places that the captain had pointed out to me on a map.

What a refreshing change it is to be near the end of student flying. We have a week more of what is called Stage C. This stage consists mostly of field problems and aerial observation of gunfire. After that, orders will come out pertaining to our new assignments.

There was a little celebration last night among the boys who passed their check rides, and your old Charlie's head is still a bit thick.

March 2, **1943** (*letter excerpt*)

Dearest Bunny,

This afternoon we sat around a hot stove and had a bull session with our instructor on the flying problems we shall encounter in the field. Everything now points toward our departure in a few days for some tactical outfit. After my fussing and stewing over my flying, I made a grade of 90 on my final check ride. That was the highest grade in P17, a class of about thirty-five officers. Of course I feel a little pleased about it, even though I was a little lucky and had a perfect day for my check.

The latest information has it that there will be no leaves granted upon completion of our course here. I'll probably be sent to some outfit that is training for overseas duty in the next four or five months or more.

I really am pleased, Bunny, to be in a position to render service somewhere now. I hope you see it that way too. You know as well as I how fortunate and how lucky I've been all my life. I have more faith and confidence now than I've ever had. All evil comes to an end, even war, and the good has a way of smilin' through.

March 6, **1943** (*letter excerpt*)

Dearest Bunny,

Bad weather keeps us from flying. Instead of graduating today as planned, we are being held over several more days to get some gunnery practice from the air. Had our party last night, and it was very much a success. P17 had as its guests all the staff and instructors who had anything to do with our class. Even the colonel joined in the singing and seemed sorry to see us go.

Enclosed is a rather clever folder distributed at the party.

The "Grasshopper" Song
(to the Music of the Field Artillery Song)

I
Over clouds, under wires,
T'hell with the landing gear and tires
We're the eyes of the artillery.
In and out as hard to find as fleas
We're the eyes of the artillery

Chorus
So then its fly, fly see
For the Field Artillery
Shout out your data loud and strong—Range Correct
So we'll give the Axis fits
With our Maytag Messerschmitts
We're the Grasshopper artillery.

II
We don't need spurs or boots
And we fly too low for 'chutes
We're the eyes of the artillery.
We don't mind the mud or sand
We don't need much room to land
We're the eyes of the artillery

III
Into action we will go
Flying too damn low and slow
We're the eyes of the artillery.
Over guns when they're fired
We won't live to be retired
We're the eyes of the artillery.

IV

Ships are full of rents and dents
We do our own maintenance
We're the eyes of the artillery.
We can find the darndest wrecks
On our periodic checks
We're the eyes of the artillery.

V

Palnuts here, safeties there
Parts go in we don't know where
We're the eyes of the artillery
Was it over, was it short
What the hell shall I report?
We observe for the artillery.

Chorus

So then it fly, fly, see
For the Field Artillery
Shout out your data loud and strong—Range Correct
So we'll give the Axis fits
With our Maytag Messerschmitts
Were the Grasshopper artillery.

CHAPTER 10

One of Patton's Boys

The 4th Armored Division was officially activated on April 15, 1941, at Pine Camp, New York. Brig. Gen. Henry Welles Baird held the reins to the US Army's newest armored division. Unfortunately, with a lack of equipment, only one tank per company, General Baird and his officers conducted their early training scenarios in a giant "sandbox" utilizing painted blocks of wood as their tanks.[1] Over a year earlier in Europe, however, Adolf Hitler had unleashed his "hounds of hell" as his blitzkrieg tanks and Luftwaffe smashed their way through Poland, Norway, Denmark, Luxembourg, Belgium, the Netherlands, and France. Even while the 4th Armored played war games, German panzer divisions were rolling through Greece and Yugoslavia.

New tactics were being developed within the 4th Armored as they moved away from horse-drawn cavalry units into tanks, artillery, and Grasshoppers. By May 1941, more than 10,000 men proudly wore the 4th Armored Division patch on their left shoulder. The soldiers followed the news abroad as well as they read of Hitler's blitzing tanks tearing their way deep into Russia in June 1941. The 4th Armored knew it would only be a matter of time before the "sleeping giant" and its soldiers would be dragged into a world war. On December 7, 1941, with the United States declaring war on Japan and later Germany and Italy, the prospect of combat overseas would become very real in a short time.

By mid-1942, the 4th Armored had a changing of the guard as General Baird retired from military service, His replacement was fifty-four-year-old Brig. Gen. John Shirley Wood. Wood had attended West Point in 1908 and shared the parade grounds with other future notable all-stars, including

Omar Bradley, Carl Spaatz, Dwight D. Eisenhower, and a rough and tough soldier by the name of George S. Patton. Because of his academic prowess, General Wood finished toward the top of his class and was bestowed the nickname of "P," for professor.

After graduating in 1912, Wood, who was promoted to major, arrived in Europe and was stationed in France with the 3rd Division.

Between World Wars I and II, Wood honed his skills on artillery and armored tactics, eventually teaming up with Patton while the two of them studied history, tactics, and strategy at Fort Leavenworth. By the time Hitler had invaded Poland in 1939, Wood was a lieutanant colonel with the 2nd Armored Division under the command of General Patton.[2] By October 1941, Wood was promoted to brigadier general and commanded the 5th Armored Division for a short time before taking over the 4th and preparing his men for war. Considered influential in armored doctrine, John Shirley Wood was an extremely forward-thinking armored cavalry-type soldier. He was considered, as history would later prove, the best-armored commander that the US Army produced during the Second World War.

March 15, 1943 (*letter excerpt*)
Camp Young, Cal.

Dearest Bunny,

Here I am finally at Desert Training Center in the heart of the California desert. Much to my surprise, Camp Young turned out to be an area thousands of square miles in extent. I'm at the camp headquarters now, but tomorrow morning I leave on a 160 mile truck ride across the desert to a Camp Ibis, where my 4th Armored Division Headquarters is supposed to be. This is a vast maneuver area, with army units scattered in all directions. I'm rather eager to catch up with my outfit to find out what is expected of me. Rumor has it that they have already finished most of their desert training here.

Camp Young is 26 miles out from Indio. I rode out there in an army truck this afternoon.

The Desert Training Center was located in the desolate southern area of California and Arizona in the Mojave Desert. The training area was established by General Patton to train American troops for battle in North Africa as the conditions in each mimicked one another. Over 18,000 square miles of desert terrain, split into a variety of camps, became the largest ever military training grounds ever built. During the war years, more than one million men trained and were housed in the eleven camps spread throughout the area. These included Camp Pilot Knob, Camp Granite, Camp Coxcomb, Camp Iron Mountain, Camp Clipper, and Camp Ibis. It was at Camp Ibis Airfield that Charles Carpenter would learn how to fight, lead, and fly off of a 4,500-foot scrub brush runway with steel landing Marston mats covering the desert terrain. The training Charles received during the simulated live-fire combat conditions provided a unique and loyal relationship with his commanding general, one which would pay lifesaving dividends later in his military career.

March 17, 1943 (*letter excerpt*)

Dearest Bunny,
I'm really out with a rough and tough outfit now and I believe I'm going to like it. The 4th Armored have been on maneuvers so much that they wouldn't know what its like to sleep on sheets or eat food without sand in it.

An armored division has about 13,000 men in it. Its commander is a major general with several brigadier generals to help him out. At present I'm with division headquarters. It will be my responsibility to fly the general hither and yon when he so desires, which is quite often, from what I hear.

I'm the first pilot officer to arrive at the 4th Armored Division. Four sergeant pilots and four planes have been with the outfit for some time. We are camped out on the desert about 20 miles from Needles, California. It's just about 10 miles from the Nevada border. I sleep on a canvas cot without any mattress or sheets. I have three blankets and, believe me, I always have to curl up tightly before morning to keep warm.

I have seen only two or three lieutenants anywhere around division headquarters. Captains, majors, and colonels are almost as common as the sagebrush. This of course is real army now, and I'm so green about everything that I'm a little ashamed of myself.

There is a spirit of comradeship existing that I have been told to expect but had never found before in my student officer days. I actually feel that I belong to somebody's gang now.

I do not know what my exact position will be yet. There are a major and captain in charge of air operations of the division, but neither is a flyer. The tables of organization call for a captain pilot and three first lieutenant pilots. None of the others have arrived at the division yet. It will probably be some time before the school at Fort Sill turns out enough to furnish more than one to the division.

I'm right up where all the action and orders originate and have a grandstand box seat for the whole show. Yesterday I flew a major out over the desert and around the mountains to look for a good place for antiaircraft units to fire at targets towed by planes. Our planes will not be used for towing targets, of course, as they are much too small. The air corps furnishes pursuit planes and dive bombers to work with our tanks. They roar by me so fast sometimes that I'm almost tempted to get out of my Cub to see if I've stopped.

Today was lots of fun. There was a big problem underway about 40 miles from our camp. Hundreds of our tanks and guns and trucks had assembled there for a big push through a valley between two mountains. First dive bombers blasted ahead of the armored forces. Then the tanks and artillery laid down a curtain of fire ahead of the advance. Tanks raced across the desert in a fan-shaped formation trailed by long streams of dust that rose several hundred feet in the air.

I got to see more of the maneuver than nearly anyone. I was overhead about 500 feet with the general, who was looking the whole situation over. The general seems to be a very fine fellow, but a mighty big one too. He shook hands with me and called me "Carpenter" thenceforth. We took off from a small rocky strip in the desert and circled our tanks and guns. He tapped me on the shoulder when he wanted to give me instructions or a new direction.

As soon as I get to know him a little better, I'm going to drop a few hints and suggestions about a bigger and more powerful plane. He weighs over 200, I weigh about 180, and our radio weighs about 60 lbs. The crew weight of our Cub is supposed to be not over 340 lbs. You can do a little addition and see why the bottom may drop out from under Carpenter and the general someday on a short takeoff over a mountain.

Headquarters sent for an air corps pilot and a larger plane to haul the general around today. The pilot made four passes at our landing strip and refused to land. The general got disgusted and finally took off with me in the Cub.

I wish you could see how beautiful the desert and mountains are in the white moonlight of tonight.

At fifty-six, General Wood was broad in the shoulders and broader in the waist and stood over 6 feet tall. General Wood did not ride in the L-4; he was literally shoehorned and stuffed into the backseat where he strapped the Cub on. With Charles manning the front seat, the L-4 employed either one of the portable SCR-610 and SCR-510 radio models the general could talk to his ground units on. Most often carried on the floor, aft of the rear seat, the radio was secured with web strappings. This location only added to Charles Carpenter's concern, especially when he carried General Wood in the rear seat. The added weight placed the CG (center of gravity) of the airplane aft. In certain circumstances, including climbs, steep turns, and stalls, this configuration could become deadly in the hands of an inexperienced pilot.

Assignment of field artillery aircraft was divided between each field artillery battalion, field artillery group, brigade, division artillery headquarters, and corps artillery headquarters. Each of the air observation sections consisted of two pilots, two liaison-type aircraft (either an L-4 Cub or Stinson L-5 Sentinel), two airplane and engine mechanics, organic transportation, communications equipment, and certain maintenance and supply equipment. In addition to the equipment, each field artillery headquarters above the battalion employed an additional pilot who functioned as the artillery air officer. Charles Carpenter would soon find his niche in this role.

March 28, 1943 (*letter excerpt*)

Dearest Bunny,
I flew up to Boulder City today with Colonel Wallace of the 66th (Field Artillery) Battalion. Of course we saw Boulder Dam while we were there. Flying around these mountains and up the Colorado River gorge is the most fascinating thing I've done in the flying line.

The colonel said he had a daughter named Carol Ann too.

April 2, 1943 (*letter excerpt*)

Dearest Bunny,

The days are steadily getting hotter here, and I shall probably be ready to move eastward and northward before another month has gone. At present I'm waiting here at the Ibis Cactus Airport (our field) for a batch of generals to show up. We will take them in our Cubs and another plane we have here for a short trip over our area. The guest of honor is a visiting General Devers, who wears three stars.

I certainly do see a lot of rank in my new job. I can remember not long ago when a full colonel really was somebody. I got bawled out by a general the other day. Was riding in a peep (jeep) with two captains when we met him on the road. He stopped his car, gave us "holy h—"for not being in proper uniform, jumped in his car, and drove on.

This afternoon I fired a .50 cal and .30 cal machine gun, a rifle, a carbine, and pistol. I didn't do so well, but this is actually the first time I've fired a shot in over a year in the army.

Although Charles's primary role was as a liaison pilot, he was still a soldier and required to not only qualify with his sidearm, a .45-caliber Browning pistol that he carried cross draw in a dark carmel brown leather shoulder holster that he wore diagonally across his chest, but also become proficient in the other small caliber weapons the artillery unit utilized. Charles quickly became familiar with the .45-caliber Thompson submachine gun, made famous by gangsters and G-men of the 1930s. He also learned how to operate M3 "Grease" guns, M1 Garand semiautomatic rifles, and both .30-caliber and .50-caliber Browning machine guns, which were either hard mounted to tanks or half-tracks, or employed with infantry soldiers on the ground. This was one weapon that Charles became very familiar with in combat. Although not a tank driver, Charles quickly learned to identify the division's tanks that he overflew.

Initially equipped with smaller M3 light tanks that shouldered 37 mm guns, the 4th Armored Division quickly transitioned to the new M5 light tank that could "run down" an enemy at 40 mph. But it was the 33-ton M4 Sherman tanks that would primarily lead the charge into battle with their 75 mm low-velocity guns. Unfortunately, their German counterparts in both the Panther and Tiger tanks had thicker armor and bigger guns that could reach out from greater distances to the American tankers and punch holes through their thinner sides.

April 4, 1943 (*letter excerpt*)

Dearest Bunny,
Was up flying this morning giving a lesson to the colonel (Neil Wallace) of the 66th. It seems as though I'll be doing lots of things that weren't in my textbooks. Tomorrow morning I'm flying down to Desert Center about 100 miles away. In the tents next to me are some movie people from 20th Century Fox. No actresses, of course, as they're only making a movie short called "War on Wheels."

As the United States was gearing up for the war in the wake of the Pearl Harbor attacks, Hollywood was called to action. On December 18, President Roosevelt appointed Lowell Mellett as the coordinator of government films. The Office of War Information (OWI) was also created, as well as its subsidiary Bureau of Motion Pictures that absorbed Mellett's department. During this time, Hollywood studios assisted in the production of training films for the US military. Some of these films were laughably ignorant of the difficulties of training and the horrors of war. *The Tanks Are Coming* (1941), for example, makes boot camp look like a summer camp and a "walk in the park." Other films took on much more serious roles. Mellett helped produce the famed *Why We Fight* series, directed by Frank Capra. Director John Ford and cinematographer Gregg Toland won Academy Awards for brilliantly capturing footage at the Battle of Midway.

The OWI played an essential role to further the war effort by opening an office in Hollywood to review feature film scripts. Most major studios supplied scripts to the Los Angeles branch of the OWI. For the Bureau of Motion Pictures, the primary question was "Will this picture help win the war?" The goal of both propaganda films as well as feature films that took on war themes was to keep up the morale of the stateside, moviegoing public. It is important to remember that movie attendance had been increasing through the Great Depression and peaked in 1946 at nearly eighty-five million people a week. During World War II, there was no better way to reach the public about their patriotic duties than to be waiting for them on the other side of the theater turnstiles.

April 16, **1943** (*letter excerpt*)

Dearest Bunny,

Can you imagine my still being held in San Bernadino by California weather? Have been here for three days now, and never once has the sun shown through the murk and mist. It was indeed an impressive sight to be flying between two towering snow-covered peaks and have the carpet beneath suddenly change from tans and browns to brilliant greens. We passed over miles of orange groves, and orange perfume extended even up to the plane a thousand feet overhead.

There is a big air-supply depot at San Bernadino. My chief mechanic, Tech Sgt. Linton, and I flew down here to get some badly needed parts for our planes. After a lot of "rigmarole" and fast talking, we got our parts all right, but then couldn't get permission to leave. I phoned my boss, Colonel Bixby, so there wouldn't be any worry about us at Camp Ibis.

It would have been amusing to have seen the arrival of our tiny plane at Marrow Field. It's an enormous place and has a mass of huge buildings still under construction. We flew around the field until we got the green light from the control tower. That's the signal to land. We landed on a runway so big that I flew from one end of it to the other so I wouldn't have to spend the afternoon taxiing in. There was a man waiting to direct us to a parking spot among a lot of huge transports and deadly looking bombers.

The air depot here is an immense thing. There are thousands of women working everywhere, on planes, driving trucks and tractors, crating parts, wielding typewriters and wrenches, and doing jobs I had seen only men work at before.

This war is going to upset our existing economic and social structure far more than most of us dream.

Many of the women that Charles observed and interacted with were re-ferred to as "Rosie the Riveter's," "Khaki Wacky," and "Victory Girl." Female workers on the home front during the war did a lion's share of important defense manufacturing tasks and work. Others worked as clerks, flight technicians, parachute riggers, antiaircraft artillery gunners, truck drivers, and aircraft mechanics and pilots. Some earlier male tasks quickly changed names to adapt to the new roles. Milkmen were now known as "milkmaids," while lumberjacks became known as "lumberjills" and streetcar conductors became "conductorettes." More than 350,000 women served in uniform during World War II, while countless others performed herculean tasks as their husbands, fathers, brothers, and uncles served overseas.

April 20, 1943 (*letter excerpt*)

Dearest Bunny,

My trip home from San Bernadino was pleasant but uneventful. I was teaching the colonel of the 22nd how to fly yesterday. He was taking off down our narrow runway in a crosswind. The next thing I knew we were off the runway on the right just clipping the tops of the cactus. I took charge then, but it was too late. We couldn't climb above them. I finally closed the throttle, and we slid along the ground minus our landing gear. We were only shaken up a bit, but the plane will need some extensive repairs. Thank heaven, it was a colonel that was learning to fly. The plane was one that belongs to his battalion also.

I'm still somewhat of a novelty around the division, and most of the officer and soldiers who want a "hop" smile on me. I do spend a lot of time after working hours giving rides. Life in the desert is so much of a grind for many of these men that I almost feel it my duty to let them get above the dust and heat for a few minutes or look down on the top of mountains.

Last night the mess tent was crowded when I came in so I was invited to sit at the staff table with the general and all the high division officers. I didn't feel too comfortable there, but the meal was good.

Yesterday it fell to me to take a visiting British colonel up to see the Boulder Dam. The British colonel was wounded in action with the Eighth Army in North Africa. He was flown over here to tell American armored force officers the results of combat experience against the Germans.

He was tall and lean and had a little mustache like you would expect a British colonel to have, and was a most interesting talker in spite of his modesty.

Although the mishap that Charles endured with the colonel flying the L-4 may have seemed minor to him, to the US taxpayer, the price of a new Cub still dug into their pocketbooks. The Piper Aircraft Company charged the army $346.50 for labor in constructing one, while $874.11 went to material costs. $433.12 was factory overhead that included employee salaries, benefits, and supervisory rates with an additional general overhead of $138.60. A built-in profit was also added to the tune of $179.23. The basic cost came to $1971.56 ($30,186.18 in today's dollars)

But Piper was no dummy when it came to a government contract. Additional equipment costs added up quickly, and these included installation of a generator, $46.00; battery box, $14.40; radio, $43.75; material for radio installation, $22.72; radio shielding on engine, $25.00; canopy and windshield covers, $20.50; a prop cover made of canvas, $3.38; and a canvas engine cover, $6.75. These costs added $182.50 to the government tab, with a fly-away total of $2,154.06 ($32,980.40 in today's dollars) for a US Army L-4. But, in reality, the cost of a Piper L-4 was minuscule, compared to the return on investment it provided for US Army ground forces.

April 25, 1943 (*letter excerpt*)
Easter Sunday 1943

Dearest Bunny,
Yesterday afternoon I flew up to Las Vegas to bring Colonel Bixby back to camp today. I'm expecting to meet the colonel here at the El Rancho soon. Las Vegas is a lurid, showy place with gambling the main business. You may have heard of this place as the spot movie stars generally elope to. Most of the establishments are gambling houses and money flows back and forth like water. I've seen people in rags here betting in two figures. Everybody gambles with stacks of silver dollars. Soldiers are everywhere. They flock in here from the desert on weekends to get a brief and expensive glimpse of the bright lights.

The Las Vegas valley region had less than 14,000 people that called it home in 1940. Two years later it had already doubled and was climbing higher. Thanks to the rapid buildup of military installations, training centers, and the soldiers that occupied them, Las Vegas began to boom. The El Rancho where Charles would drop his boss Colonel Bixby off was like a desert flower with a swimming pool, tall slender whitewashed spire with attached windmill, casino, restaurants, and a parking lot big enough to land a Cub on. It was also the first resort to be built on the infamous Las Vegas strip and housed tables for roulette, blackjack, craps, and slot machines where visiting Hollywood stars and soldiers plied their luck.

April 29, **1943** (*letter excerpt*)

Dearest Bunny,
Returned from a long 180 mile truck ride to Indio, California, about 1:30 a.m. We now have four new planes in crates out at the airport. Don't know whether to unpack them and put them together or leave them in the crates. It's pretty definite that we move in a few weeks. We were told we would be moving to Camp Bowie, Texas.

The 4th Armored seems to have been ready for action for some time, but as yet there has been no call for them. No place to use an armored division in the Pacific theater yet, and no need for them in North Africa. Perhaps, if a second European front ever opens up, we will be the first to go across.

April 30, **1943** (*letter excerpt*)

Dearest Bunny,
I'm still getting along pleasantly as Division Air Officer. In fact, I really believe I wouldn't trade jobs with anyone in the division, including the general. Tomorrow I shall inspect the tents, the planes, and the equipment. It's a regular Saturday morning procedure. Last week one mechanic had even washed the tires on his plane and polished the propeller hub. I pick the best appearing soldiers, best tent, best plane, best vehicle, and best soldier at drill. The competition is slightly more than mild, even though the difficulties of dressing up in the desert are great. I'm certainly glad the men do not get a chance to inspect my tent as I strut through theirs looking for an article of clothing out of place or a stray match stick.

According to the instruction memorandum of the Organic Field Artillery Air Observation manual, section d, as it relates to Charles's role as division air officer:

The senior pilot assigned to the division artillery or to an artillery brigade functions as the artillery air officer on the staff of the division artillery or brigade commander. In addition to his duties as a pilot, he will, under the direction of the division artillery or brigade commander, inspect the pilots and airplanes of the command from time to time and make recommendations as to their training and maintenance. He commands the air observation section of the division artillery or brigade headquarter battery.

Charles felt right at home with these duties as he acclimated himself to army life and leadership.

May 7, 1943 (*letter excerpt*)

Dearest Bunny,

Suddenly today I realized that Sunday was Mother's Day, and that you are now eligible to be honored especially on that day. I think you are and shall be a wonderful mother in addition to the job you had to being a real sweetheart to me. Please don't let your new job crowd out very much of the old one, because I think I need you as much as a sweetheart as Carol Ann needs you as a mother.

I like the desert here very much and shall miss it, I know, when we move, I like the reproachful cactus plants, the melancholy mountains, the silken night and cheerful dawns. A dish of ice cream tastes so good here, and a glass of ice water is a wonderful experience in the heat of day. It's hot, but the dryness of the air whisks away the perspiration as fast as it gathers.

Today I went for a walk back to camp and threw rocks at long-eared jack rabbits and saw a desert fox drift by. Sometimes when I come into the tent at midday, there's a tortoise resting here out of the sun for a little while, before taking up again his painful travels. The other day a coyote came out on the landing strip to inspect a plane. He shot away in great amazement when I climbed out of the thing. I saw a horned rattlesnake, too, and he buzzed a warning and there was no trouble. The desert seems so lonesome most of the time, but I guess there's almost always someone looking me over from behind a cactus bush.

For a change once in a while, I cross the dead mountains and skim up the Colorado River a couple of feet above the water. There's always a duck or an awkward crane to chase, and once I've seen a fish try to dodge me. Flying is pretty tricky here now at times. There are many up and down drafts in the hot part of the day. Sometimes when we can't get over the mountains and it's too far around, we search for a rising current of air and go up on it like a leaf. Our passengers are often greatly startled at the bumpiness of the air, especially when the bottom suddenly drops out for a hundred feet or so. However, the pilots have grown used to it and have learned to depend very little on the fickle air that supports us.

My latest flying student is Major General Wood himself. He's in his fifties and doesn't expect to get his wings. He tells me he only wants to be able to get the thing down and walk away in case something happens to the pilot. Yesterday he gave me three books on flying that had been autographed by the author himself. General Wood is a rough, gruff fellow with a roaring voice. I imagine I'm the only fellow in a good while around here who has been telling him what to do and getting by with it.

Incidentally, Colonel Bixby, (The "Old Man"—meaning my boss) tells me that he has signed a recommendations for my promotion to captain. A captain is tops in my line of work, but I wouldn't trade jobs with the colonel himself. Colonel Bixby has been so fine to me that I'm just about ready to settle down and work my head off for him. Right now I am concerned with the problem of getting my Air Observation Section moved about 1,200 miles or more eastward. Took a trip of about 80 miles this afternoon with Colonel Bixby down to the 7th Armored Division. Everyone envies us because we are moving out of the desert.

As a division commander, General Wood did not suffer fools lightly and had little respect for soldiers who did not take training seriously. Charles Carpenter had much in common with his boss and back-seat student. Both men were not afraid to express their ideas and moral courage, although Charles stuck to military protocols and its respect of rank, both men were natural leaders in their own right. Both of them were active in sports, having played football in college, and both of them now enjoyed the game of tennis as their sport of choice. If Charles had not realized it at the time, any outside observer would have surmised that General Wood had taken a shine to his Grasshopper pilot.

May 21, **1943** (*letter excerpt*)

Dearest Bunny,

Another soft starlit evening is passing quietly away. All the time since supper I have spent talking and laughing, first with the men who are under me at Ibis Cactus Airport, and then with those who are above me at division headquarters. Such sessions at the close of day are one of the truly enjoyable features of army life. Men learn to rely a great deal upon the companionship of other men.

Tomorrow I shall probably make my last trip to Las Vegas. The colonel leaves for our new camp next week. He told me that we "Grasshoppers" would probably arrive at Camp Bowie about June 15. I expect to get home not long after that.

Did you ever stop to think that the friends that you and I have are the greatest asset by far that Carpenter Inc. has? May it always be so.

May 24, **1943** (*letter excerpt*)

Dearest Bunny,

El Captain writes to you tonight. It was hotter than h—today, but still it was a very nice day. There was a letter in the mail addressed to Captain Charles M. Carpenter, so I pinned on pair of bars, bought a few drinks for the boys, and thus became a captain.

I'm still the same fellow, of course, but I suppose I should grow up a little more and perhaps work a bit harder. I don't know what has become of Weaver. When I last heard of him he was on his way back to Stuttgart from Waco, having failed to get into the Liaison Course at Fort Sill. The whole glider program seems to have been folded up rather quietly, as being rather impractical on a large scale.

Little did Charles know that his statement about the glider program could not have been further from the truth. Less than a year later, in preparation for the invasion of France, thousands of paratroopers, aircraft, and gliders would participate in the largest invasion force the world would ever witness. And Dempsey Weaver would have a front-row seat.

May 26, **1943** (*letter excerpt*)

Dearest Bunny,

Today our air section left at dawn on maneuver problem of moving forward from one hastily prepared landing strip to another. At best this is a rather trying type of problem, but today had more than its share of shaky moments. I am not referring to my flying but to the responsibility of taking planes and crews out across the desert and mountains and getting them safely there. Our only mishap was a broken propeller.

Most of the traveling today was done in a "half-track"—an unusual vehicle half truck half tank that can negotiate the most difficult terrain imaginable. Tomorrow morning I have to aid in a search of our vicinity for a missing air corps plane. We'll send out all the "Grasshoppers" but really can't cover many miles of this territory, as rugged as it is.

June 4, **1943** (*letter excerpt*)

Dearest Bunny,

There are just a few of us left here at division headquarters. We're packing things up at the airport and getting everything but five planes ready to ship. The general has moved out already too along with Colonel Bixby and most of my other bosses. The general gave me a cap that other day, just like the one he wears when he goes flying. Naturally now, I put mine on too when he comes out to take a hop.

We've been having a little tough luck lately in our flying. Last night one of the boys flew our newest plane into some telephone wires over the river. After looking at the plane, especially the wing that had hit the wires, I decided that perhaps we were still one of the luckiest "Grasshopper" crews in the desert.

All of us are keenly interested in our trip to Texas by plane. Although it has been done before by small planes, it is still considered quite an undertaking. I'll be vastly relieved when I get all of them there in one piece at the same time.

June 10, 1943 (*letter excerpt*)

Dearest Bunny,

I'm sitting in one of the tents out at the landing strip. The day has been hot but not unpleasant. In a few minutes I'll call the boys together for last minute instructions for the cross-country flight that begins in the morning. We plan to take off at sunrise and make our way leisurely to Phoenix or Tucson, Arizona, where we expect to spend the first night.

All other men are traveling by troop trains. It takes 36 trains to move our 4th Armored Division from California to Texas. Tomorrow it will be "Good Day!" from Arizona or New Mexico

Love and Kisses, Charlie

Unfortunately, less than a week later, there would be only "sad days" for the Carpenter family. The hope that Lois and the rest of the Carpenter clan had held out for their beloved Gene faded in an instant the moment Lois digested the typed words on the piece of paper handed to her. In a telegram received on Wednesday, June 16, 1943, from the War Department in Washington, Lois Carpenter officially learned the fate of her youngest son Eugene; he had died at the age of twenty-seven in a Japanese prisoner of war camp, Osaka Main Camp, Chikko, Osaka, on June 11, 1943. That information was later rescinded and updated by the War Department via a letter dated November 29, 1945. The body of that letter stated:

I am writing you relative to the communication from this office in which you were regretfully informed that your son, First Lieutenant Eugene H. Carpenter, 0396376, Air Corps, died as a result of acute enteritis. The distress you have suffered since you received the sad announcement of his death is most understandable. As stated in my previous letter, the initial report received in his case disclosed that he died in a Japanese Prisoner of War camp, but failed to give the exact date of his death. Now that our forces are in control of all former Japanese-held areas, authentic information has become available which reveals that his death occurred on 28 January 1943. The report further states that the cause of his death was acute colonic catarrh.

My continued sympathy is with you in the great loss you have sustained.

Sincerely yours,
Edward F Witseil
Major General
Acting The Adjutant General of the Army

Lois Carpenter had become, like many other mothers before her of loved ones killed in combat, a "Gold Star" mother. In due course she placed the gold star atop one of the blue ones that hung in her window that represented Gene's military service, showing the world and her neighbors that one of Reynolds' own had paid the ultimate sacrifice. She held out hope that her oldest son Charles's star would forever remain blue.

June 17, 1943 (*letter excerpt*)

Dearest Bunny,
Here are a few hurried lines to let you know that I'm well and happy and heading home at midnight tomorrow night.
   The trip by plane from California to Texas was pleasant indeed, but uneventful. The countryside here has trees and grass and looks something like Illinois. But the humidity makes the heat more oppressive than the greater temperatures of the dessert. I surely am eager to see my two darlings in Moline, even if one does cry and shrink back when I come breezing in.

It had been almost fifteen months since Charles had held Elda in his arms. Now back in Moline he had to share those loving hugs with a complete stranger—his daughter, Carol Ann. Charles wasted no time reacclimating himself with his family and his mother. Catching up on all the news, the conversations usually turned toward the death of his brother Gene and what a tremendous blow it was to the family. But as a Carpenter, they did not wear their emotions on their sleeves and showed no sentiment publicly.
   As he visited old friends and colleagues, those that had not left for military service, Charles began to settle back into a routine. But it was the day-to-day dose of news found in the *Moline Daily Dispatch* that caused him to question some of the unpatriotic events that were occurring in our country. While Elda made a grocery list, thanks in part to the latest A&P Super Market ad that reminded shoppers to avoid the July 7 ration rush and the expiration of blue ration stamps K, L, and M. Other important dates on

rationing included the limited availability of meat, processed fruits, and vegetables, shoes, sugar, coffee, stoves, and gasoline. Charles focused on the headlines. One front-page item proclaimed, "Coal mines shut again!" with another disturbing, attention-grabbing title of "Race Riots in Detroit; 7 dead, 200 hurt" right under it. Charles Carpenter, who had been caught up in his duty to serve this country, was utterly disgusted by some of its citizens. The only real news that brought any sense of joy to him were the war reports. These included several articles, like "Soviets hammer Nazi airdromes," "Germany can be defeated in the air this year," "Red planes raid enemy railheads," and "Reports 14 Nazi U-Boats sunk in last two weeks."[3] He had hoped the war would end by the time he had to return to his unit and L-4 Cub airplanes he oversaw. But that was not to be. His challenges ahead were unknown. The only thing Charles did know was how lucky he truly was to have such a lovely wife and baby daughter. Those memories would be like cherished souvenirs that kept him focused on why he was a soldier, the duties he performed, and the enormous responsibilities it carried with it to ensure the freedoms of his family and his country would never be jeopardized.

CHAPTER 11

Sharpening the Sword

July 3, 1943 (*letter excerpt*)

Dearest Bunny,

I'm waiting at the station in Fort Worth. The trip has been rather tiresome, but that is partly because I'm leaving so many good times and sweet memories behind as the wheels click off the miles. I'll miss you and Carol Ann more than ever now that I've spent several weeks at home with you. I do expect to be quite busy for a while though and that will help keep my mind from straying homeward too much so that the "Blues" pester me.

July 6, 1943 (*letter excerpt*)

Dearest Bunny,

Just got a phone call saying that the general will be out in a few minutes to fly. He comes out almost every day to look over some problem or maneuver from the air. He expects me to pilot him each time, so that is probably one of the more important features of my job here.

Our airport is quite a busy place most days. We dropped over 200 lbs. of flour in paper bags yesterday to simulate a bombing attack on the Red forces in a problem here. Flew out in a plane and landed near Lake Brownwood in a pasture and had a ticklish moment or two on the take off when I thought a herd of long-horned cattle were going to charge me before I could get off the ground. They seemed to resent the plane a great deal.

From the way conditions are right at present, it appears that the 4th Armored will be at Camp Bowie for some time, perhaps as long as six months.

July 10, 1943 (*letter excerpt*)

Dearest Bunny,

The 4th Armored Division held a big review this morning and the general spoke to us afterward. I had never seen all our men assembled in one group before. Needless to say, 14,000 men is quite an impressive group, at least so far as size is concerned. I marched by in review as one of the members of the Division Artillery Commanders staff.

Today I flew above the clouds again for the thrill and beauty of it all. Once the shadow of the plane was right in the center of a rainbow on top of a cloud. I'm looking forward to taking you with me someday. There are castles in the air and fairylands below that you must see.

July 18, 1943 (*letter excerpt*)

Dearest Bunny,

My duties are somewhat the same as in the desert-managing an airport and handling flying missions for eight small planes. This morning, I flew in a three-plane formation that bombed one of our own Field Artillery Battalions while it was on the march. Of course the bombs were only paper sacks filled with flour, but they had to react as if we were real enemy planes and the bombs real bombs.

Some days we are the enemy and try to catch our troops napping. Other days we fly missions to aid our battalions in every possible way—letting officers see how their outfits look from the air, adjusting the fire of the big guns, dropping and picking up messages on the go, running errands, and lots of other jobs.

Sweetheart, I am one of the luckiest guys in the whole world. One of the best breaks I ever got was when I captured you and later, through you, Carol Ann. If my luck doesn't wear out I'll have you both for a long time yet too.

August 16, **1943** (*letter excerpt*)

Dearest Bunny,

Have been working on a course for training aerial observers. Colonel Bixby visited the opening class today and complimented me on it. He said that he even got interested himself in spite of the heat and burning sun.

We are being tested and checked a lot lately in many ways. I don't know what it all amounts too, but it does keep us on the move. Thank heaven that I drive an airplane instead of a tank under these conditions.

Just finished taking a carbine apart and putting it back together for the first time. Went out on the range and fired my new pistol several days ago. I've been issued field glasses, compass, pistol, mess kit, shelter tent, and lots of other small items that I can scarcely keep track of, and some of which I do not know how to use very well yet.

Last evening I went through the infiltration course for the first time. It is an imitation battlefield with trenches, barbed wire, TNT exploding beside you, real machine gun bullets whizzing just above your head, and choking dust and smoke everywhere. It looks like some movie set Hollywood would fix up for a battle scene.

September 6, **1943** (*letter excerpt*)

Dearest Bunny,

Rumors are in the air again about us moving. Gee! Just returned from my evening flying chores. Demonstrated methods of air-ground communications to a group of officers over at the parade ground. First we gave a smoke signal and were answered with smoke. Then we used flashing lights, read panels on the ground, communicated by radio, shot off flares, and dropped and picked up messages. The whole demonstration went off very smoothly.

Flew both Colonel Bixby and General Wood on missions. Some days I'm practically nothing but a chauffeur. Flying is much smoother and more pleasant of late, although it is beginning to bore me a little occasionally.

The message pickup that Charles demonstrated from his low-flying L-4 Cub was performed using a braided, 40-foot rope that was attached to a large, three-pronged, barbed grappling hook. As the L-4 dove below the tree line, Charles set his sights on the soldiers ahead of him who were holding two 12-foot poles spread 15 feet apart. A thin black wire was strung between the poles with a small canvas message pouch attached to it. With bomber pilot-like precision, Charles held the Cub rock steady as the observer in the back lowered the hook and snatched the message skyward, and wound it up into the back of the L-4.

September 30, 1943 (*letter excerpt*)

Dearest Bunny,
Just at this moment I'm riding along about 400 ft. above the ground heading for Fort Sill. I'm taking the inspector, Captain Hatch, to Sill by plane. He has been doing the flying. Since most of the scenery looks the same here, I got bored after about 2 hrs. flying and so this letter.

We landed back some distance and poured 5 gallons of gas that we were carrying, into the plane.

The field we landed on had about 20 planes there already with women pilots from the school at Sweetwater, Texas. One of them tried to crank our airplane when we left, but didn't have quite enough "oomph." We just flew through a shower of rain, but now are out in the sunlight again.

The women fliers Charles met that day were known as Women Airforce Service Pilots (WASPs). In 1939, Jacqueline "Jackie" Cochran, a world-record-setting air-racing pilot, who many considered the best female pilot in the United States, proposed to the Army Air Force the use of female pilots in noncombat missions. Turned down by the all-male airforce, Cochran set sail for Britain to immerse herself and study the Air Transport Auxiliary (ATA), where civilian pilots, including women, were already ferrying military aircraft for the Royal Air Force (RAF).

When the United States entered the war, Cochran's proposal to recruit and train women as pilots became the Women's Flying Training Detachment (WFTD).

A fellow female aviatrix, Nancy Harkness Love, had also foreseen the need for more pilots. Love proposed the idea of an elite group of America's best and brightest female aviators, who could quickly be trained to fly military airplanes for the various branches. Beginning with just twenty-eight pilots, Love's proposal became the Women's Auxiliary Ferry Squadron (WAFS). In 1943, the two programs merged to become the WASP.

Motivated by a desire to serve their country and fly, more than 25,000 women applied for the WASP program between 1942 and 1944. Criteria were stringent as only the "best of the best" were desired. Of the 1,830 that were accepted, 1,078 completed training. WASP recruits came from all walks of life. From millionaires to teachers, clerks, students, office workers, and dirt-poor girls who worked very hard just to buy an hour's worth of flight training. They all had one thing in common, the love of flight.

As civilian employees, every WASP had to pay her way and had to buy most of their equipment. In contrast, their male counterparts were supplied most of their equipment from Uncle Sam. Beginning in 1943, recruits were trained at Avenger Field in Sweetwater, Texas. Though all of them had earned pilot certificates before enlisting, they were taught to fly "the Army way," receiving advanced training in navigation, meteorology, aircraft mechanics, and other aviation subjects. WASP recruits were subject to the same military regulations and training as their male counterparts. None of them, however, were trained to be combat pilots.

The WASPs flew more than 60 million miles, crisscrossing the United States in a variety of military aircraft for the US Army Air Forces before the last class graduated on December 7, 1944. Less than two weeks later, the program was terminated.

October 23, 1943 (*letter excerpt*)

Dearest Bunny,

It has been a good week for our air section. Today we had what amounts to a final exam for our air observers. We have been training them for about six weeks. Almost without exception, they did a fine job of firing their problems from the planes. Colonel Bixby was very pleased and therefore I was pleased also.

My sergeant pilot (Roy) Carson is away on furlough. He is the other pilot in the Division Artillery Air Section besides myself. He will be commissioned a second lieutenant soon. The other six pilots belong to their Field Artillery Battalions.

The half dozen other pilots that Charles oversaw including Roy Carson, who hailed from San Francisco, California, along with a fellow by the name of Robert Pearson, originally from Toledo, Ohio. Pearson, who had enlisted in the army in January 1941, was deemed unfit for pilot training due to being colorblind. Pearson recalled his earlier days in the military and how he overcame that obstacle:

> I couldn't be an officer or a pilot. So of course I had those two goals in mind for my military career, but they sent me to Aerial Photography School, which at least got me off the ground. But when I finished that, I realized that riding as a passenger and clicking a camera was not my idea of what I wanted to do. So I saw on the bulletin board that they were looking for glider pilots. So apparently glider pilots can be colorblind, so I almost finished the course before they canceled it. They had many more glider pilots than they needed, so we went in a pool of hundreds of "almost glider pilots." And then I saw that they were looking for liaison pilots in the artillery. I signed up for that and had about two hundred hours before they discovered that I was colorblind. I convinced the surgeon that I hadn't had any accidents up to that point, and that I should be allowed to fly, and that it would be a big expense on the government to waste all that time and money on me. So they OK'd me and I joined the 4th Armored Division, 22nd Armored Field Artillery Battalion, in the Mojave Desert.[1]

And like Charles Carpenter, Pearson and Carson would soon make names for themselves in England and France. Another California flier, Harley Merrick, from Richmond, California, would tag-team with Carson and Pearson in England on fitting their Cubs with "a defensive weapon" and utilize their experiment to the fullest in France. A Charles Damon from Ames, Iowa, followed a similar path to the sky, including attending glider training in Stuttgart, Arkansas, in early 1943, then, like Charles Carpenter, transferring to Fort Sill to become a liaison pilot before joining the 4th Armored Division. There would be more hair-raising adventure—some good, some bad—for Damon in France the following year, including being chased by a gaggle of German Me 109 fighters who blasted away at his slow moving L-4. Other pilots included another hailing from Colfax, Iowa, named John Maher, who later christened his L-4 Cub with the nose art of "Dizzy Lizzy." Eventually, two other pilots, lieutenants Wade and Bower, rounded out Carpenter's rag-tag bunch of Grasshopper fliers.

But before the Cub pilots could successfully enter the war zone, they needed to teach a new observer corps the "do's and don'ts" of spotting artillery. That was an art in and of itself. The first step was to get the observer used to flying. Some of the men would lose their sense of direction even after a few gentle turns, so it was important to allow the observer to become accustomed to this. If the pilot felt comfortable, then the pilot would fire several artillery missions allowing the observer to study techniques. Some of these included a thorough understanding of "no-fire line," location of infantry front lines, and proposed attacks or counterattacks. The observer was also responsible for understanding the purpose of the mission, looking for enemy tanks, enemy batteries, targets of opportunity, or firing an artillery mission. Even if no targets were discovered, the observer had the responsibility to be aggressive in all things observation. That meant he had to assert himself and his aerial platform with the offer to fire direction control to go hunt for targets. As one officer stated, "We can't win the war squatting in the shade under the wing of our planes."

November 5, 1943 (*letter excerpt*)

Dearest Bunny,
About 4:30 in the morning I shall find my way to the airport. There Sergeant Pearson and I shall take off along a row of lanterns to chase a hydrogen-filled balloon across the sky. With the aid of thermometers, a barometer, and other items, we shall compute the wind direction, wind velocity, temperature, relative humidity, and the density of the air. This information will be radioed to the guns ten miles away and used by them in firing on an unseen target over the heads of our own troops.

December 2, 1943 (*letter excerpt*)

Dearest Bunny,
Another day passed and I'm still waiting for something to happen. Was down on the range firing my pistol this afternoon. I was real "hot" and won sixteen bottles of beer from my fellow officers. I have a fine new pistol and I'm proud of it.

December 6, **1943** (*letter excerpt*)

Dearest Bunny,

My old bones are pretty stiff and sore today. Was playing touch football yesterday and fell pretty hard on the rocky ground several times. Some days I feel every one of my 31 years.

Colonel Bixby has already departed for our next destination. It will probably be a matter of a week or more for the rest of us now.

The prospect of going to war does not yet bother me in the least; I have been playing and loafing so long with the army that I feel I owe some hardships and discomfort in return. I have been such a lucky fellow for so many years that I have no reason to expect my luck will change now.

The end of a lot of things is in sight, most of them bad, a few of them good. Each time I see you, you have been steadier and wiser. May you always keep the firm grasp on life that I think you now have.

Utilizing twenty-two trains to transport the division, the men began to board their respective train cars for their journey to the East Coast and their destination of Camp Myles Standish in Taunton, Massachusetts. Not all the trains, however, took the same route. Some of them traveled north before turning east, while others headed south before turning back to the northeast. This was to confuse any foreign spies that may have reported back on the 4th's movements.

December 17, **1943** (*letter excerpt*)

Dearest Bunny,

I have been traveling quite a bit. After a four-day train ride through sunshine and snow, I finally ended up in one of the New England states. Don't be too disappointed at my telling you that our train passed right through Moline about 7:30 p.m. last Tuesday evening. It did bring a lump to my throat to almost see the lights of home and yet be so far away in other respects. So much secrecy attends troop movements that practically no one of the train knows where it will end up. In fact, of all the trains it will take to move our outfit, scarcely any two will follow the same route. At present writing is a problem. Do you know that I'm not even permitted to use X's for kisses because it might be used as a code message?

The use of V-mail was introduced during World War II not only to reduce the weight of mail from soldiers outside the United States but to once and for all deal with censorship concerns. "Loose lips sink ships" was a rallying cry here in the United States, warning its citizens, especially those in the service or working as government employees or contractors, that any divulgence of secrets or unit locations could cost lives. The quarter-size envelopes and letters known as V-mail took away and circumvented soldiers from writing home in code. Some tried the use of milk, Coca-Cola, diluted aspirin and water, sugar water, and even urine to write secret messages home that could be read under ultraviolet conditions or heat. The censors soon found themselves overwhelmed until V-mail was created. When a soldier wrote a letter home, the original was microfilmed and shrunk. The original was burned—therefore no remnant of secret writing remained.

CHAPTER 12

Strangers in a Strange Land

As Charles and his fellow 4th Armored Division soldiers boarded one of the five ships anchored in Boston harbor (HMS *Britannic*, and *Queen Elisabeth*, SS *Oriente*, SS *Exchange*, and *Santa Rosa*), that would take them across the North Atlantic on a very similar route that the *Titanic* had taken several months before Charles was born in 1912. This time, however, the enemy was not only icebergs but Nazi U-boats that operated in "Wolf Packs" and stalked the frigid waters where the Allied ships plied. For the next eleven days, the convoy of ships endured heavy swells and almost constant zig-zagging. As an officer, Charles was crammed in a cabin with other officers, while the enlisted men slept in hammocks below decks as each ship was stuffed to the gills with men and equipment. To pass the time, dice and card games were about the only entertainment besides betting on who would get seasick next. Freshwater was reserved for cooking and drinking only, so if a soldier wanted a shower, it was a cold saltwater rinse at best. The only thing the men had in common after eleven days at sea was their rancid body odor as the coast of England came into view.

January 9, **1944** (*letter excerpt*)

Dearest Bunny,
Arrived safely after a pleasant but rather dull trip; we've been at anchor almost a day already. I really don't know why we haven't left the ship yet. The air is damp and misty, just about as I had expected to find it. This moment I have exactly two cents to my name. After tipping the steward and our table waiter, I had two dollars and two

cents. I just lost the two dollars in a poker game, and yet I still have the problem of disposing of the two cents to face. Everyone has so much baggage and equipment to carry that I can't even give my two pennies away.

January 16, 1944 (*letter excerpt*)

Dearest Bunny,

At last I am able to write to you again. You and mom are just about the only correspondents I have these days. That is all right too, because writing is certainly a problem with all the "dos" and "don'ts" attached.

My latest roommates are a Major Pickard from Texas and a Captain Smith from Ohio. Our living conditions are rather rigorous, far better than what I expected to find. It's cold and damp and foggy nearly all the time. But still this part of England is as beautiful as anything I have ever seen. Every block has its picture-postcard scene. The garden's thatched cottages, ancient churches, dark forest, and rolling green hills are more beautiful than the pictures I've seen. The people are extremely intelligent and courteous, even though a bit tired and worn looking.

We are fortunate enough to have a radio, and the programs broadcast by the Germans and British are comprised almost entirely of wonderful music played by symphony orchestras and sung by opera companies.

Our diet is going to take a bit of getting used to, featuring as it does, mostly canned and dehydrated products. Still I'm hungrier at mealtimes than in the USA. So everything tastes just as good. How true it is that thirst is the best wine and hunger still the best sauce.

Someday I'll tell you a million things that I'd better not right now. Among them will be some of the better ways of saying I love you than with pen and ink oceans away. Yours is still the hardest job. But how you have stood up to it.

Good night, sweetheart.
Charles

Besides the symphony and opera music Charles enjoyed, if he tuned into the German radio programs, he also had to endure the likes of "Lord Haw

Haw" (William Joyce) and "Axis Sally" (Mildred Gillars), who spewed out
Nazi propaganda to its Allied listeners as well as American songs. Determined
to break the spirit of the Allied soldiers by claiming inflated combat losses
of airplanes shot down, ships sunk or men killed on the battlefields, most
of the soldiers paid little attention to their lies. Although homesick, many
soldiers simply enjoyed the music that reminded them of home and the
loved ones they were fighting for.

January 31, **1944** (*letter excerpt*)

Dearest Bunny,
Life has become full again. And I was flying this morning and fog so
thick that I had to stay down at treetop level to see the ground. It isn't
necessary generally that we fly under such conditions, but sometimes
we get caught a little ways from the home field.

We have an air raid alarm occasionally, but haven't seen anything
more than Searchlight scanning the sky. I've had opportunities to see
that part of England within 20 or 30 miles of where we are located.
What I've seen has been beautiful and most interesting indeed, especially to a history instructor.

March 7, **1944** (*letter excerpt*)

Hello, Bunny:
I know several British officers quite well now and enjoy their company
very much. The difference between the two peoples are much smaller
that many believe. In general are every bit as small as those between
a person from Vermont and a person from Alabama.

Outside the planes are droning in the sky as they do day and night.
Last night an enemy plane crashed in flames not far from us. We see
many indications of the war, but, as yet, seem to play no part in it.

Thousands of Allied airplanes of all shapes and sizes, some with single
engines, some with two, and others with four massive radial engines that
could haul several thousands of pounds of bombs from England deep in to
Germany were spread out across the entire English continent at hastily built
airfields. B-17 Flying Fortresses, B-24 Liberators, A-20 Havocs and B-26
Mauraders, shepherded by P-51 Mustangs, P-47 Thunderbolts, P-38

Lightnings, Spitfires, and Hurricanes joined their British counterparts in de Havilland Mosquitos, Lancasters, Blenheims, and Wellingtons as they flew around the clock on either deep penetration missions to industrial targets and military targets located deep inside Axis held territory, or to the shores of Normandy and several miles inland where they pounded German rail and troop concentrations.

But it just wasn't a one-sided battle as the German Luftwaffe, still stinging from huge losses of fighters and bombers during the Battle of Britain, continued to send German night raiders and V-1 rockets over populated areas as they continued their torturous destruction and harassment of the stoic and battle-hardened British subjects.

March 19, 1944 (*letter excerpt*)

Hello Bunny,
London is probably the most interesting and amazing city in the world. Soldiers of all nations, but mostly Americans, throng the streets. The bombs still fall, the blackout is a thing of wonder, but the antiaircraft and protective system is more than a match for the weakening efforts of the Germans to retaliate for the terrible air blows we are striking at the Reich.

March 28, 1944 (*letter excerpt*)

Hello! Bunny, Sweetheart:
I used up a lot of my luck this morning—two or three bad landings, a close takeoff and a near collision in the fog. Don't think it's like that every day because most of my days are uneventful. Everything seemed to be all wrong except my luck. That has been right for as long as I can remember.

April 1, 1944 (*letter excerpt*)

Hello! Bunny:
Got lost in the fog the other morning and I climbed above it into the sunlight. Cruised about for more than two hours looking for a hole to come down through. I was in radio contact with our ground units the whole time. I finally landed in an ammunition dump about 50 miles away. I still had 10 minutes of gas left.

Flying in England during wartime in clear skies was dangerous enough for an L-4 pilot. With fighters and bombers operating at countless bases across the island nation, an L-4 pilot had to have his head on a swivel. Add the fact that steel cables tethered barrage balloons near military bases, intended to keep any low-flying Luftwaffe airplanes at bay. But when the haze and fog rolled in, which at times seemed more frequent than not, the pilots flying in it, were at its mercy. There were far more aircraft downed or destroyed by accidents, weather, or training than there were in combat.

April 5, 1944 (*letter excerpt*)

Dearest Bunny,
I'm actually writing to you sitting in one of the planes. Since the wind is blowing rather hard and since there are cattle in this field, it seemed best that I stay with the plane. I'm waiting for Major Hasselback to return from an official visit to another artillery headquarters located not far from us.

Just a few minutes ago, I refused a ride to a small boy who came running out. Once in a while I take them for a short ride, but it was too windy this afternoon.

It seems that I have been away from home so long this time. I hope everything is still well with you and Carol Ann. Other than you two, I have scarcely a care in the world. When you are well, all is well with me.

Before leaving for England, Field Artillery Air Sections left their aircraft stateside and were assigned new aircraft by the artillery air officers when they arrived in England. The Piper L-4 was the primary liaison aircraft assigned to the European theater of operations (ETO). Piper L-4A and B models began arriving in England in 1942, followed by L-4Hs in 1943 and 1944. One particular Piper L-4H (Piper J3C-65D) bearing serial number 11717 and a military registration of 43-30426 was given the fuselage serial number 11543. It was built on April 10, 1944, at the Piper plant in Lock Haven, Pennsylvania, with standard equipment that consisted of a 65 hp Continental Motors A65-85 that swung a Sensenich wooden 72C-42 propeller. The round wooden wingtip bows were handcrafted by the local Amish carpenters as they provided their talents for the war effort.

Because it was an army aircraft, it came furnished with a standard military instrument panel. This included a B-16 compass, C-11 tachometer, B-12 altimeter, and B-8 airspeed indicator.

Its total empty weight came in at 722 pounds. After its test flight by a Piper pilot, the Army Air Force completed the necessary acceptance paperwork for the L-4H to become the property of Uncle Sam. Most L-4s were disassembled and placed in large wooden crates for overseas shipping.

Piper 43-30426 was transported by train to the port of New York, where it was loaded on a ship and departed the United States on April 21, 1944. Bound for England, this L-4H arrived in early May, where it was assigned to the Army Ground Forces and assigned to the 4th Air Division where it was given a fuselage code of 53-K. This particular L-4H was eventually assigned to one Maj. Charles M. Carpenter.

April 27, 1944 (*letter excerpt*)

Hello! Bunny:
Troops must be coming to England in large numbers. One could scarcely toss a stone in a large part of England without hitting a soldier or military vehicle. I just returned drawing my rations. It included seven packages of cigarettes, a package of gum, two candy bars, several magazines, and a package of cookies. The English are generally very much impressed with the attention given to the American soldier insofar as food, clothing, and morale are concerned.

By January 1944, there were over 750,000 US military men spread out across England. By late May that number doubled to over 1,500,000 soldiers and airmen as they prepared for the invasion of occupied France. Tanks, Jeeps, planes, trucks, ships, weapons, and assorted supplies littered the countryside. The British certainly took notice of the "overpaid, oversexed, over here" soldiers that mingled with the British citizenry. Most American soldiers' salaries were as much as five times greater than those of their British counterparts. British women became the center of attention for many American soldiers and by the time the war ended, more than 70,000 of them became GI brides.

May 3, **1944** (*letter excerpt*)

Hello, Bunny:
Just returned from a training flight to a nearby unit. We are giving
instructions to air observers who may have to ride with us later.

I suppose you will notice my new way of signing my name—major.
It doesn't make me feel at all different, and my job is still pretty much
the same.

May 14, **1944** (*letter excerpt*)

Greetings, Bunny, Dear:
Today is Mother's Day. I found out just a little while ago. Carol Ann
was pretty lucky I think in getting the mother that she did. As far as
her father, I sometimes have my doubts about him.

I take quite a few trips by plane and spend considerable time on
field problems. I flew across the mountains of Wales all the way to
the sea. On the return trip we crossed about 12 miles of open water
between England and Wales.

May 16, **1944** (*letter excerpt*)

Dearest Bunny,
The rain is puttering on the office roof now, and it seems quite cozy
here inside. In view of the weather now, I'm glad that my proposed
flight with the General did not come off. The General (Woods) invited
me to lunch yesterday and chatted with me about the Air Section. The
Air Section still comes in for its share of attention from him, but he
doesn't fly as much as he did in the U.S.A.

Gen. John Wood was of course, as all generals were, slightly eccentric. He
lived in a tent, in the same manner that any lieutenant, sergeant, or private
would. It was somewhat embarrassing to other generals who outranked him,
like Patton, or Montgomery, who had their own railroad cars or chateaus.
While fighting in Europe in October 1944, witnessing his primitive conditions, an air force general had sent General Wood a house trailer van that
other senior general officers used in the field. General Wood, however, chose
not to sleep in the said trailer and instead remarked, "My people are living

in the mud, and if they can live and fight in it, I can do work in it as well." General Wood was a soldier first and would live in a simple two-man tent like the men he oversaw—mud, rain, cold, snow, and all.

May 24, 1944 (*letter excerpt*)

Dearest Bunny,
I guess I haven't been thinking very far ahead lately. Invasion time will be sure to be rough on plenty of soldiers and, of course, I could be one of them. I any case I want you to be sure and do what planning you can now for yourself and Carol Ann in case something unfortunate did happen to me.

June 5, 1944 (*letter excerpt*)

Dearest Bunny,
We've moved out of the barracks into tents. I live at the airfield for the first time since joining the Division. Our airport is a beautiful green cow pasture without any cows. Our barracks will be a hospital during invasion time. Naturally I'm not looking forward to any return trip here. Damon, my assistant, has just received his promotion to captain. He is a good man and does my work and his too very well.

While Charles sat in relative comfort writing his latest letter home, his former glider training companion, Lt. Dempsey Weaver, sat strapped at the control of a large Waco CG-4A glider, many of them hastily painted with black-and-white-colored zebra stripes that ran vertically along the wings and fuselage to distinguish friend from foe. Lt. Weaver's glider was tethered to the tail of a twin-engine C-47 transport that would act as its mother ship and tow the glider over the English Channel from its base in England to its intended drop zone somewhere near Normandy. Behind him sat a handful of airborne division troops, all slinging half their weight in combat assault gear and equipment. By the time Dempsey's glider was cut loose from the C-47, German antiaircraft shell bursts, and small arms fire filled the sky. Dempsey later remarked:

We landed okay in spite of the terrific Nazi gunfire. We put all our stuff in a jeep and trailer that we took over with some paratroopers in a ditch—and just in time too. A German 88-millimeter gun made a direct hit on the jeep and the whole thing went up. After that, we went around with the paratroopers knocking off Nazi machine-gun positions until we got relief from amphibious landing forces.

Three days later, Dempsey and the remaining surviving pilots returned to England where they would later be presented with the Air Medal for their role during D-Day and began preparing for more glider missions, including one over Holland as part of Operation Market Garden. Perhaps the earlier friendship Dempsey had developed between himself and Charles instilled the confidence and mental toughness he needed to overcome anything that was thrown at him. Dempsey Weaver proved to the skeptics and the world that he had what it took to be a soldier and a fearless man. And that same fearlessness also engulfed Charles Carpenter, as he would soon prove his significance as a soldier in a little over a month.

Thursday, June 8, 1944 (*letter excerpt*)

Bunny, Sweetheart:
Of course you know that the big invasion has started. What happens to me in the near future depends on the progress made by our troops. Being an armored division, we are not likely to be employed until a good foothold has been established.

Most of our outfit are pretty tired of practicing war and would like to get in the thick of things if it meant bringing the war to a quicker end. At this particular moment, I'm sitting high on a windy hill in Wales. There are mountains in most directions and sheep everywhere. Periodically the ground shakes with the roar of artillery fire. The sheep are so used to the sound of the big guns they no longer lift their heads.

In several more days we will be back at our own camp again. There of course we are living in the open too. Before we move off, I'll have to get rid of some of my clothes and other possessions. Carrying all my belongings in a bed roll and bag you know will be quite a sacrifice for me. Little did a I dream when I purchased them about six years ago for a camping trip that I would be going to war with them.

You have been a darling as a war wife and mother. I suppose I have done less actual thinking and worrying than you. I've raised hell on occasions and spent more money than I used to make. My luck has always been good but war is a silly mess at best.

When the Allies landed on scattered, heavily defended beaches in Normandy of June 6, 1944, the 4th Armored Division and its men were still firmly planted in England, training for war and anxiously awaiting their orders. The evidence for the soldiers on the ground that "something big" was going on was evident when they saw returning C-47s with tow wires dangling from their tails with nothing attached—for the pilots of the gliders, like Charles's friend Dempsey Weaver, it had been a one-way trip.

July 6, 1944 (*letter excerpt*)

Hello, Bunny:
The war on the continent seems to be going well from our standpoint. At the rate the Russians are advancing it cannot last many more months in Europe.

July 11, 1944 (*letter excerpt*)

Hello Bunny!
Have just completed over six months in England and still kicking up English dust and going nowhere. Haven't heard from you lately, of course, the reason is that none of us have been getting any mail since we moved.
    Fighter planes leave this base every day and generally return without firing their guns for lack of opposition. Still, we seem to be running into plenty of opposition on the ground. I don't see how the Germans can hold out much longer. They might be just mean and stubborn enough to make the European phase of this war last another winter. How's that pretty baby of mine? It's hard to realize I'm a father so many miles from her.

Love and kisses,
Charles

While making last-minute preparations for himself and his cadre of other Grasshopper pilots, including working with the mechanics to make sure the

My Creed

I have resolved to exert all my efforts toward being a nobler and stronger fellow, a gentleman, a scholar, a friend, and a real man. To the best of my ability, I will ever strive for self-control, self-improvement, freedom, wisdom, courage, generosity, truth, and true nobility before gods and men. I will be better.

Charles Marston Carpenter

Charles Carpenter's personal creed, written when he was only seventeen years old, was his guiding light throughout his life. *Courtesy of Carol Apacki*

Poor and proud, the Carpenters used a horse-drawn wagon to move themselves and all of their belongings. *Courtesy of Carol Apacki*

The Carpenter clan. *Back row, from left to right*: Mildred, Margaret, Charles. *Front row, left to right*: Merle, Eugene (Gene), and Helen. *Courtesy of Carol Apacki*

The whitewashed iron gates to the Reynolds Cemetery, where Charles and his young friend encountered "the monster." *Courtesy of Jim Busha*

A proud and stoic Charles Carpenter poses in his Roosevelt Military Academy uniform. *Courtesy of Carol Apacki*

The "Prayin' Colonel," Carpenter was a natural athlete in every sport he played. *Courtesy of Carol Apacki*

Charles Carpenter, *bottom left*, attended four years of Citizen's Military Training Camps (CMTC), earning the title of second lieutenant. *Courtesy of Carol Apacki*

Elda Fritchle strikes a "movie star" pose. Elda soon caught the eye of Charles at a local dance. *Courtesy of Carol Apacki*

The Coliseum Ballroom, on the Davenport, Iowa, side of the river, was where Charles and Elda first met. *Courtesy of Jim Busha*

Newlyweds Elda and Charles traveled to Chicago for their short honeymoon before beginning their lives together in Moline. *Courtesy of Carol Apacki*

A lovestruck Charles and Elda dated for only a short time before they were married. *Courtesy of Carol Apacki*

A confident Charles Carpenter leans against a side-by-side Taylorcraft airplane. The fledgling aviator cut his teeth in this airplane while a member of the Rockets Inc. Flying Club. *Courtesy of Carol Apacki*

Charles received training as an army aviator in a variety of aircraft, including this PT-17 Stearman he is strapped in the back seat of. *Courtesy of Carol Apacki*

Fellow army aviators, *from left to right*, Charles and Dempsey Weaver pose with one of their glider instructors. *Courtesy of Carol Apacki*

Charles, standing in front of an Aeronca L-3, would hone his skills at the control of the light airplane. *Courtesy of Carol Apacki*

Charles, *on the right*, poses with one of his instructors, a Mr. Diehl, alongside the Aeronca L-3s used in training. *Courtesy of Carol Apacki*

The Piper J-3 Cub was a docile, yellow-fabric-covered, tandem two-seat trainer that helped a nation learn to fly. *Courtesy of Jim Busha*

The L-4 Cub was basically a civilian J-3 with a coat of olive drab paint. More like a wolf in sheep's clothing, the L-4 was one of the most feared Allied weapons by the Germans. *Courtesy of Jim Busha*

As part of the 4th Armored Division, Charles's front office was at the controls of the L-4. Here he poses while on desert maneuvers. *Courtesy of Carol Apacki*

As a liaison pilot, the men who earned that honor wore silver wings with a large L on them. These L wings are the actual ones worn by Carpenter. *Courtesy of Jim Busha*

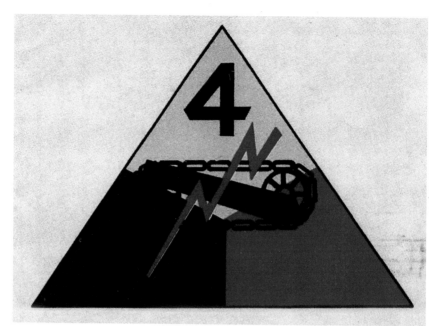

The 4th Armored Division emblem did not carry a nickname, since their commander, Gen. John S. Wood, stated, "They shall be known by their deeds alone." *Courtesy of Carol Apacki*

Carpenter poses next to the pilot board at Ibis Cactus Airport. Located in the barren desert California terrain, this was a perfect location for training large armies. *Courtesy of Carol Apacki*

The front office of an L-4 Cub. Although spartan and utilizing only basic instruments, in the hands of a capable pilot they were deadly fighting machines. *Courtesy of Jim Busha / EAA*

The rear deck area of the L-4 carried an assortment of radios, headsets, microphones, and antennae, all of which used to communicate with artillery units or other army ground forces. *Courtesy of Jim Busha / EAA*

Posing high atop a windswept hill during his desert training days, Carpenter had no idea what he would encounter when he entered the French combat zone in mid-1944. *Courtesy of Carol Apacki*

Carpenter oversaw other liaison pilots, including one named Robert Pearson, standing in the middle wearing dark coveralls. Robert Pearson mimicked Carpenter, on a smaller scale, by mounting two bazookas to his L-4. *Courtesy of Carol Apacki*

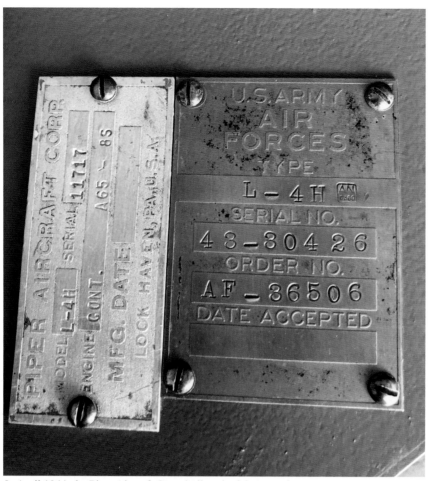

In April 1944, the Piper Aircraft Corp. built one of the most famous L-4s ever produced. Beginning as serial number 11717, and US Army Air Forces serial number 43-30426, this L-4 was later assigned to Carpenter and christened as "Rosie the Rocketer." *Courtesy of Jim Busha*

US Army ground crew members attached three bazookas to the struts of an L-4 while stationed in England. Note the small ferry fuel tank suspended from the roof of the L-4. These were actually modified oxygen bottles used on B-17 Fly Fortresses. *Courtesy of Carol Apacki*

A very stoic-looking Carpenter poses alongside his L-4, "Rosie the Rocketer," in between frontline action. Note the cross-draw shoulder holster with .45-caliber pistol that Charles neglected to leave in the cockpit when he encountered German troops. *Courtesy of Carol Apacki*

Powered by a Continental A65 engine, the L-4 sipped less than 5 gallons an hour. This wartime poster depicts a bazooka-equipped L-4 destroying a column of German trucks. *Courtesy of Jim Busha / EAA*

Carpenter carried a photo of his wife, Elda, and daughter, Carol, while flying his L-4 "Rosie the Rocketer" in combat. *Courtesy of Jim Busha*

The M1A1 bazookas attached to the struts of "Rosie the Rocketer" were loaded with M6A3 HEAT (high explosive antitank) rounds. *Courtesy of Jim Busha*

A rare wartime shot of "Rosie the Rocketer" with six bazooka tubes attached to her struts along with black-and-white "zebra stripes" on the fuselage and wings. These stripes assisted in identifying friend from foe by Allied gunners. *Courtesy of Carol Apacki*

Carpenter poses alongside his six-bazooka-equipped L-4, "Rosie the Rocketer," somewhere in France, in late October 1944. *Courtesy of Carol Apacki*

Carpenter was awarded the Silver Star for his acts of bravery, including leading the charge on top of a Sherman tank while engaging German troops. This is the actual medal presented to Charles Carpenter. *Courtesy of Jim Busha*

Carpenter was also awarded the Air Medal by General Wood for his heroic actions against the Germans. This is the actual medal presented to him. *Courtesy of Jim Busha*

As a frontline liaison pilot, Carpenter did not live like many of the fighter pilots stationed in England, who slept on comfortable beds and lived in large chateaus. Carpenter poses in front of "Rosie the Rocketer," his small canvas tent, and a 4th Armored M5 Stuart light tank along with its crew. *Courtesy of Carol Apacki*

The expression on Carpenter's face show the aging caused by war and its atrocities, which took its toll on the former history teacher. *Courtesy of Carol Apacki*

While French children inspect the interior of "Rosie the Rocketer," Charles and a 4th Armored sergeant pose in front of the L-4. *Courtesy of Carol Apacki*

From left to right: An unknown officer, Lt. Gen. Omar Bradley (*holding map and wearing glasses*), Maj. Gen. John Wood, Lt. Gen. George Patton, and Maj. Gen. Manton Eddy study a map as they determine their next battle order. *Courtesy of US Army*

Carpenter wearing his leather flying helmet, *in the middle*, is flanked by a military policeman on the left and one of the 4th Armored Division chaplains on the right. *Courtesy of Carol Apacki*

A freshly restored "Rosie the Rocketer" rests on a recent blanket of New England snow after a postrestoration flight at the Collings Foundation museum. *Courtesy of Joe Scheil*

Charles and his daughter, Carol, intently look over one of the many books Charles acquired during his lifetime. *Courtesy of Carol Apacki*

A beaming Elda enjoys dinner with her husband, Charles, and daughter, Carol. *Courtesy of Carol Apacki*

Urbana High School history teacher Charles Carpenter poses in front of a map of the United States. *Courtesy of Carol Apacki*

The Carpenter family, Elda, Carol, and Charles, pose for a Christmas card with their furry pets. *Courtesy of Carol Apacki*

Several young boys enjoy the calm waters of the Current River as Charles mans the outboard engine of the flat- bottom boat near his Bay Nothing Camp. *Courtesy of Carol Apacki*

The exuberance of summer youth is captured by Charles as he witnesses some of his Bay Nothing Camp attendees enjoy a cool dip along the Current River. *Courtesy of Carol Apacki*

Carpenter's daughter, Carol, cradles some of the insignias worn by her father during his career in the US Army. *Courtesy of Carol Apacki*

A much-different-looking "Rosie the Rocketer" in civilian colors flies off a grass field in Austria after World War II. *Courtesy of Carol Apacki*

A proud Colin Powers stands alongside his latest warbird restoration, "Rosie the Rocketer." *Courtesy of Ryan Brennecke / EAA*

Carpenter's granddaughter, Erin Pata, re-creates the nose art of "Rosie the Rocketer," which her grandfather flew in World War II. *Courtesy of Carol Apacki*

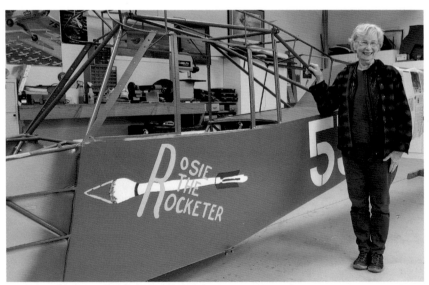

Carol Apacki comes full circle as she physically touches her father Charles's past while admiring her daughter Erin's handiwork re-creating the nose art on "Rosie the Rocketer." *Courtesy of Carol Apacki*

A restored "Rosie the Rocketer" awaits its final placement in the Collings Foundation Museum while surrounded by just a small sample of the collection. *Courtesy of Jim Busha*

Charles Carpenter returned home to his final resting place at the Edgington Cemetery in Illinois. *Courtesy of Jim Busha*

L-4's were mechanically ready to make the jump across the English Channel, Charles gathered many of them at Grove, England. Grove, located west of London, had been turned over to the Ninth Air Force as a repair and modification center.

Several modifications were made to the L-4's before they made their flights across the English Channel. The first was to install an auxiliary fuel tank or a ferry tank. Utilizing an oxygen bottle from a B-17 Flying Fortress, it was determined that this new fuel tank could hold approximately 8 gallons of fuel. Positioned above the observer's seat and fashioned with a Y-clamp and copper tubing, the L-4's were ready to tackle the over 100 miles of the English Channel and any potential headwinds or diversions they may have encountered along the way.

Another modification consisted of installing Plexiglass wing root fairings and a new, rounded bulbous rear upper "turtleneck" that provided the pilot with better visibility from possible rearward attacks by German fighters. Charles also added a rearview mirror, obtained from a twin-engine Lockheed P-38 Lightning, and had that attached directly above the front windscreen, above the cockpit, so he could glance up while flying and spot any incoming threats from his six o'clock.

The final modification was to paint the black-and-white "zebra stripes" on the upper and lower wings and on the fuselage sides to identify the L-4s as friends and not a foe by trigger-happy Allied fighter pilots.

But Charles had also gathered his pilots to determine if it were feasible to mount a bazooka to an L-4 Cub without blowing oneself out of the sky. One of Charles pilots, Robert Pearson, recalled that earlier experiment and stated:

> When we were in England, all the pilots gathered and were discussing, "Could we mount bazookas on our L-4s?" And if we did, would firing a bazooka ignite the tail of our airplane? So we went out on the level ground, away from the camp, landed our Cubs, lifted the tail up, installed a bazooka, used black electrical tape to secure it to the struts, and fired it. Lo and behold, the rocket flew away and we didn't see any fire from the tail end of it. So several of us mounted at least one bazooka, and when we went to the air corp field, awaiting orders to go to Normandy, several of us mounted extras. I mounted a second one, and Charlie Carpenter installed a total of six. To fire them we ran a wire from the bazooka to a battery igniter located in the cabin. A shoulder-fired bazooka on the ground produced a fair amount of

recoil and blowback. But up in the open air, there was nothing. Charles Carpenter and I use to kid one another that we were going to win the war by ourselves—me with two bazookas and him with six.[1]

Unbeknownst to Charles and his pilots, Captain Haynes had earlier tried this same experiment at Grove with an L-4. Installing three 2.3-inch antitank rocket launchers (bazookas) to both the left- and right-wing struts, Haynes coaxed his L-4 high above the English countryside. To hit his intended target, an old abandoned British tank, Haynes had to push the nose of his L-4 almost straight down as he activated the bazookas. Scoring hits, Haynes remarked that "it was a good way not to live through the war."

But Charles and his pilots thought differently. Convinced they could help shorten the war, and defend themselves against the unknown German armor and infantry that waited for them to arrive somewhere in France, Charles sought some last-minute permission from Maj. Charles LeFever, artillery air officer, 1st Army Group. Asked to approve the modification of the at-tached bazookas, Charles explained his reasoning to LeFever and assured him the feasibility of an L-4 Cub as a ground-attack aircraft could be fruitful.

Not simply taking Charles's word for it, LeFever took off in the bazooka-equipped L-4 and found that although the rockets would not "blow the tail off" the L-4 after he fired them, and that they did have some accuracy, he could neither approve nor disapprove their installation.[2] That role fell on Charles and his resilient bazooka-toting pilots.

CHAPTER 13

Leading the Charge

July 23, 1944

Dear Elda,

I'm finally down where the shooting begins. We took a longer hop than usual when we "hopped" the channel to France. It's a good thing that there's a lot more shooting than hitting here, or some of the liaison pilots wouldn't be feeling as good as they do. Most of us have drawn enemy antiaircraft fire on several occasions, but with no other damage than several holes in the fabric. Once, one of the boys was chased down the other day by a German plane. Other than that, we have seen practically no enemy aircraft activity. Our own planes are almost always in service, and always in evidence. The hail of antiaircraft that comes when an enemy plane does appear is indeed something to see and hear. I had a sponge bath and change of clothes yesterday for the first time in over two weeks. It is indeed a thrill and probably shall continue to be so for several days. Although the front is about a mile to two miles ahead of our landing strip, there are still many reminders of fighting. I am well and still have loads of luck I haven't used. Happy Birthday to Carol Ann.

Love, Charles

On the ground, units of the 4th Armored Division began their race across France. As American tanks engaged German armor near Avranches, Major Carpenter and his fellow L-4 pilots directed deadly artillery fire from the air as a bloody slugfest engulfed the French countryside. Two of his pilots, lieutenants Merrick and Carson, attached to the 94th FA (Field Artillery) utilized the effectiveness of surprise and altitude.

As two German cargo trucks were retreating and racing back toward the Fatherland with Sherman tanks hot on their heels, the intrepid aviators, with bazookas strapped to their wing struts, destroyed both of them before they even knew what hit them.

"We figured we ought to have something to shoot with," said Merrick. "And since a machine gun was too heavy for our type of small plane, we got four bazookas from an Army Ordinance depot and went to work."

By August 1, 1944, the 4th Armored Division had already captured more than three thousand German prisoners. Gen. George S. Patton was now at the tiller of the entire Third Army, which comprised the 4th Armored Division as they found themselves at the tip of Patton's spear. Because of their speed and tenacity, the road into Brittany, and more importantly the heart of France, was laid open as Allied ground forces roared inland. The 1944 Armored Command Field Manual stated the following about the armored division:

The armored division is organized primarily to perform missions that require great mobility and firepower. It is given decisive missions. It is capable of engaging in most forms of combat but its primary role is in offensive operations against hostile rear areas. The most profitable role of the armored division is exploitation.

For Charles Carpenter, no truer words were written as his next combat action would forever change who he was as a soldier, man, and husband.

As the division's air artillery officer, Charles was tasked with locating the next suitable landing site for his cadre of 4th Armored Division L-4 Cubs. On August 1, 1944, the German left flank at Avranches began to disintegrate. The 4th Armored, following their Command Field Manual doctrine, knew it was time to exploit the ensuing chaos. As he drove forward in his peep (jeep) scouring the countryside for a patch of land that could accommodate the short-field operations of the L-4, Charles knew that a field with cows grazing on it was more than ideal—that was a telltale sign that it was probably void of German land mines. At that same time, the 6th Armored Division was running parallel to the 4th while the 2nd Armored Division was also close by, all persuing a withdrawing enemy. Confusion and pandemonium ran high on both sides of the line, as artillery rained down on the fleeing Germans, while high- and medium-altitude Eighth Air Force bombers and low-level Ninth Air Force, close-air-support P-51 Mustangs, and P-47 Thunderbolts unleased bombs and rockets on their prey. But some of the Germans did not simply turn tail and run. Several of the battle-hardened units stood their ground against the American and Allied onslaught.

As a pilot, Charles's primary mission was in the air, spotting artillery and scouting the countryside ahead for any trouble. Although he wore the "L" wings of a liaison pilot and operated a fabric-covered 700-pound airplane, he was still a soldier, wearing the same uniform as his brother GIs. Maybe that was why he did what he did without hesitation when he saw the problem ahead.

War correspondent J. Wes Gallagher, writing for the *Stars & Stripes* newspaper, detailed what happened next and how Carpenter kicked a hornet's nest:

> The legend of Carpenter started near Avranches when Patton's army made its first big breakthrough. The major at the time was scouting for a landing ground for observation planes attached to the division when he came upon a tank and infantry formation stymied by 88 fire before a vital town they were supposed to take. Carpenter jumped on the leading tank, grabbed a .50-caliber gun on the outside, fired a burst, yelled, "Let's go," and ordered the attack. Although technically Carpenter had no authority, sheer drive and the .50-caliber got the attack underway and the town was taken in a matter of minutes. It was discovered its only defense was a couple of 88s. Carpenter pushed on the trail of the fleeing Nazi tanks. Every time he came to a corner he stuck his head in the turret, yelled, "Let her go," and the crew cut loose with a 75, which drove the German tanks back to the next corner. As the ground force that Carpenter had been exploiting was not his division, he was placed under arrest and threatened with a firing squad until he was rescued by his own general.[1]

For Charles, there was nothing but confusion and anger. In his mind, he had always done "the right thing." Now the entire playbook and rules had been changed while the "game" (battle) raged on. That great Carpenter luck that had been steadfastly part of his makeup had vanished like a puff of smoke. As a tenacious and ferocious competitor, especially as an athlete, Charles for the first time in his life felt like he had been benched. By the time he had written his letter on August 5, 1944, back home to Elda, he had reached the pit of misery, despair, and hopelessness. As a man of great moral character and a belief he was destined to do great things, the only thing Charles was certain about at that moment was that because he was facing a court-martial and potentially worse, he would probably never see his wife or daughter again. With his character now in question, bruised and battered, Charles was unrecognizable, even to himself. But all of those thoughts swirling around his head while a world war raged hundreds of yards away only added to his bewilderment. His last sentence before saying his good-bye to Elda foretold his belief in that horrible war. *However, the individual should no longer count for much when so much else is at stake.*

What Charles did not realize at the time was that his heroic actions spread like wildfire among the soldiers. It ranged from privates to corporals, corporals to sergeants, and on to lieutenants and majors. Even full-bird colonels smiled at the valiant undertaking of a liaison pilot who many began to dub "the Mad Major." But when word of Charles's folly reached Gen. John S. Wood, Charles's longtime back-seat companion, the general was outright flabbergasted that "his pilot" who had displayed untold courage was being held back from the war because he commandeered another division's damn tank! General Wood had even greater plans for Charles and was not about to let his star player sit out the war.

By August 6, Carpenter, licking his emotional wounds, was back at the controls of his L-4 Cub reporting to only one person—Gen. John Wood. Charles did not waste his time feeling sorry for himself. He had a renewed fire burning in his stomach and focused on only one thing—getting this damn war over as soon as possible. With his past escapade now spreading like a prairie brush fire, Charles soon endured the wrath of several nicknames that the Allied press corps began to earmark him with.

Several reporters referred to him as "Lucky Carpenter" or "Bazooka Charlie," while others gave him the title of "the Mad Major." Charles, never one to seek acclaim or notoriety, shrugged off the remarks and focused on his task at hand. On one such early reconnaissance mission, Charles was accompanied in his L-4 Cub by a *New York Sun* reporter by the name of Gault Mac Gowan who was also writing for the *Stars & Stripes* newspaper. As they circled at treetop level over the inland port of Quimperle, halfway between Quimper and Lorient, Mac Gowan reported the following passage:

Carpenter came low over the city, skimmed rooftops, flew down city streets, zoomed over the wharves, waved his hand to the gendarmes on traffic duty. People tumbled out of their houses, "Les Americaines, Les Americaines," we know they were saying. They had recognized our markings. They knew we were friends.[2]

But not everyone on French soil was friendly or welcoming of the American liberators. Several of Charles's fellow 4th Armored Division GIs, including A Company, 8th Tank Battalion, Sherman tank commander Len Kylie from Massachusetts, along with L-4 pilot Robert Pearson, who was assigned to the 22nd FA (Field Artillery) whom Charles oversaw and supervised during their time in Texas while on maneuvers, witnessed firsthand the tenacity of German armor and its vulnerabilities to a bazooka-equipped Cub. Both Len and Robert recall one incident in early August where both armor and air-power worked in unison to destroy their targets: "As far as I was concerned the guys I respected the most were the FOs (Flying Observers)," said Len. "Those guys use to do one hell of a job."[3]

Len recalled one incident when he saw a "little L-4 Cub" with a pair of bazooka's tied to its wings:

As a Sherman tank commander, I along with several other Shermans were called up to take care of a problem. The problem was two German Panzer tanks that were coiled near a farmyard. The Germans definitely held the advantage over us as they were on higher ground while we sat on the low ground figuring our next move.

Unable to advance, knowing the Panzer's longer guns and higher muzzle velocity had a farther reach than that of the 75 mm gun carried on the Sherman, Len called for artillery to take care of his little problem blocking their company's advance. Expecting to see incoming artillery shells exploding in the farmyard, Len was surprised by what he witnessed next:

Suddenly this L-4 came low over my right shoulder, flying at full speed heading for the German tanks. Almost instantly at the same time, I saw smoke and heard an explosion, and I thought, "that's him, he's had it." And the seconds seemed like hours when miraculously this L-4 came back toward me over my left, and I wondered, "What the hell is going on up there?" Then there was a second explosion.

4th Armored Division L-4 pilot Robert Pearson picks up the action from here:

I got a call from a fire direction center that there had been a request to shoot at some tanks in a certain area. Center could not give me exact coordinates, but I was told to look at the area and find them. Once overhead, I found two German tanks that were sitting by a big barn. As I gave them the once-over, I realized that since I'm already here, I decided it was now or never to use the two bazookas I had strapped to my wing struts. I crossed over the top of the tanks quickly, as quick as the 65 hp engine would give me, and made a quick turn with the L-4 and came back around to shoot. Beforehand, me and Charlie (Carpenter) figured if there was any way a bazooka was going to hit a tank, the best shot was low and from the rear.

As I made my 180-degree turn, I came in low. I was between 25 and 35 feet off the ground. Low altitude was a big advantage to us because by the time we go by a problem it was harder for the Germans on the ground to lead us. I aimed for the first tank, toggled the electrical switch in the cockpit, and watched the first bazooka round streak towards the target. I cranked the Cub back around and made a second pass at the other tank. At 100 yards or so away, I fired my second bazooka and got the hell out of there because I was in dangerous territory. The thing to remember in combat is that when you are shooting at somebody in enemy-held territory, you take the shot and leave. Some guys forgot that lesson as they made multiple passes and got shot down by small arms fire. My motto was, "Shoot these bastards and get out of there!"

As I zoomed away, I was convinced at the time that I had missed both tanks. When I called in the coordinates to our fire direction center, I was told simply that the mission had been canceled, so I went about my business looking for other trouble. The only person that ever got upset with me was my mechanic. He accused me of wasting government money because we couldn't see what we'd had done.[4]

As Lieutenant Person climbed for altitude in his L-4, Len Kylie was ordered to move forward toward the tanks:

As we approached the area there were two distinct German tanks, both burning from the rear. They were about 50 yards apart from one another and one tank had been hit in the left rear while the other tank had been hit in the right rear. I was surprised not only by the accuracy of the bazooka shooting L-4 but more so what a little L-4 Cub could do to a German tank. I remember word spread quickly, and when I reported to my battalion commander, Major Irzyk, and said, "Jesus, did you see that guy get those tanks in that little airplane?"

As word spread quickly among the GIs on the ground, the use of the bazooka-equipped L-4's with the 4th Armored Division began to take on a life of its own. As the 4th Armored advanced across occupied France in early 1944, Charles had originally begun using only two bazookas, then four, and eventually strapped a total of six of them to his L-4 "Rosie the Rocketer." But hunting German armor and infantry brought about its own set of hazards. No longer did the German soldiers hold back from firing on the L-4s. In fact, the German hierarchy placed a bounty on them and awarded their soldiers up to a week or more off the front lines if they brought down one of the Grasshoppers. Charles soon encountered the persistence of German gunners while on a reconnaissance flight near the occupied and heavily defended port city of Lorient.

Once again *Stars & Stripes* reporter Gault MacGowan found himself strapped in tight to the back seat of Charles's L-4 as he witnessed and documented the following extract of a battle scene near Lorient, which housed the dreaded U-boats of the Nazi wolfpacks that were the scourge of the North Atlantic:

The American forces have tightened their cordon around this great U-boat base here, but the Germans garrison is still holding out. Fires behind the ramparts suggested that the port's more valuable assets were already being liquated to prevent our using them when the port falls into our hands. A group of Germans marooned in an outpost by our defenses frantically waved white sheets from the upper windows of a charred and blackened building as a token surrender.

I couldn't stop to accept their offer. Maj. Charles Carpenter, "Lucky Carpenter," they call him, was rushing me around the outer defenses at the speed that an unarmored artillery grasshopper airplane can go at its best.

Ahead of our advancing troops, we saw the German's frantic surrender signal and the only sign of life in a blackened, ghost city, once full of the picturesque, old-world, Brittany homes. Going on toward Lorient, we saw the tall cranes along the wharves still standing and the bridge across the river still intact, and nearby there was still smoke rising from the recent visits of allied bombers, which blasted at the concrete roofed U-boat pens.

We soared higher to get a better view, but the German gunners resented our curiosity and some of that famous flak that has made Lorient a hell hole for pilots came cruising across the skies after us. "Lucky Carpenter," that is why they call him Lucky, laughed and wriggled into a river valley, between the trees and over hedges, "My lucks a tradition," he said. "I hope you don't mind my way of flying. They're firing 88's at us, it's less risky down low," Carpenter said. "They won't shoot; it will give away their positions—besides the nearer the ground we are the harder it will be for the gunners to hit us."

We hedge hopped to safety, but it seemed worth the risk. It was a privilege to see that last phase of the battle of the Atlantic, smoking out the undersea rats from their lairs.[5]

August 12, 1944

Hello! Bunny:

I'm taking it easy for the first time in days. I'm still in fine health. Since my refusal to return to Div. Artillery Hq., I've been assigned to Div. Hq. to work for the general. I'm still a major, although I would have become a private before returning to my regular job. In fact, it might even have been thrown in jail.

However, I have the reputation of being a good soldier when the going is tough. I expressed my opinions quite freely when I thought certain superiors were bungling their jobs. This of course made no friends in certain circles.

Lately I have been taking quite a few chances, but my luck has been marvelous. Yesterday I got one bullet hole through the wing and hit a church steeple with one wheel. It was very little for what might have happened under the circumstances.

I travel light these days and alone most of the time. I have acquired a Frenchman who speaks English, French, and German for a partner and interpreter. My job for the time being is to handle special missions for the general, consisting mostly of observation and reconnaissance trips for information.

I have become a very bad risk as a father and husband. At times I am so restless and impatient that I scarcely know myself.

If my luck goes all the way through the war with me, I know I won't be a teacher in Moline High again.

When I told you, I didn't think I'd be home again. I meant that the war has changed me more than I realized until recently.

Please don't worry about me, needlessly.

The pictures of Carol Ann are wonderful. I shall carry them with me.

I don't write much lately, but I still keep you posted on the big things until life slows down.

Love, Charles

CHAPTER 14

Fistful of Rockets

Around August 21, 1944, Charles once again carried the *New York Sun* reporter, Wes Gallagher, aloft with him in his L-4 and reported the following passage:

> At Lorient he put two bazookas on it and gradually increased their number to six. Some of his fellow pilots tried it out, but found that driving their frail craft into a hail of German small arms fire was extremely unhealthy and returned to their observations duties.
>
> Some people around here think I'm nuts, Major Carpenter says, but I just believe that if we're going to fight a war we have to get on with it sixty minutes an hour and twenty-four hours a day.[1]

Inspired by his earlier coaching days at Roosevelt Military Academy, Charles reached deep into his playbook and reunited himself with the term "deception." With bazookas firmly attached to his Cub's struts, Charles Carpenter was even more determined to end the war as quickly as he could, even if he had to do it all by himself.

Most of his missions, operating at between 800 and 2,000 feet, Charles was very aware of the dozens of eyes that looked skyward, tracking his route over occupied France. Focusing on the olive drab, zebra-striped, tandem two-seat Piper L-4 Cub circling overhead, the German soldiers on the ground remained frozen, clutching rifles and machine guns, not daring to fire on the predator above. Their Panther tanks and armored vehicles were concealed under overhanging trees and brush near a French church. Their fear was not from the petite, tube- and cotton-covered, unarmed reconnaissance aircraft; it was from the occupant inside. If the American pilot spotted the infantry and convoy below, there was a great chance that he would radio a nearby US Army artillery unit as hundreds of high explosive shells would be unleashed and rain down upon them.

As the little 65 hp Cub zigzagged overhead, it suddenly began to corkscrew down from its 1,500-foot perch. Had the Germans studied the L-4 closer, they would have noticed six tubular objects, three on each side, attached to the wing struts along with words "Rosie the Rocketer" painted near the nose, as a tribute and a play on words to the "Rosie the Riveters" he met back in the states. As the Cub stabilized in its shallow dive and drew closer to the targets below, a mere hundred yards, the first two M6A3 HEAT (high explosive antitank) rounds were launched from their M1A1 bazooka tubes. Multiple explosions shook the area below as one armored vehicle took a direct hit; thick black smoke began to pour from the burning shell. Those that weren't disoriented by the surprise attack, shouldered their rifles, and began to fire on the L-4. As the Cub clawed upward, turning and jinking, the soldiers on the ground stared in disbelief as the L-4 came roaring back and fired four more bazooka rounds at them before scurrying off after delivering its death and destruction below.

The M6A3 rocket that Charles carried was 19.4 inches long and weighed 3.38 lbs. It had a blunted, more curved nose to improve target effect at low angles, and a new spherical fin assembly to improve flight stability. The M6A3 round was capable of penetrating over 3.5–4 inches of armor plate (88–101 mm). During the 1944 Allied offensive in France, Charles began to encounter the heaviest German tanks such as the Panther and the Tiger Ausf. B, or King Tiger, the Nazis' deadliest tank. Unable to penetrate the thick armor from the front, the bazooka rounds would bounce off like a rubber ball. The true weakness lay in the fact that these models used thinner 40 mm or 45 mm armor on the tops of their turrets and hull superstructure. That is what gave Charles Carpenter the advantage, especially from above because the M6A3 bazooka rocket warhead could easily penetrate that thinner area.

Charles Carpenter held the ultimate advantage over any infantryman who had to face down the Panther tank from the front. Traditionally tanks are built to have very thick armor. The Panther tank was designed with thick armor from between 70 mm and 130 mm on the front side, but the armor was angled at around 35 to 40 degrees. The angle that armor faces an incoming round is very important to its design and survivability because it will deflect the energy of the round away from the tank. That slanted armor concept was alien to American tanks, especially the Shermans, until the Pershing came out toward the end of the war. An infantryman shooting a shoulder-fired bazooka at a Panther could knock it out by stopping a road wheel or blowing a track off. The German suspension was very delicate, and it could be easily damaged. But from his aerial perch, Charles Carpenter didn't have those limitations in that he was shooting from above and generally behind, so he could shoot into the engine compartment or into the aft section of the turret, where the armor was much thinner and the round could penetrate. He and his fellow Cub pilots could easily knock out a tank from above and behind. The bazooka rounds they fired were exceedingly powerful and deadly. But not nearly as powerful as the horrors of war Charles observed daily. Elda saw in his letters home that her husband, father to her infant daughter, Carol, was not the same man she had seen off to war as his character and spirit began to change.

September 5, 1944

Dear Elda,

It has been a long time since I've written to you. I hope that this letter does not upset you or hurt you as my previous one did.

The terrible part of war includes much more than the wounded and the dead. The tearing down of old values, the coarsing of the human character, the wearing away of their veneer of civilization—these are casualties too.

Colonel Bixby spoke to me yesterday about your letter to him. He told me he would leave his answer to me.

My military career is in no state of change after all, I guess. When I returned from my several days rest with the medics, I reported into the general and asked for a transfer in any grade, from the division. He refused to consider it and ordered me to be attached to division headquarters as his personal pilot and special agent. Since then I have lived in the general's section and taken orders from him alone.

As you seem to know already, my reputation for sanity is rather doubtful in some circles. Several of my actions have reflected discredit on higher ranking officers, but in no way have I dishonored myself or you, or any of my friends.

It's true that my outlook on many things has changed. A certain wildness and restlessness has been uncovered in me. I cannot see myself in the old life, however, peaceful and content it might have been. I never intend to willfully break your heart or faith in the more practical obligations. A man's spirit cannot be taken or given any more freely than his religion. In my case, it is my religion. I have never yet cried for help because of bewilderment or fear. In many tender little ways you changed me and I loved it. In some of the big ways, I only held myself in check, or gave outlet and some of the forms of physical endeavor that used to puzzle and worry you so. As a woman, you naturally desired a home and security and contentment. My home has been where I am; security for myself has not appealed to me; and the possibility of sleek contentment sometimes actually frightened me.

It is not "good-bye" or anything so dramatic between you and me, unless you should so desire it. There are probably not many who love me as you do, or whoever will. My love for you has not diminished. I just do not think I can make the concessions the rest of my life that your happiness and welfare rightfully deserve.

When the war ends, I do not know what I'll do or where I'll go. I do intend to work for myself if at all possible. You and Carol Ann would still share any good fortune of mine and perhaps bad fortune too.

It was only fair to tell you, though, that I intend to keep going and expressing my free opinion. So long as I desire.

Please write to me and I'll promise to answer all the questions I can. Talk to my mother. She is the sanest person I know. She might possibly even understand me. Whatever you do, don't make me ashamed or bitter unnecessarily. I ask nothing more than the finesse and spirit you are capable of. You have already faced much without me. My letter told you that there might be much more.

Good-bye for now. Don't let tears hide all the smiles or I could never come back.

Love, Charles

September 6, 1944

Hello Bunny,
The end of another busy day is here. The mist is creeping up the hillside and the wind is making a lonesome sound through the struts

of the plane. Most of the time now I even sleep in the plane because of the damp, cold nights that are getting all too frequent.

I hope that you are not too upset by events of the past few weeks. I am in good health and in good standing here with the people that count most.

I do not believe that I am a Red Cross case. Any investigations that you may have started about me can only cause embarrassment to either or both of us. Please don't invite the outside world in on our troubles. I know you want to do something, but all there is to be done concerns only yourself and myself.

The European phase of the war will end soon. What happens then, I do not know. If you go to pieces I don't believe I'll ever come back. Recent months have put considerable strain on my former ways of thinking and living. It has nothing to do with God or a nervous breakdown. When I get myself set on solid ground again things may or may not look different. I am not bothered by any "hero" complex. The clippings are a surprise to me.

I'll always love you. Be strong. Call on your God and face up to life.

Goodnight, Charles

September 8, 1944

Hello! Bunny:
Not much news these past several days. Summer has gone from France I believe. The cold rains and gusty winds on this hill top are several more good reasons for this war ending soon.

Our division has taken life easy for several days, mostly because all the bridges are out across the next river. The Germans are making it quite difficult for us to build a new one.

We are now occupying territory that was a famous battleground of the last war. The battle scars and trenches of a quarter of a century ago are scarcely hidden by the all-conquering grass yet. Not far from us, on a high hill, is a beautiful monument to the American dead of that campaign.

The futility of war has seldom ever been more evident to me.

Last evening, the general gave me the Silver Star. For what I am not exactly sure. The bravest moments I have known in this war are mine alone. There'll be no medals for them—perhaps only skeptical head shaking. They have given me a confidence, though, and a fine scorn of many things that have definitely marked me—perhaps too much.

Tell me your worries and troubles and heartaches, but don't tell them to the world. "The silly old world has troubles enough of its own." Even the pain and misery I've seen have made me feel that all of us do not get our share of such things. Except to those who see clearly—the brave and the generous—happiness as a gift, almost an accident.

If you aren't able to take a few steps forward and upward without me, then your happiness was an accident. If your kind of faith is worth having, then it will surmount any present difficulties that you or I may be having. If not, then your life was built on a fragile foundation at best.

Carol Ann is a pretty and intelligent child. She is endowed with far more than most children ever know. I regret never having known enough of home and family life to feel like a father should feel. I do know that I cannot yet return to the settled existence I knew. I do know that you'll never be quite happy out of it. You have not failed me. It is I who failed you.

Most men I know in this war are not fighting for a better world. The old world was good enough for most of them. They are now fighting to return to it.

Hurting you as I have is probably the worst thing I've ever done. Whether or not it is a purely selfish thing, time alone can tell. The knowledge that I could see you without wading through a vale of tears and pleas would bring me home sooner than anything else.

The sun is shining justice in the moment. It comes sometimes when least expected. Mine is not the death of a love. It is a death of an accepted, standard, way of American life that obviously can't be designed for all people.

Think of a happier moment. Show me some pride, without which life is absurd. A bit of cheer and understanding from you now would go a long way toward proving me wrong.

Words are such idle things many times. Love is a many-sided thing too—but I do love you.

Charles

What Charles did not share with Elda, who read it later in the Moline, Illinois, *Daily Dispatch*, was the narrative with his Silver Star Citation that read in part the following passage:

For gallantry in action in France on August 1, 1944. The forward elements of the division were holding the north bank of the river when a half-track came back to report a strong German counterattack that was pushing the entire line back and had recaptured the bridge. Major Carpenter took command of the vehicle, returned to the bridge, and with great daring and fortitude engaged a strong German force of 88s and machine-gun posts. His attack with a single vehicle was so ferocious that he scattered the enemy forces and retook the bridge. His actions saved a difficult situation and served as an inspiration to all members of his command.[2]

Knowing that her husband did not seek notoriety and was already embarrassed and exasperated with the amount of press he was receiving, Elda took it upon herself to contact the newspaper and told them in no uncertain terms, "Please don't make a big deal about it, and please don't print his picture again."

September 17, 1944

Dear Bunny,
Out of ink again! The rain has been beating down on my plane roof all morning.

It's a cold persistent rain, but I have a much better place than most to hide from it.

Last night, the AA boys shot down a German plane overhead. Today the big guns are rumbling several miles away on my right. The Germans are being hard-pressed, and we are doing quite a bit of damage to them lately. I'm half expecting to see some of them come running out of the woods nearby that is being shelled. I'm here alone this morning because the clouds are right down on the ground and I couldn't move forward with the rest of the outfit.

The general gave me the Air Medal with one Cluster this morning before he left.

I've been behaving very well of late and have been in no trouble for several weeks. The last incident was when I shot the six rockets mounted on the plane near camp and badly startled some of the big-wigs who thought the Jerries had finally gotten back to them. The general thought it was rather funny, so I was only requested to announce the next target practice.

I hope that you and Carol Ann are baring your end of the war not too uncomfortably.

War is hardest on those who wait and wonder.

Good-bye, for now with love,

Charles

One witness to Maj. Charles Carpenter's use of his bazooka-equipped Cub "Rosie," was a US Army paratrooper with the 101st Airborne, from Iowa. Sgt. Frank Freestone wrote a letter home to his old flight instructor, Howard V. Gregory, Des Moines Flying Service, and described one epic flight and diving attack by Carpenter and "Rosie the Rocketer":

It's still muddy and the mud is hell. I saw the sun about two weeks ago, but since that time it has been raining from day to day with little or no respite. Funny about those little Cubs—you know, when I used to look at them I'd wonder just what could a Cub do at war? Well, I found out. As artillery spotters, they have done a lot of fine work. A few of these brave little ships have died, but it has been a glorious death. From time to time I have seen tail feathers fly. It was funny because neither the ships nor the pilots were injured aside from a few scratches.

A few minutes of flying at about 300 feet then a big black puff of smoke would appear near the Cub. For a while it seemed that the ship must crash; then, at the last possible moment, it would come out of its dive and either land or resume its former altitude.

There is a major (Carpenter) who, not to be outdone by the roaring Thunderbolt and its rockets, had mounted on his tiny Cub four bazookas—well if you know the bazooka, you know it is a tough customer in any language. The major waited for the day when he would have the opportunity to use those weapons. One day he was cruising along at 200 feet when suddenly, off to his left, his eye caught a tiny

147

movement. It wasn't much at first, then the dust began to tell the story—an enemy tank was moving into position to attack and there were others.

The sun had disappeared behind a huge curtain of dark clouds as the tiny Cub started its dive—a dive that had a huge Tiger dead to rights. Five hundred yards, four hundred, three, two, one, seventy. Fire! Two thin white streams of smoke and two dark shapes hurtled toward the helpless tank—then the explosion, shortly before the Cub passed over. Not much of an explosion, thought the Major, who had never seen the bazooka fired before. He didn't know that the force of the explosive carried the projectile inside the tank before the blast, but upon circling, he saw the tank, its guns stilled, emitting a heavy pall of smoke. For the tank and its crew, a little Cub had placed the finger, and for a Cub, brother, that's rich![3]

Sergeant Freestone had his own brush with history back in 1930. As a seventeen-year-old high schooler, he wanted to make a name for himself. He announced to his parents that he was going to set the "world's champion tree-sitting record." On July 16, 1930, after selecting a fine, sturdy tree in the yard of his home on S.E. Sixteenth Street and Bell Avenue, he proceeded to lash a mattress to a handmade platform secured on some tree limbs. Supplied with food and water by his parents, he stayed on his lofty perch for over 1,318 hours and 28 minutes until he came down on September 9. Unfortunately for Freestone, that wasn't the only brush with history he would encounter. After witnessing the exploits of Maj. Charles Carpenter and his Cub, along with slugging it out with German infantry and armor alongside 4th Armored units and others, Freestone would face his uncertainties at a small town in Belgium called Bastogne during the Battle of the Bulge two months later.

On September 19, 1944, the Germans found themselves with an advantage; the heavy fog had rolled in and they were using it as a shield. They quickly organized and began a counterattack against the 4th Armored Division near Arracourt. The fighting below was ferocious as Sherman's and Panthers dueled and slugged it out with one another with early victories going to the heavily armored Panthers. Charles, aloft over the battle scene in "Rosie," was helpless as he listened on his radio to the raging battle below like he was a sideline spectator at a football game. With fog preventing him from locating the enemy, all he could do was wait for it to lift.

By noon his patience paid off as he spotted a company of Panzers on the move heading toward Arracourt. But Charles also noticed something else below, a half-dozen GIs of a water point crew who were now jumping into the neck-deep water to hide from the advancing German armor. As he radioed the situation back to his headquarters, Charles realized that the German tanks would quickly overrun the stranded GIs.

As he jammed his left boot down on his rudder pedal and muscled his control stick forward and to the left, "Rosie" began to dive on the tanks below. From less than 100 yards, Charles launched two rockets that impacted near the tanks but missed them completely. Clawing his way back skyward, he held "Rosie" in a steep climb, with the full-throttle being pushed full forward. Leveling off, he repeated his maneuver, but this time he steepened his dive. Launching two more of his bazooka rounds, he watched them streak toward the German tanks, before jinking his stick back and forth to avoid the intense ground fire that was arching its way for the Germans on the ground. Not knowing it at the time, one of his rounds impacted into its intended target as the German tank began to burn.

As he pushed "Rosie's" throttle forward once again, Charles brought the stick back to his gut as he clawed his way back for another pass. With the GIs still hiding in their watery sanctuary, they watched as "Rosie's" nose was pushed over and began to dive once again. With only two bazooka rounds left, Charles chose his target and virtually ignored the incoming rounds that were being thrown at him and "Rosie." With the final toggle of his switch, the two rounds ignited and launched from their tubes as they screamed earthward toward their target. A fire soon engulfed another vehicle as Charles found his mark yet again. Charles would land and rearm twice more that day as he fired a total of sixteen bazooka rounds at advancing German armor.

He later told a *Stars & Stripes* reporter, "I did not claim any, because everyone seemed to be shooting at me and I had to get the hell out of there!"[4] But once back on the ground, Charles was congratulated for not only knocking out German armor but also halting the German advance.

September 24, 1944

Dear Bunny,
Another busy and exciting day has just ended.
   This is the latest. I have been up for a long time. It's after midnight now. Yesterday I took a blow torch off a wrecked German tank. Now

if I carefully close all the holes in my tent, I can use it for heat and light. Your letter came with the snapshots or photos of you. Thanks a lot, even though they do not do justice to your looks at all. Also a box of Fannie May candy arrived in fairly good shape.

The weather has been miserable lately, but I have managed to keep my generally "good disposition" in spite of it. Just a few minutes ago, I had to leap and brace myself against the tent pole to prevent the wind from taking my tent away from me.

We have had some exciting tank battles lately. The Germans have turned on us and taken the initiative. They must be some of Hitler's own schoolboys because they fight to the end often against great odds. On two occasions, the fog lifted just in time for us to beat them off.

The other day we "knocked out" 44 German tanks. The doughboys from their slit trenches gave "Rosie the Rocketer" and me credit for two.

I have been very mean to worry you and mom, the way I have. Your letters have been very sweet. Goodnight and Love,

Charles

September 27, 1944 (*letter excerpt*)

Dear Bunny,
Today has been the quietest day in months; the general has not called for me once. The sun shone long enough that I worked up courage enough to wash my uniform and take a bath out of my helmet.

Jerry has been giving us much fiercer resistance lately and actually has us on the defensive now. We have been in the same spot several days. The end of the war here does not look quite as immediate to me now as it did when we were racing through France. Some of our men are beginning to show signs of mental and physical strain. It is a new experience for us to be the ones under attack.

The psychological effects of combat were staggering during World War II; 504,000 men were lost from America's combat forces due to psychiatric collapse. At one point in World War II, psychiatric casualties were being discharged from the US Army faster than recruits were being mustered in. With uninterrupted fighting occurring day and night, with men on both sides of the lines suffering continuous pressure, and witnessing death and destruction daily, some sought solace by accepting the fact that they were already dead.

September 29, 1944 (*letter excerpt*)

Dear Bunny,

The war drifts along of late without much progress on our part. The Germans have been ruthlessly attacking us almost everyday and have managed to keep us on the defensive for a change.

I hear the P-47s overhead now. When they appear, life is much more complicated for the Jerries. It's on the bad days and foggy mornings that we have our most trouble with German counterattacks.

An army public relations dispatch in late September 1944 provided a detailed description of what it was like to fly with Charles and "Rosie" over the battlefield of occupied France:

Headquarters
European Theater of Operations
United States Army
Number 26759 (Censored)

With the 4th Armored Division, France-A flight in Major Charles Carpenter's bazooka-shooting Cub observation plane is something like a ride in a roller coaster equipped with skyrockets.

The thirty-two-year-old liaison pilot, who taught history in Moline, Illinois but now hunts tanks with six bazookas mounted under the wings of his tiny aircraft, sometimes takes a passenger, although it cramps his gunnery.

"I can't get down to within 75 or 100 yards to shoot because my plane isn't as maneuverable with two people in it," he explains.

As we flew over the front where the 4th Armored tanks were blasting German positions with 75s and machine gun tracer fire, the major pointed out a burned vehicle.

"That's a German armored car I hit the other day," said the flier, who has also bagged at least two Nazi tanks and an ammunition truck.

"There's a German tank down there, right next to that building in the village, and another hidden under that tree," he pointed out and dipped a wing to circle the positions.

"We'll go down for a try at the one in town," he shouted and shoved the nose of "Rosie the Rocketer" down.

Diving almost vertically to less than 300 yards off the ground, Major Carpenter squinted through the sight, then touched a switch firing two of the rockets—one from each wing.

There was a dull boom and a flash of flame. "Rosie" stuck her nose up in a steep climb that would be called evasive action if she were a Thunderbolt.

Tiles on the roof of the house next to the German tank disappeared in a cloud of red dust.

"Allowed too much wind," the Major grinned. "Anyhow our tanks will know there's something there to shoot at. Next, we'll try for that tank under the tree."

Again the Cub dived and two rockets flashed groundward. Dirt spouted from the ground near the tank—apparently a massive Panther.

"That's another one marked for the boys on the ground," the flying artilleryman said as he wheeled "Rosie" about for a parting shot at the tank in the village.

The last two rockets roared from the launcher tubes in one explosion and blasted the ground 15 feet from the tank. Major Carpenter climbed and circled above the tanks, critically examining his work.

"I don't expect to get them very often, especially from this long range, but I imagine I worry them at that."

German gunners then attempted to prove that the worry should not be one-sided. Black puffs of antiaircraft shell bursts spotted the sky.

"They usually don't shoot at a Cub for fear of observation and artillery fire, but when they see it shooting bazooka they cut loose. Aggravates them some, I guess."

And with that "Rosie" turned leisurely back to her hillside pasture landing field for another load of gas and rockets.

CHAPTER 15

Death Is My Copilot

On October 1, 1944, General Patton visited his dear friend and confidant-General Wood at division headquarters. Patton was quite pleased with the advances of his 4th Armored Division and instructed General Wood to pass on to all of his men his observations that "I consider the 4th Armored Division the finest armored division in the United States Army." Although complimentary to all of Patton's GIs, Charles could not help but feel the pain and misery of the French people who had to once again endure a world war. His letters home that month expressed his forlorn observations and actions, some of them captured in poetry as well as Charles's own personal "dance with death" on several occasions.

But his documented actions brought surprise fan mail as well. Two specific letters addressed to Elda, who was literally in shock with all the "movie star"-like attention, attention that she knew her husband would not welcome nor acknowledge openly, especially around strangers, made her inwardly proud of her brave husband's achievements.

October 2, 1944 (*letter excerpt*)

Bunny Darling,
I found a bottle of ink in an abandoned German tank yesterday, so I will be writing a few lines to you in ink again.

We have been in one place for several weeks now. German resistance has been stronger and our supply lines longer, temporarily at least.

This part of France has had many wars waged over it. The people have about as many German traits as French. Most of them look rather tired and discouraged. It is a pathetic sight to see them leaving their villages one day with a few belongings and returning to smoking ashes the next. If we occupy a town, the Germans shell it. If the Germans occupy it, we do the destroying. There is little left to the natives of those towns and villages that happen to be in the path of war, especially where the fighting is severe.

The discomforts of life in the field are not many for me, but the comforts of life at 724 do look like a bit of heaven from here.

October 7, 1944 (*letter excerpt*)

Hello! Bunny:

Thanks for the newspaper clippings. I look at them and wonder about myself. My publicity in the papers at home is a surprise to me. The incidents are merely part of the war until I read about them.

My job is actually very easy now. I chauffer the general around occasionally and take a few special missions for him on call.

The artillery on both sides rumbles all night long. I'm far enough back of the lines now though, that it seldom distracts my sleep.

The sun is shining brightly this morning, and the Jerries will again be catching the devil again from our planes. The battle is much more equal between us when bad weather prevents our air power from being used.

October 13, 1944
Letter from TS. W. C. Roberts
2532 AAF Base Unit
Sec I
Randolph Field
Texas

To Mrs. C. M. Carpenter
724-21 St. "A"
Moline, Ill.

Dear Mrs. Carpenter,
Thank you so much for forwarding my letter to your husband. When I mailed it I was somewhat apprehensive as to its ultimate delivery.

Since you were kind enough to advise me that it has been forwarded, I do indeed feel grateful to you.

What your husband is doing is probably the most unorthodox type of fighting that either the Allies or the Germans have ever witnessed or are about to witness. But regardless of what the general opinion of other pilots is, I for one feel that he knows what he is doing. Major Carpenter very audacity in such an attack is probably his greatest protection. The information that I wanted him to review was a different way of mounting the Bazookas on his ship. The method that I suggested was as unorthodox as the type of fighting your husband is doing. I sincerely hope that he sees the benefit there that I have visualized. Because I feel that it will enhance the chances of surprise. Which to my way of thinking is one of the most if not the most important factor in protecting the major.

Last July I gave an idea for mounting bazookas on liaison aircraft. The officers who decide upon ideas submitted practically threw me out for having the unimaginable gall to waste their time with such a proposal. When I read the newspaper accounts of your husband's exploits I was not only surprised but pleased because I was able to confront those same officers with proof that the idea was not only practical but deadly effective. I even offered to post a bond to cover the equipment necessary to prove the idea but I was again refused. This time because they probably didn't want to admit their error. Hence I wrote to your husband. You must be terribly proud of him. Not so much for his daring but more importantly because of his love for country and you that drives him fiercely ahead. I doubt if there is a man in Europe who wants to come home as badly as Major Carpenter does. I know that there are a few who would fight as bold for that privilege. I would sure give anything to be helping him.

Sincerely,
Technical Sergeant W.C . Roberts

October 17, 1944
Letter from Sgt. Wayne Flatt
1st Cook, Troop C, 34th Cav
Fort Riley, Kansas.
To Mrs. Carpenter

Dear Mrs. Carpenter,
After reading of your hubbies adventures overseas, I can't resist sending my regards and best wishes to him. Due to fact that I know of no other way to contact him, I am going to prevail on you to relay my message.

I have admired him since I played football for him at R.M.A. (Roosevelt Military Academy) and sure wish I was on his team now. But I guess I will have to be content being a water boy.

Respectfully,
Sgt. Wayne Flatt

October 18, 1944

Dear Elda,
This time the rains have come to stay all week, it seems. My tent has become such a welcome home to me that I often wonder why men go to so much trouble to build mansions. Of course, everything is relative here. When I say that we had a fine dinner of dehydrated potatoes and corned beef hash, you know I am telling you how hungry I was.

The privations and hardships of war are not all that some of us would have you believe. A canvas cot can be a glorious luxury. Black coffee without sugar tastes like wine some mornings, and white bread becomes cake after a couple of days on K rations. A slit trench can look positively beautiful at times, and the sun breaking through the clouds invokes more awe and gratitude than a rainbow would at home.

Lately I seem to have attracted some bit of attention at home over the tank episode. Although it might be news there, it brings me little credit here. My real mission is reconnaissance and the general is generally more concerned over my getting back with the latest information. Probably such events stem from my inability to sit and watch when there is a chance to play.

You know how I used to exert so much more effort at games than at jobs. That is why I try to regard the war as a game. It helps too to keep me apart from hatred and bitterness. It is a game dangerous to the mind and character if taken too seriously. A good part of our casualties have never been touched by enemy shells or bullets. It is a game often laughable, filled with absurdities, and sometimes attaining the pandemonium and hysteria of a goal line stand. Once in a while it even approaches nobility when someone plays with both courage and generosity. Often I cannot help but feel that the conquerors and the defeated, even the spectators, file out the same gate. Thus, to me, it seems best to take part in the game, and foolish to try and play it other than gallantly.

Several weeks ago, I delivered a message by plane across a stretch of enemy-held territory. The trip took me over a green valley with high wooded hills on the far side. Men were fighting below and hiding behind drifting curtains of smoke from artillery shells. It was a beautiful late-summers afternoon, with fleecy clouds, piled high against the blue and gilded on top by a retreating sun.

Generally I fly alone. This time though I had the feeling of being accompanied by some quiet, friendly personality. I'm sorry, but it wasn't the fellow you think. This one made no promises, and no provisions for me to fulfill. I believe he just happened to be going my way.

I arrived over my destination with a wealth of altitude to spend. In a mood of exhilaration, I squandered it recklessly in spins and loops and dives.

When I landed at the end of one last swoop, men stopped digging their holes to stare at me.

Strangely, during the trip I don't believe any shots were fired at me, even though I saw numerous enemy vehicles and our troops had been unable to penetrate that area.

Later, these lines kept running through my head, so I took my pen and chased them out.

If we agree that it is foolish to play the game other than gallantly, the title is obvious.

"For Gallantry"

It seemed, I spoke with shining Death today. I walked beside him toward a valley green. He took my hand and smiled at me, and quietness gathered near the scene.

He rode with me through trembling clouds. We built a palace there from sunset glow. We played wild music across the skies, and laughed at frantic Life below.

We strolled on dark-stained grass, among the torn and trampled flowers. Men cursed and fled, and hid from us, to linger but a few more hours.

From muddy holes they shouted "Fool!" At me who did not shun him so. Then tearful life appeared again and whispered that I should not go.

Death smiled and turned away toward home, as would a friend who would return for me. Across the lovely valley rose the mountains, and beyond the mountain stretched an endless sea.
Love, Charles

October 24, 1944 (*letter excerpt*)

Bunny, Darling:
Recently I took an army photographer out to make some battlefield movie shots. Enclosed are several snapshots he took of me as a favor. Could you get me some reprints made of the negatives? I would like one of each with the exception of the picture of the tank crew and myself. I would like to have four reprints of that as I promised one to each of them.

During one mission in October, Charles and "Rosie" had been shooting at German armor, in concert with American tanks, artillery, and 9th Air Force Thunderbolts. As he overflew the still-burning carnage below, Charles eased the throttle back on his Cub and began a gentle descent as he set up for a landing. With his Cub's wheels kissing the tattered French foliage, Charles eased "Rosie" to a stop. Turning his mag switch off, he opened his right side window and door and placed his well-worn boots onto the fiery battlefield, bordered by some woods.

Before him lay burning hulks of German tanks and armored vehicles along with dead German soldiers scattered about the area. As Charles began to inspect the battle-damaged vehicles, he had an uneasy feeling he was being watched. Charles was not alone. Sensing something was not right, he reached his right hand across his chest and upward toward his shoulder holster and the .45-caliber pistol nestled inside. Charles closed his eyes for a second and shook his head; he had left his sidearm inside "Rosie."

Suddenly fewer than a half-dozen German soldiers appeared in front of him. Quickly grabbing a discarded German rifle, Charles shouldered it and pointed the weapon at the advancing enemy soldiers. But the German soldiers were no longer in the mood to fight. They, like Charles, had had enough of this terrible war, as they raised their hands in surrender. As his prisoners sat on the ground, Charles studied their faces and realized they were not that different from himself, and wondered if they too had loved ones waiting for them at home. Charles marched his captured detail a short distance to approaching Allied soldiers and turned them over. He thought they were the lucky ones, for them the war was over.

Back inside "Rosie," Charles reflected on his near-fatal mistake as he fitted his shoulder holster over his leather flight jacket. To recount the episode, Charles wrote the following poems.

October 1944

Incident in the Woods.

The other day I met one of those who fought. In a dark and shattered wood. I had come to see what death our fire had wrought and face to face we stood.

Flames crackled from the wreckage all around. The stench of burning flesh was in the air. His rifle near him was cast upon the ground, and I, surprised could only stare.

Wild shots rang out and stilled my heart. This time, my foolishness must cost. He smiled that I so easily should start from heated bullets whose aim was lost.

Bright ribbons shown upon his coat, to speak of war in other lands. His broken spirit forbade me gloat for empty glories in wretched hands.

He nodded wearily at my stern command and bent to search his soldier's bag. He tossed aside a knife, a pistol, a shining band, and his face lit up at one small rag. The soldier dead. The man had returned to save some seeming trifle. It was a baby thing, blue, and partly burned. He folded it and kicked his loaded rifle.

I had led him from that torn and stinking spot; may tire and grassy time soften memory. Willing guards took him at the prison lot, and smiled, and wrongly guessed me free.

October 1944

Late Autumn Toast

Now nights are much too long, And days drag slowly by.

The birds are without a song, And gray clouds hide the sky.

Soft greens have turned to brown.

A silent chill is on the air.

The leaves have fluttered down, And trees stand dark and bare.

Come! raise the cup and let us drink, to brighter days that once we knew.

To youth and maid with love the link, To flaming blood and friendship true.

CHAPTER 16

Rain, Mud, and Misery

There was hardly anywhere in France that a soldier could find respite from the rain, which quickly turned the French soil into a quagmire. Most of the time, Charles would fold himself into the front seat of "Rosie" to catch up on his letters home to Elda. As he scribbled, bits of cold rain would enter his sanctuary from his leaky glass rooftop and trail down the back of his neck. What may have been annoying to some men, Charles welcomed the distraction while the war on both sides took a short reprieve from death and destruction as Charles began to focus on a possible new job back home once the miserable war was over.

Friday, November 3, 1944

Bunny, Sweetheart:
If there had been any pumpkins around, the frost would certainly have been on them this morning. There has been lots of rain and chilly weather, but we have had much more comfortable living accommodations also than usual. Our division headquarters is in an old French Chateau—the kind that has old armor and swords and guns hanging on the walls.

Thanks for sending me the clippings. I try to send back to you the ones you ask for. Right now I am unable to find the one from the *Denver Post*, but I expect to locate it somewhere in my tent.

All the clippings that I have are on the way to the Piper Aircraft Company. I'm interested in a job with them after the war. They, of course, have asked for any publicity for their planes that they can obtain.

My Christmas shopping is a problem to which there seems to be no traditional solution. It won't seem like Christmas at all this year. At least all the other holidays have been just days of the week to me.

Love, Charles

Fall 1944 (*enclosed poem*)

The Soldier Song

O, I'm a jolly soldier O.
When at the bar I stand
I roar and blow and curse the foe,
And squeeze my girlies hand.
But when the foe comes shootin', O
That isn't any fun.
I dig myself a bit below
And wish the war were done.

November 7 , 1944

Hello! Bunny:
Today I heard one reason for our not getting any mail lately was that ammunition and rations were getting top priority. That of course is only a temporary situation, and I'll be hearing from you soon.
    The picture and publicity about the bazookas still go on. Enclosed is a clipping from the *Stars & Stripes*, the service paper that we get here.

(Elda, setting Charles's letter aside for the moment, began to read the following excerpts about her husband's latest wartime exploits.)

The Stars & Stripes
Thursday, October 5, 1944
Now comes the one-man air force
1 Cub plus 6 Bazookas equals bad news for Panzers
By J. Wes Gallagher

Alsace-Lorraine

"Bazooka Charlie" Carpenter used to teach history. Now he is making it on the western front. "Bazooka Charlie" is a former American football player, and until he entered the army he taught history at Moline (Ill.) High School. He is fast becoming a legend in Lt. Gen. George S. Patton's army, where eccentricity is not unknown and bravery is commonplace.

At present he is making history in a little muslin and wood cubicle of a "cub" reconnaissance plane, which he has armed with six bazookas fired from the cockpit. His assignment is to pilot the commanding general of an armored division and to carry out personal reconnaissance on the general's behalf. But this passive assignment was not enough; he wanted something with which he could shoot back when he was shot at. Hence the bazookas.

Carpenter, a major, has already been credited with two tanks, several armored cars and some highly startled Germans who never expected to be bitten by a war rabbit such as a "cub" plane.

Carpenter shot up German staff cars and in general carried on a one-man war. His big day came north of Nancy recently when the Germans launched a tank attack and overran a waterpoint.

Carpenter came on the scene with his cub and dived into the barrage of German fire in a series of attacks, firing all six bazookas. During the day he fired sixteen shells, returning to the ground only to reload. Engineers at the waterpoint credited him with two tanks.

No target too small. He even fired at some scattered Germans walking toward a wood.

His favorite headgear is sort of a jockey cap. He is inclined to underrate his fighting ability, but looks the part with sharp features and a football player's neck, shoulders, and legs.

"Some people around here think I am nuts" is the way he puts it.[1]

(Folding the *Stars & Stripes* paper carefully, as she did with all of Charles's clippings and letters, she placed it in a large box already swelling with other assorted papers and writings, preserving them for not only when Charles would return home, but saving them for Carol as well, to digest when she was old enough to understand and comprehend the triumphs and tragedies that her father had to endure during his time as a soldier. Elda continued with Charles's letter.)

A couple of days ago, I visited a nearby armored division and got my pistol and the holster back that they took from me a long time ago. Most of the time since then we have been several hundred miles apart. My relations with them seem to have improved quite a bit since we have had little contact. In that episode, I did lose my leather jacket, air mattress, and bed roll. Since then I've been able to acquire substitutes for everything but the air mattress.

Air mattresses are precious items here, more because of the protection they offer from the wet ground then their softness.

The rain has been coming down so hard today that the whole top of the tent is dripping. When we go on to action again, the mud will be a tremendous problem. The temperature here is reputed to drop as low as 20 degrees below zero. We have had nothing like that yet of course, and I hope that we don't in the future. I sleep with my clothes on now, sometimes even my shoes. We'll be issued another blanket soon, and some new clothes came in the other day. I still marvel at the exceptional care and equipment given to the American soldier. The people at home have done a finer job than they are generally given credit for.

Good-bye for today.

Love, Charles

By the time Charles woke the following day on November 8, 1944, the Third Army was back on the offensive as the skies over France began to clear. But the ground was like a soupy mud hole, especially for the Sherman tanks who dared not deviate from hard surface roads, or for those like Charles, operating light airplanes from unimproved fields where an airplane would be easily damaged during such conditions. Living close to the front lines, most of the time all Charles could do was listen to the booming sounds of the battle which lay only a few miles ahead. When his fields became firm enough, Charles was back in the air, as an overloaded "Rosie" waddled into the skies with General Wood occupying the rear seat as he directed the movements of his division for the sky.

November 14, 1944

Dearest Elda,

About four days have passed since I have written to you. Life has become a little hectic again after a period of idleness. The days are short, and evening generally catches me fumbling in the dark for something or other. Of course we're rather careful about lights after dark in our present position.

Some nights are so black that I have gotten lost in our own bivouac area, going from one tent to another.

The war situation looks brighter to me again since we are on the move. I have seen quite a few dramatic episodes in the last several days. It might ease your mind a bit to tell you that I was merely a spectator to most of them. My principal duty now is to make reconnaissance flights several times a day to keep the general posted on the changing situations of our combat elements.

If there should be gaps in my correspondence for a while I hope you will understand. No news must be taken as good news in wartime. If anything were to happen to me, you would be notified more quickly by the army than I even could do myself. Life is not very tough yet on me living at division headquarters, even though my tent does leak and I haven't had my clothes off in several weeks.

You know, of course, that I am in the Third Army. That should help partly in keeping track of me.

The weather is much colder now. We had our first snow yesterday, although it is raining again today.

I don't get much mail either lately. That is because deliveries are held up at the present time. So the space can be used for food and gas. Of course that is only temporary, and that mail will come through again.

This is a poor letter but it is written under rather difficult circumstances. I'll write you a better one later.

Love, Charles

Sunday, **November 19**, **1944**

Dearest Bunny,

I ever had a grand stand seat for the war for the past week. Last night, even our antiaircraft defense downed a German plane over our headquarters. Yesterday afternoon, I saw one of our P-51s crash and the pilot come floating down by parachute. Our tanks have been battling it out with the German tanks and antitank guns. We do not always come out as well as the newspapers and radio reports would have you believe. They seem to give the enemy's losses but not always our own. Yesterday, I saw the doughboys advancing across an open valley under enemy shell fire. Theirs still seems to be the most uncomfortable and trying job. Yesterday, too I had seven bullet holes patched in "Rosie." Once in a while I get in a rather warm spot, myself. I flew the longest 2 miles of my career yesterday when the Jerries let me get well over their lines before they "opened up."

I did everything but turn myself inside out before I got across our own lines again.

The weather has been much better the last 2 days. Our tanks are once more able to leave the roads without mirring down. That means our advance should speed up a little again. Conditions are such that it is difficult to write regularly. So don't think too much of it when the postman misses you. I'll write twice some other day.

You'll probably have to take care of the Christmas remembrances mostly by yourself. I may even have to end up by only writing a Christmas note to you and Carol Ann. Carol Ann should be old enough this Christmas to get a real thrill from Santa Claus time.

There are no civilians in this battle area now. I've put my French phrase book aside and carry a German phrase book instead. All the signs and directions are in German now. If I don't do any better than I did with the French, I won't get beyond "Good day" and "Good-bye."

In French it's "Au revoir"; in German, "auf Wiedershen." Otherwise it's just "So long" with love for now.

Charles

Unable to give Elda any details of his combat experiences in letters home, the only way she found out about his exploits was by reading them in the newspapers. On Monday, November 20, the *Stars & Stripes* reported a short write-up on page 4 with the following headline:

"Cub Ace Blasts Ammo in Snowstorm Flight"
With Fourth Armored Division, Nov 1944

Maj. Charles Carpenter, the bazooka firing cub ace from Moline, Ill., doesn't let weather interfere with his operation ahead of his advancing division. Yesterday he took off from a muddy landing strip in a snow fall, blew up a German ammo truck, fired several times at a Panther tank, and returned.

"I'm not sure that I got the tank," Major Carpenter said. "The weather was too thick."[2]

Back on the ground, Charles found solitude with a pen and paper as passages of past battles and experiences were transformed into poetry:

November 1944

Revolt

You speak to me of God above, you say he plans what is to be.

By the millions you shout of him, And still I ask, "Where, is he?"

I have heard the wounded curse Him

And remember not what he replied.

I have heard the innocent plead And remember only they died.

In the eyes of starving children I have seen the light grow dim.

I, myself, have walked with fear and not cried out to him.

In the dark of night I wondered, when he passed the faithful by, and asked in bitterness, "Whose hand shaped him, that built the sky?"

"Faith! Faith!" they cried to me.

"Have faith and faith alone.

Love and reason rule not the world, and only thus can man for sin atone."

Then, and only then, I cried in anger What once I dared not say,

O Yahweh! jealous War-god of the past, Beseeched by Thy hosts, night and day, endlessly praised in thy Myriad temples,

On trial in scarcely one, still are thy people on the Cross where once they crucified thy son.

Bred in man's fear, fostered in his pain. Opiate to his misery for a fee, promising the world to the meek.

What prayer can my foe offer up to thee?

Through the ages of your bloodstained rule, the greed of nations casts yet a mightier spell.

Flames of war rise higher and hatred roams afar.

O God! A mortal might have done as well.

Unseen force! behind the universe. Give me a God who laughs with men, who leads against the wall of darkness and glories in creating once again.

I'll kneel to him who dares to show His hand, were brave men grapple in the fight, who speeds with justice at Mercy's call where the aged weep, and children moan at night.

Until then, life is a gift, Reason the candle; Honor is my shield, Nobility my creed.

Goodness is wisdom sought in Beauty's temple, sin but stupidity, and Nature the book I read.

Happiness is only of this world.

Hell does not wait for men to die.

Death is, but Life at rest. All else is silence—A last "good-bye."

And now my angry heart is still.

I lose my torturous way alone.

Yet he would walk with me, must still step down from off the throne.

There are yet those dim horizons, beyond which I do not hope to see; but all the stars fling down their challenge and call me from Eternity.

Thanksgiving Day, 1944

Dearest Bunny,

It isn't quite like Thanksgiving used to be. I had two fresh eggs for breakfast and there's going to be Turkey for dinner. Still there's something missing.

I can truly say I'm thankful for a thousand things. The prices I've paid have been ridiculous for the lovely things I've gotten from life. I'm so far ahead in the game, I feel I cannot lose.

My tent is still my home, but our headquarters are in another Chateau. Before this, we were in a railroad station. Last night, I stayed so late playing chess at the headquarters that I couldn't find my way home in the dark. After stumbling around in the mud and rain for a while, I found the Chateau again and slept on a bench there until daylight.

Most American women, I'm sure, would find the French Chateaus I've seen very barren and inconvenient. They seem much more attractive from the outside. The furniture is generally uncomfortable, the furnishings and pictures stern and gloomy, and the plumbing hopelessly inadequate.

No mail has come to me for over a week now, but most everyone is experiencing the same thing. You and I were always grateful for many things. I feel that most of our treasures are still there. Love, Charles.

November 26, **1944** (*letter excerpt*)

Dearest Bunny,

There has been so much rain that our advance is grinding hindered against new enemy action. The Germans destroy the bridges as they retreat. The rivers are so swollen that building new bridges is much more difficult than usual. The chief of staff told me this evening that I had been awarded the Silver Star again. After the first award, the second and subsequent awards are distinguished by a cluster Oakleaf, which is attached to the medal ribbon.

You'd be surprised to know my official title in the division. I'm assistant G 3 and Division Orientation and Education Officer. The latter means that I would be in charge of educational training in the division when the war ends while the men are waiting to be demobilized.

Love, Charles

Charles wasn't the only one receiving an award for his flying feats. His passenger, Maj. Gen. John Wood, was awarded an Air Medal by General Patton. For a ground officer, this was an unusual honor, but General Wood was no usual soldier. By placing himself over the battlefield while strapped in the back seat of Charles's L-4 Cub, he could direct his troop's movements with ease, while surveying enemy positions, most of the time, on the receiving end of antiaircraft fire. This was General Wood's fourth medal he had received since landing in France. Unfortunately for him, this would be one of his last with the 4th Armored Division.

CHAPTER 17

Nothing to Cheer About

Those who have long enjoyed such privileges as we enjoy forget in time that men have died to win them.
—Franklin D. Roosevelt

December 3, **1944** (*letter excerpt*)

Hello! Bunny:
The war in this section has slipped into a grinding, destructive sort of thing. Our progress is seriously delayed by mines, blown bridges, and determined opposition. Seldom do I hear or see the French language used now. Everything is now characteristically German from here on in. Landing fields are so soft and the weather so bad that I do not fly much these days.

Please don't worry about those letters you get from people who write because they have read something about me in the papers. There is nothing secret now about the rocket-carrying liaison planes. You don't have to engage in lengthy correspondence with strangers who write, but I think it best not let suspicion lead you to treat them discourteously.

Patton is the commander of the Third Army of which our division is a part. I get a chance to see him quite often when he visits our division. He is a personal friend of Maj. Gen. John S. Wood.

Gotta close for now for a little business.

Unfortunately, Charles's latest letter home was cut short, perhaps due in part to the tragic news that was sweeping through the 4th Armored Division headquarters and surrounding units; Gen. John S. Wood was relieved of his command. The news sent a shock wave through the entire rank and file as grown men, many witnessing and inflicting the ultimate horrors of death and destruction upon their fellow man, wept openly as their faithful and tireless leader was taken off the line and ordered to return home to rest due to "battle fatigue."

No one within the 4th Armored Division would argue the fact that there was no greater leader, tactician, or man with the highest moral character than Wood. History would later paint a clearer picture as to Wood's dismissal. If Wood was guilty of anything, it would be his undying love and admiration for his men. From privates to colonels, Wood at times was outspoken, especially to superior officers when he felt that their decisions were the improper ones and would likely cost the lives of his own men. On several occasions in the fall of 1944, Wood had disagreements with his superior, Gen. Manton Eddy, about deployments of his armor. Eddy had reported these to his superior, General Patton, and claimed that Wood was encroaching on insubordination.

As a longtime friend of Wood, Patton wrote the following personal journal entry about Wood's latest encounter with General Eddy:

General Eddy said the division was not fighting hard, was not living up to its capabilities, and would have to move faster. General Wood angrily disputed these charges and Eddy retorted that he, Wood, had promised to be out of the Seventh Army zone in a couple of days, and it was still blocking the 44th Division's roads after more than a week, and General Haislip was calling him every day to find out when Wood was going to get moving. To which General Wood, who rarely swore, replied, "God damn it, Matt, my boys have bought every foot of this ground with their blood, they have done everything humanely possible and I will not ask any more of them. We will get out as fast as we can but no faster."

General Wood then turned on his heel and stalked out leaving a very angry General Eddy behind.[1]

With no other recourse left, Patton begrudgingly ordered his longtime confidant, a soldier he had long considered the "tip of the Third Army spear," back home to the states to rest.

Wood was quickly replaced with Patton's longtime chief of staff, Gen. Hugh J. Gaffey, who would not only lead the 4th Armored Division but would also, on occasion, occupy the rear seat of one "Rosie the Rocketer" as Charles chauffeured his new commander over the battle lines.

December 5, **1944** (*letter excerpt*)

Dearest Bunny,

I flew for the first time in several days today. It was good to be up in the air and see our tanks making real progress for a change. With the mud problem, many of our vehicles bog down as soon as they leave the highway to attack or maneuver.

We've had a change in division commanders. I flew my first mission for the new commander today. From first impressions, the 4th's record will continue to be good under his guidance.

About eight of the P-47 pilots who fly in support of us are with our division to get acquainted. They all sleep in the same room with me, and things are a bit crowded at present. They are fine fellows though, and it is enjoyable comparing "Grasshopper" and "Thunderbolt" experiences.

One of the P-47 Thunderbolt pilots that flew top cover for the 4th Armored Division, and their L-4 Cubs, was Robert V. Brulle of the 366th Fighter Group, 390th Fighter Squadron, Ninth Air Force. Operating nearby and in coordination with the 4th Armored Division on the ground, these "Angels of Death" were the scourge of German armor and infantry. Lieutenant Brulle's recollections give a short glimpse of what it was like during those hectic days leading up to the Battle of the Bulge on the ground and in the skies over Belgium:

The mission briefs seemed to become shorter and shorter: search and destroy German barges, trains, and armor. Trains had their own set of problems because the Germans were camouflaging flak guns on flat cars that were hidden behind canvas sides. When we came roaring in to attack, the sides came down and the flak came up. Although the P-47 could take a tremendous amount of damage, we continued to lose many good men and aircraft to the murderous German antiaircraft fire. Once a German convoy was spotted, our initial attack was to drop our 500-pound bombs and then set up a pattern to strafe them. I was taught early on to focus on one target and not try to strafe the whole column. The trick was to give it a short burst. With eight .50 caliber machine guns focusing on one place, it was a tremendous amount of firepower that was sure to be unsurvivable.

The month of December ushered in fog, rain, and heavy snow—a perfect cover for the German push toward the Ardennes region of Belgium. While the German Panzers on the ground pushed forward, creating a bulge in our front lines, we could only hope and pray the weather would clear so we could assault their advance. The day before Christmas Eve, the weather cleared as the sky was filled with fighters and bombers from both the Ninth Air Force and Eighth Air Force as we slugged it out with the Luftwaffe in the sky and the Panzer troops on the ground. Around this same time, P-51 Mustangs of the 352nd Fighter Group of the Eighth Air Force, known as the "Blue Nosed Bastards of Bodeny," were temporarily assigned to Y-29. Their job was to provide top cover for us while we performed our dive-bombing and strafing missions around Belgium and Germany. Our tempo only increased as we flew multiple missions each day, forcing the Germans to give up the ground they had gained. The New Year was right around the corner as we held out hope that the war would be over soon. But we also took no day for granted because we knew there were surprises behind every corner.[2]

December 14, 1944 (*letter excerpt*)

Dearest Bunny,
Unless last minute changes occur (quite a likely thing here), I'll leave for six days of school in Paris beginning Sunday. Of course Paris in these wartime days is probably not the same Paris the tourists see.

When Charles wrote his latest letter to Elda, he had no idea that the German army was amassing its tanks, armor, and infantry among the dark forests of the Ardennes, with its sights set on sweeping across Luxembourg and Belgium and taking the Belgian seaports of Antwerp. On December 16, German tanks and infantry quickly thrust forward through American lines holding in the dense forests of the Ardennes in Belgium and Luxembourg as if it were a repeat of their blitzkrieg of the same area in 1940. By December 18, the adverse weather conditions, along with the fast-moving columns of German armor, made air observations by the L-4s and L-5s practically impossible, which only hampered the ability of US artillery units to direct fire on the advancing Germans. Although the 4th Armored Division was still well south of the advancing German onslaught and ordered to move north to meet the Germans head on, the "Carpenter Luck" continued as Charles was sent even farther south to Paris to begin six days of officer training.

December 18, 1944 (*letter excerpt*)

Hello, Bunny Darling!
As usual I got all the luck when I got sent to Paris to this six-day course. Paris itself is as amazing and impressive as the things I have read and heard about. Paris has anything in the world beaten for beauty and interest that I have seen. The people are very friendly, and many of them can speak enough English. The city still puts on a brave front, although there are bitter shortages in many necessities.

But while Charles was engaged with his studies and lectures in the relatively safe city of Paris, there would be no luck for paratrooper Sergeant Freestone, who two months earlier had witnessed firsthand what an L-4 Cub could do to a German tank and sent a letter back home describing the bazooka shooting exploits of Charles and "Rosie the Rocketer." Sergeant Freestone, who had been fighting nonstop since landing on enemy soil in the spring of 1944, found himself on death's door at a town called Bastogne.

As part of 101st Airborne, Sergeant Freestone was part of a much-smaller band of soldiers, desperately trying to hold the town of Bastogne from an overpowering and overwhelming advancing German army.

Sensing that the odds were not in his favor and that he would never return home, Sergeant Freestone wrote what he thought was his last goodbye to loved ones back home in Iowa and England and to the home's owner, Countess Rene Greindl. Utilizing an old typewriter that he found in Countess Greindl's Chateau that fellow American soldiers were occupying, Sergeant Freestone wrote the following requiem:

As I write this I regret to say that the situation is extremely bad. I also dislike telling you that we, your allies, are at a critical disadvantage, for we are completely surrounded by the enemy … completely cut off from supplies.

I dare not tell you this now, but someday you will learn, someday you will know. You must forgive us for barging into your home as we have done. Believe me, it has not been due to our desire to do so …no, it has been due to conditions of war.

When peace has again arrived and it is possible for you to convey a message to those at home, will you please write my mother, Mrs. Edith Freestone, 4520 N. Twelfth Street, Des Moines, Iowa, and to my wife, Mrs. Frank Freestone, 123 Greenham Road, Newbury, Berkshire, England.

Just tell them that I love them very much and that I am terribly sorry to have to go out in this manner. Tell them also that I deem it a privilege to have fought and died for this country…as well as my own country.

Now to you and your family, may I extend a handclasp over the years to come, may God be with you forever and ever. I remain your uninvited guest.

Sergeant Frank Freestone
Paratrooper, US Army

After concealing the letter between two magazines (which were found by the Countess six months later), Sergeant Freestone joined other scattered soldiers who were attempting to make their last stand and link up with other members of the 101st Airborne. With darkness approaching, Sergeant Freestone concealed himself near a monastery and later recounted the following: "On the perimeter of the monastery grounds, I met a soldier in an American uniform with an American gun. He put the gun to my stomach. It was over."[3]

Taken to a prisoner-of-war compound by the German soldier in disguise, Sergeant Freestone would eventually be liberated by Free French forces and survived the war, returning to civilian life in Iowa.

December 23, 1944 (*letter excerpt*)

Dearest Bunny,
I miss you more than ever now with no airplanes and clouds to fly in, no rush of everyday army life to speed the hours by.

Christmas is just a few days away, and it might as well be the Fourth of July for all the lack of Christmas feeling within me.

On Christmas Eve everyone is closely restricted and there'll be no hanging up the stockings.

Christmas 1944 (*enclosed poem*)

Christmas Greetings

I'll not be with you this time when falls the seasons glow.

No bells shall peal or sweetly chime across the stained and muddied snow.

Here the flames out shine; the empty manger seeks the King.

The Wise Men wander still afar, and cannons war where angels were to sing.

Here, the sword can't be sheathed. This strife has bought a single end.

Psalms of life are scarcely breathed, and duty bars the way from friend to friend.

Still homeward, through wings the heart, where firelight falls on silvered pine, where children's lips in wonder part, and love and laughter come to dine.

There, opening doors frame the candles gleam, and carolers serenade the Holy Night.

To you we send this Christmas dream; for it, we carry on the fight.

December 26, 1944 (*letter excerpt*)

Dear Bunny,

School in Paris is over for me and now I'm trying to find my outfit again. The ground has a light covering of snow and it is quite cold. The war is getting more involved than ever it seems.

December 26, 1944 (*V mail excerpt from a letter*)

I'm back where things can happen again. Have been looking for my outfit since yesterday, but finally caught up with them this evening. They were almost a hundred miles away from where I left them. When I reported into the old headquarters, I found it absolutely deserted. I had to go all the way to army headquarters to find their new location.

It is a beautiful moonlit night outside. The weather is crisp and clear, and fighting is heavier than any we have seen for a long time.

The details that Charles could not share with Elda were one of despair and hopelessness. One soldier who did document the rapidly evolving events around Bastogne was a Sgt. Saul Levitt, attached as a staff correspondent to *Yank*. Sergeant Levitt had been part of a B-17 Flying Fortress crew with the 100th Bomb Group, which was based with the Eighth Air Force in England. While stationed in England, he was injured in a vehicle accident, and after recovering he was taken off of flight status and assigned to *Yank* magazine. Sergeant Levitt's excerpt described the following unfolding battle of Bastogne:

What went on around Bastogne until the 26th of December was a crazy—quilt of battles. The Germans—yes the same Germans, who some people said had no Luftwaffe reserves, material, or morale, but only those V things—broke through our most advanced lines with great speed and power on December 16. They were marching through an area which had been the scene of their victorious breakthrough in 1940. And until the 26th of December, the ghosts of German invincibility rode riot once again. In its first great surge, the German power overran, rolled back, and broke some American units. Make no mistake about it, we took a whale of a beating as they cracked through.

Two days later, December 18, astride three of the main roads to the east of Bastogne, elements of the 10th Armored met the Juggernaut head on. They could not prevent the tide of the German power from rolling on around them, but they did not crack. They stayed put.

On December 19 the 101st (Airborne) pulled into Bastogne and was immediately committed to battle. On Dec. 21 it was, with the 10th Armored, sealed off completely from the outside, within a circle around Bastogne. On December 19, the 705th TD (Tank Destroyer)

Battalion, attached to the 101st, fought its way south to Bastogne to get into the major actions of the Bastogne pocket. But eight of its tank destroyers did not get back to Bastogne until the Fourth Armored had finally broken the pocket. And far from merely slugging through on the 26th to establish a lifeline for the defenders, elements of Gen. Hugh J. Gaffey's 4th Armored Division and the 80th Division were in the battle for four days. They smashed through only after four days of bitter fighting, and you can still see their road markers along the way, particularly around Assenois and Clochamont, in the form of burnt-out tanks, halftracks, and the bodies of the dead. Air support from the Ninth Air Force and the 19th TAC (Tactical Air Command) finally got into the picture on December 22.

These were the men and these were the units that got in front of the thundering herd of the German Army, slowed it down, blunted its momentum, and finally deflected it so that larger groupings might afterward contain it.

By December 26, the Germans still did not have Bastogne. The 4th Armored was going north. Stopped cold at noon of the 26th by heavy resistance and with further movement possible only at the heaviest cost, they decided to force through at once. They knew it would have to be a very fast and continuous movement. The armor took off, playing machine-gun fire on the woods and surrounding hills. In that drive through Bastogne, lasting more than four days, they killed, captured, and took prisoner more than two thousand Germans. But they did not come through easily. The straight rush though the German ring cost lives.

The Fourth Armored seems to span the history of this war. In France, you met the division as it made its first big play in the hot summer days, going through Coutances in our big breakthrough after St. Lo. Again you ran across the outfit in the fall as its big tanks lumbered through the mud of Vollardingen, near the German border, with its tanks out of contact across the mine-covered hills where neither man nor jeep could follow them.

And now they showed the Bastogne, lumbering through the snow with the men of the 80th Division, against the blooming green of pine trees and into the town itself…

The battle of the Bastogne pocket ended at 1645 on December 26, 1944.[4]

After the war, Sergeant Levitt became a successful author and playwright with one of his plays, *The Andersonville Trial*, turned into an Emmy Award–winning movie.

December 29, 1944 (*letter excerpt*)

Dearest Bunny,

The weather has been so bitterly cold lately that we are forced to seek shelter indoors. The people are very cooperative but often the space is so limited that the poor natives are almost shoved out into the cold themselves. However, the German menace is so great lately in this area that they are very glad to see us arrive. Everyone is busy tonight because of a reported counterattack on the way.

The harsh winter weather that descended upon the scattered Allied lines stretched thin across the Ardennes Forest in mid-December 1944 was a bittersweet triumph for Adolf Hitler. His ground troops used the horrible weather conditions to their advantage, concealing buildups for their eventual forward thrust into the overwhelmed GIs. His once vaulted blitzkrieg Luftwaffe sat helpless on the fog-covered frozen ground as the Battle of the Bulge commenced. The Luftwaffe was not alone, however, as Allied fighters and bombers along with their crews, deployed throughout England and on forward bases scattered about the continent, sat similarly frustrated and helpless as their wings collected ice and snow while heavy, thick fog blanketed their bases.

The original plan, codenamed "Wacht am Rhein" (Watch on the Rhine), called for coordinated ground and air attacks forecasted to cripple and destroy Allied airpower that had decimated the Luftwaffe in recent months. If this plan could be accomplished, the Allied ground push to Germany would be halted in its tracks, and without protective air cover, the Allies would be thrown back into the channel. It was all wishful thinking on the Fuhrer's part. Hitler lived by the sword and now he was about to die by it.

The Führer had to wait for something he had no control over—clearing weather conditions. By the time the fog and low clouds had lifted, the Germans were advancing to the rear with the Allied army hot on their heels. As the New Year approached, Hitler used his final trump card and unleashed more than eight hundred of his Luftwaffe fighters, Me 109s, Fw 190s, and Me 262s, in a frantic act to save himself and his homeland. "Operation

Bodenplatte" (ground plate) was a desperate attempt by a desperate man to turn around the course of the war.

Convinced of overwhelming success, Luftwaffe planners and pilots prepared for what was hoped to be Germany's victorious start of the new year: the low-level surprise attack by German fighters on western Allied airfields in Europe. The bad news was in the making as the Luftwaffe losses were colossal. Two hundred eleven pilots and more than three hundred aircraft were lost. The damage the Luftwaffe inflicted seemed minimal compared with German losses in proportion. This would be the Luftwaffe's final large-scale operation on the Western Front as the Axis fliers held out for as long as they could.

One of the Luftwaffe pilots that participated on that January 1, 1945, mission was an Fw 190 pilot named Feldwebel (Flying Sergeant) Oscar Boesch, who flew with Sturmstaffel 1./JG 3 "Udet." Sergeant Boesch recalled in great detail his mission that day:

Our wake-up call came at 5:30 a.m. A top-secret mission, Operation Boden Platte, was laid out for us at the morning briefing.

We, pilots, studied detailed maps of our route and target area, Eindhoven airbase, Holland, and listened to last-minute instructions before making the short walk to our Fw 190s.

I was surprised how calm my nerves were and felt somewhat refreshed knowing that it was now our turn to attack allied aircraft that were hopefully still on the ground. Finally, I thought of some payback and our day for revenge against the bothersome allied escort fighters. They called us "targets of opportunity" when they left their bombers and dropped down to go looking for us. We were always outnumbered as we took our daily beatings.

Every day we had to endure attacks by Mustangs, Spitfires, Lightnings, Thunderbolts, and Typhoons.

They shot up everything they saw; even a man on a bicycle was not safe on the streets! As I strapped myself into the 190, I believed this important mission would bring some much-needed reprieve from allied superiority on the western front. I also knew, however, if this mission failed, it would spell disaster for all of us and the tactical end of the Luftwaffe.

Shortly after 8:20 a.m. our Staffel (squadron) of nineteen Fw 190s quickly lifted off from the snow-covered field at Guetersloh and disappeared into the western sky. We quickly rendezvoused with the rest of the Geschwader "Udet" near Lippstadt and formed up with other 190s, as we became a strike force of sixty Fw 190s. To prevent detection by enemy radar, our flight level was on the deck. We flew between chimneys and around church steeples to avoid detection.

Leading us to Einthoven was our "mother goose," a Ju 88 that did all of the navigating and communicating; radio silence was mandatory until we reached the target. With good visibility and flat terrain, we flew over the front lines undetected by antiaircraft guns. Fifty km behind allied lines, we dropped our belly tanks, charged our guns, and I tightened up my straps as Einthoven airbase came into view.

In front of us was a huge parking lot full of Spitfires and Typhoons. Hundreds and hundreds of allied aircraft were right before my eyes, and this time they were all on the ground! I saw four Spitfires being fueled at a gas booth, and I aimed for the center one as my cannon rounds tore into them. Huge explosions ripped the Spitfires apart, and they all began to burn.

All around me were black and red fireballs where allied aircraft once sat.

Streaks of cannon shells zipped through the snow and mud into burning aircraft as Einthoven airbase was chewed to bits by our Fw 190s. I made pass after pass on the fully engulfed field and saw Typhoons and Spitfires trying to taxi through the chaos. Other Fw 190s sealed their fate as cannon shells found their mark and ignited the allied fighters before they could get airborne. The heavy antiaircraft fire began to arch in my direction as the British defensive gunners tried to retaliate. It was like flying in a damn hornet's nest as tracer rounds swirled everywhere!

On my fourth and last pass over Einthoven, I ran out of machine gun ammo and my cannons jammed on me.

I was just above the treetops as the fires from the burning aircraft threw thick black clouds of oily smoke into the air completely limiting visibility. Suddenly, out of the smoke and haze, came a fellow Fw 190 right in front of my nose! A fraction of a second sooner and we would have collided. That's when I thought, "Oh boy, it's dangerous. Time to get the hell out of here!"

With my cannon still jammed and my machine guns out of ammo, it was a wake-up call for me to leave. On the deck at full throttle, I turned east for home. Like so often after a battle, I was all alone. About five minutes flying time from Einthoven, I saw a low flying aircraft ahead of me and thought it was a fellow Fw 190. As I got closer to my newfound wingman, a chill ran up my spine. This was no 190; this was a hostile Typhoon!

I was right behind him, 100 feet away, and lucky for me, right in his blind spot. The Typhoon was one of the Luftwaffe's most hated and feared allied aircraft. It had done so much damage to our ground units, particularly our armor. It was fast and when heavily loaded with rockets, it turned our tanks into Swiss cheese. I recharged my jammed cannon and got a green light!

The Typhoon made a 30-degree turn to the left as I stayed with him out of sight. I had him bull's-eyed in my gunsight, and at this close range, how could I miss? I pulled the trigger on the 30 mm cannon and hoped he would fall with the rounds I had left.

I squeezed the trigger again and again… Nothing! The only thing that worked was that damn green light!

I was 50 km behind enemy lines on the backside of a ferocious tiger. He had superior speed, firepower, and probably lots of ammunition.

Had I been over Germany I may have rammed him or chewed off his tail, but over his lines, I had no chance to survive a tangle with him. The Typhoon went into another turn as I followed him through it, still unnoticed.

I had a ten-second window of opportunity to leave before I became a Typhoon victim.

I carefully maneuvered myself out of harm's way and the golden opportunity for the Typhoon pilot to get an easy kill. I wish I knew his name to let him know how he and I got away then we could both celebrate!

There was no celebrating when I returned to Gutersloh. The bad news was in the making, as the Luftwaffe losses were colossal. Two hundred and eleven pilots and more than three hundred aircraft were lost.

The damage we inflicted seemed minimal compared with our losses in proportion. This would be the Luftwaffe's final large-scale operation on the western front as we held out for as long as we could.[5]

Charles Carpenter was also airborne that day in a slow-flying, unarmed L-4 and found himself an "unwilling" participant among his trigger-happy compatriots.

January 3, **1945** (*letter excerpt*)

Dearest Bunny,

I haven't flown much lately. The day before yesterday (January 1), as I was being flown to Luxembourg by another pilot to pick up "Rosie the Rocketer," we were almost shot down by a German in one of our own P-47s. At first we thought he was just playing until he opened fire. Then we took him more seriously and scooted down over a friendly town as he took off into the sun. It's a strange war now with Germans driving our American vehicles and wearing our American uniforms at times.

January 8, **1944**

Dearest Bunny,

The snow is drifting down again. Already it is so deep that I am unable to get my plane off the ground in its present location. Flying is almost out of the question, and our division is practically at a standstill.

This morning I rode up to one of our advance command posts. The winter setting was more beautiful than I have ever seen. The forests of Luxembourg and Belgium are unbelievable. They look like stories in children's fairy-tale books. Now festooned with ice and snow, and with the tops of the tallest trees rushing into the winter mist, the scenic splendor is breathtaking and war seems far away.

Men cluster around tiny fires and sit huddled next to the big guns and tanks. Most of the scars of war are hidden beneath a blanket of snow. Even the burnt-out vehicles and wrecked homes look less harsh beneath their white coverlet. Someday the coverlet will be green, and other soldiers in another war will probably muse as we have over the half buried wounds of the last war.

The saddest part of the picture is the remnant of the population that still tries to cling to what is left. There is no cheering anymore—just vacant stares and hopeless scratching around for bits of firewood.

Goodnight, Charles

January 26, **1945** (*letter excerpt*)

Dearest Bunny,

Its lovely and quiet here now and I have time to think a little bit. I know you love me and that your love overlooks many faults of mine. After several years of being without you, I have to fight against the feeling that you are the dream and this life is grim reality.

Some of the days are ages long now, and the nights remind me that those moments, when our bodies and souls were locked in embrace and awakenings were tender moments stolen from sleep, can exact a price for loving you.

January 29, **1945** (*letter excerpt*)

Dearest Bunny,

At present I am permitted to say I am somewhere in Luxembourg. In recent weeks you might have read of our division in connection with the relief of Bastogne and the stopping of the German breakthrough.

Bombers are droning by overhead now. It must be tough on the German these days. The tremendous Russian offensive has all of us here discussing that end of the war. I don't see how the German can hold out much longer.

February 1, **1945** (*letter excerpt*)

Dearest Bunny,

The weather has changed now. Outside a south wind is blowing and the snow is melting everywhere. I don't think spring has not as come yet, but the soft breeze does remind me of spring.

We have been in one place for almost three weeks now, well behind the lines. I do not like my new job and may not be doing very well in it. I know myself well enough now to realize that I am not a staff officer. I loaf a great deal and make no pretense of being busy. Sometimes that is not good.

War is hard on ideals as it is on human beings and homes. Drinking is common place here now. Language is generally pretty rough, and the senses often become dulled to actual beauty and culture. I do not know if it is good to relax ones standards. Many of those who have fought against it are no longer with us.

That is, the mental casualties seen to be more plentiful among those who only sit and think about home and what they are missing there. Religion is probably a help to many, but I guess I do not happen to know them. There is one chaplain I know who leaves me with an impression of sincerity. The other chaplains fear and distrust him because of his disapproval of them.

Of course war seems always to have had this effect on the finer things. The physical damage and injuries may be long healed before the mental and moral senses of value have scarcely begun to recover. Do not worry about me. Somedays the gray clouds are so low I walk among them.

February 4, **1945** (*letter excerpt*)

Dearest Bunny,

The news is coming in over the radio now. It certainly does sound encouraging with the Russians less than 60 miles from Berlin.

Just now I'm leaving to the see the doc about a swelling on one side of my neck. It doesn't bother me now, but still, the doc wanted me to go to the hospital to have it checked. He's here now so I will say "Adios" for a while

CHAPTER 18

A New Enemy

February 6, 1945 (*letter excerpt*)

Dearest Bunny,

This time I'm writing from an army evacuation hospital. I have never felt better. However, there is a swelling in one side of my neck that has the doc puzzled. In the morning I start on a round of X-rays and blood tests. There's nothing serious about my case, but it does look as though I might get several weeks' vacation with pay.

In army language, I'm probably "goldbricking" now, except that I was picked out and sent up here without any effort on my part.

The hospitality of the people of Luxembourg is beyond belief. They wait on Americans hand and foot and splurge with their last resources to entertain us. They suffered much mentally and physically under the German occupations. Now their gratitude knows no limits. Normally the country is prosperous and progressive, and its people more like Americans even than the British.

When Charles arrived at the 38th Evacuation Hospital with excessive fatigue and a lump in the right side of his neck, the doctors there realized it appeared much more serious. He was sent to the 108th General Hospital in Paris, where on February 14 a gland was removed. The examination revealed a uniform spherical mass on the right side of his neck. According to the doctor, the mass was smooth, freely movable, and accompanied by slight enlargement of several other lymph nodes in the neck. The pathological report on the gland removed was suggestive of Hodgkin's disease. For Charles, the war was over but a new battle against cancer was about to begin.

February 15, 1945 (*letter excerpt*)

Dearest Bunny,

I've moved again. This time I'm in a magnificent big hospital in Paris. Yesterday the Doc took several glands out of my neck to look at under microscope—they may do some operating tomorrow.

My roommate is a major too. He has one leg gone and naturally feels a little blue.

We just now had a air raid warning. The German air strength has diminished that few people are much concerned any longer. The buzz bombs are a different thing though.

Charles attached the following poem to his latest letter home:

February 1945

Escape

O! come along and merry with me be.

We find a lonesome shore besides some sunlit sea.

There with song we'll fill the air where none will care.

And let our dancing hearts go free.

Enough of war and greed and hate.

We fought their battles long and late.

Now live with me beside the sea.

Grief will always be, but youth and laughter will not wait.

March 5, **1945** (*letter excerpt*)

My operation was a success but my case is still quite a puzzle to the doctors. My case is of the type that could be very serious or could be almost nothing. A growth was removed from beneath the muscle in the right side of my neck. As you would guess I am relatively undisturbed.

The army doctors determined that Charles would need further treatment back in the states. Charles was flown by military transport across the Atlantic, a trip he had endured for almost two weeks at sea going the other way on his journey to England, a little over a year ago. This time the journey by air was much shorter for him. Upon further examination at Walter Reed General Hospital, doctors observed that the operative scar was noted to have considerable enlargement and diffused swelling under it. Charles neglected to tell his wife that according to several doctors, he was given only a year to live.

March 14, **1945** (*letter excerpt*)

Dearest Bunny,
Just a note to tell you that I am on your side of the Atlantic again. The doctor in Paris recommended that I be sent to Walter Reed Gen. Hosp. in Washington, DC.

Outwardly I don't believe I have changed much. Inwardly I seem to be moodier and more restless. Being away from home has robbed me of the sentimentality you had awakened in me. I hope that I didn't lead you to expect me home right away. It looks as though I am in for quite an extensive course of treatments yet. I feel fine, although I get tired more easily than I used to.

April 5, **1945** (*letter excerpt*)

Dearest Bunny,
My neck is getting a little sore now. I hear it gets a little worse later on. It's hard to realize I have been away from home three years now in the army. That is as long a period as our married life together. The world has certainly been turned tospy turvy in that time.

Because the pathologist was unable to make a diagnosis of Hodgkin's disease, doctors determined a course of radiation treatment to the right side of Charles's neck because of the clinical pictures of Hodgkin's disease. Charles began a series of ten 4,000 r treatments between March 22 and April 11, which resulted in over a 60 percent shrinkage in the size of the mass in his neck. Perhaps due to his treatments, the following letter Charles sent back home to Elda had the outward appearance of a man fraught with guilt, anger, and despair.

April 10, 1945 (*letter excerpt*)
Walter Reed General Hospital
Army Medical Center
Washington, DC

Dear Elda,
Yesterday, almost a dozen of your letters arrived from oversees. They carried your same story of faith in me and in our future. There were several extremely justified but gentle reminders of my own shortcomings as a correspondent and absentee husband in the past few months.

Your reception of this letter will have much to do with how I write to you in the future. Although my mind has been filled with inner conflict, this letter in no way stems from a mental lapse or breakdown. The war may have hardened and coarsened me, but I have never for a moment suffered in it. It was an "idiot's delight," an absurd and tragic farce that the world has yet to pay for. I fought impersonally and without hatred. Many times I was filled with admiration for the courage and skill of the enemy. My greatest moments of pity were not for my fellow man, but for helpless and innocent people ground to bits between the opposing armies. It was largely a question of whether our brand of stupidity or that the enemy was to be predominant in what was left of the world. Selfishness ruled both sides, but I preferred ours to what the spectre of defeat held for the loser.

Present previews of the fumbling toward peace indicates that selfishness is still enthroned, and that the winners will match if not excel most other winners in history in stupidity.

Enough of that. The point is that I have changed more than I let you know. For my part, much of my idealism has slipped through my fingers and disappeared. I have made friends that you would find difficulty in accepting. I have been unfaithful on more than one occasion and thought scarcely anything of it. Money has run through my fingers like dirt.

You and Carol Ann have often been little more than a dream out of my past and little part of my future. Despite all your missionary spirit, your God is less my God than ever before. I gave the lovely Bible you sent me to someone who will use it. The thought of nothing after death but dreamless sleep is pleasant to me. I am not interested in trading it for a brighter heaven.

Once I thought to go to the Pacific war and prolong the lovely illusions I believe you have of me. Now that is gone. I shall probably be discharged from the army to a future of uncertain health and longevity. I may spend it in the manner of what the world calls a "bum," at least certainly not as a saint.

Now that my return to you and home draws near, I had to write these things. I do not expect to return to the old life in Moline. I could not teach young people feeling this way. This period is a clean break in my life. I expect to find a new life somewhere. This is not the "eternal triangle." Any woman in your position with me could I be writing tonight. If I break your heart, look about you and see that you are not alone. If I break your spirit with a letter such as this, then it would have broken one day anyway before another storm of life. If you have dreamed me into some sort of hero, I must disappoint you sooner or later. Why not now when there is more time for healing? Pray to your God. This is not mocking. Your faith should be stronger than my selfishness—my unwillingness to dedicate the rest of my existence to you and Carol Ann. Tears or hysterics or entreaties from your friends and mine would hurt but not soften me. I did not write this letter on a moments prompting. This is the cruelest but fairest thing I have ever done. Perhaps I am no longer a refuge, a rock to build upon—but I am far from a liability.

If possible I might stay in the army. That does not lie with me now, however. Otherwise I expect to go West or South and start something new. You may follow if the new terms of my existence are acceptable to you. It is reasonable to assume that the monthly allotment of the present time may not last long.

I am hungry for the loveliness of you and home. There is a deeper hunger and pain that I am sure cannot keep me there. I am no hero, war or otherwise, and I dread any appearance in Moline in that role.

This letter will probably hurt you more than it should. You have not failed in anything. I am in conflict with life myself and telling you about it so you may be forewarned and take steps to look out for your own interests as well as our common interests.

April 12, 1945 (*letter excerpt*)

Bunny, Dear:
It is quite hot and sticky here now. The trees have their new green cloaks and the cherry blossoms are falling like snow. I certainly am feeling low these days.

I do hope that my actions haven't upset you too much. It isn't worth it. Compared to the troubles all about me, my own are not much. I do know that I don't give a damn about a lot of things that used to be very important to me.

You have turned out to be a much more reasonable person than myself. I hope that you can still be master of your emotions, else I might drive you almost to distraction.

After writing his latest letter home to Elda, Charles would soon encounter, along with not only the rest of the nation but the Allied world as well, a new heartbreaking distraction. President Franklin D. Roosevelt, the thirty-second president of the United States, had died. The sixty-three-year-old had been resting at Warm Springs, Georgia, since late March and passed away at 3:35 p.m. with a cerebral bleed. As a nation grieved and mourned the loss of its leader, the fighting across all fronts of the war continued.

What Charles Carpenter did not realize at the time was that his earlier actions and exploits in combat, those encounters while using "Rosie the Rocketer" that was later highlighted in *Yank* and *Stars & Stripes*, along with a variety of other stateside newspapers, actually inspired other liaison pilots both in Europe and in the Pacific theater. One of them was a Marine observation pilot named Lt. Thomas Rozga:

The Marine Observation Squadron's (VMO) were the eyes and ears of the commanding officers of the various Marine divisions. Able to communicate via a two-way radio, we could tell the troops on the ground what was happening on the front lines, scout out targets of opportunity, and then direct artillery fire onto enemy positions.

Unfortunately, all of this was performed in an unarmed, two-place tandem fabric-covered Warbug called the Stinson OY-1 (L-5). The Stinson was constructed utilizing Chromoly steel tubing and fabric covering with a wraparound Plexiglas greenhouse giving the pilot and observer an unobstructed view. The OY-1 was powered by a six-cylinder 190 hp Lycoming O-435 engine, giving it ample power to get in and out of most short-field situations. Some models carried an observer in the back seat, and others carried a stretcher behind the observer so we could fly our wounded away from the battlefield. I have to admit that the first time I saw this airplane; I scratched my head and wondered out loud, "We're flying these in combat?"

By January of 1945, I was the new CO (commanding officer) of VMO-4 when we flew our L-5s to Iwo Jima. Unfortunately, the Japanese were concealed at the other end of the runway and pounded us with motor rounds and machine-gun fire as our Stinsons landed. The fact of the matter was as a Marine observation pilot, droning around above a battlefield talking on the radio calling in artillery; most of us were frustrated fighter pilots. We wanted in on the action, and with only a .45-caliber pistols slung on our hips, we knew we had to come up with something bigger to do any damage. One of the pilots in our squadron had the mind-set of an ordinance man and came up to me one day and said, "Skipper, how's about we mount some bazookas on the airplanes?" I laughed and said, "do you think it can be done?" He shook his head up and down like an excited boy and said, "I know it can be done!"

My concern was that the fabric-covered tail section or elevator on the OY-1 would be burned completely off from the flame that exited the rear tube of the bazooka. The smile from the pilot's face departed and he became more serious, thinking about the question I posed. "I guess it's possible skipper, but we won't know unless we try it out. Want me to mount one on each side?"

I thought about it for a second and said, "Hell, if we're going to do this right, then let's put three bazookas on each side. Now go find some bazookas!"

Finding bazookas on Iwo Jima was like a kid finding candy on Halloween. We mounted three of the bazooka tubes to the wing struts of both wings on an OY-1 that was adorned with the nose art of "Lady Satan." We had installed six toggle switches on the instrument panel to fire each of the bazookas. By that afternoon it was ready to try out. Our engineering officer, Lieutenant Kelly, asked if he could be the first to try it out. Before I could say anything, he was already airborne.

He fired one bazooka, looked back, and saw that his tail wasn't on fire, so he cranked off another round. Satisfied, he fired the remaining four rounds and came back in to give his report: "The handling was beautiful, no adverse yaw effect whatsoever and no fire exiting the rear tube. Once the projectiles have left the bazooka, it becomes a hollow tube with no resistance and excellent airflow. It's time for some Marine Observation payback!"

From then on, the biggest problem I had was breaking up the fights between the pilots because they all wanted to fly "Lady Satan." Thankfully rank has its privileges, and even I got into the action with our lone bazooka equipped OY-1.

The procedure was to get up to altitude, never really that high, select a target below, and then push the nose over into a shallow dive. Most of the time I fired all of them at once as they zoomed toward their target below. The Japanese learned to keep their heads down as the Marines on the ground waved and cheered us on. Honestly, they weren't that accurate, but they made a hell of an explosion when they hit and it sure made us feel like fighter/bomber pilots for a while! I found out later that the brass in the Pentagon had spent an ungodly sum of money trying to figure out how to properly mount a bazooka on an airplane. We wrote them a letter, and it read, "From VMO-4.

Reference to our bazooka-mounted OY-1s. It didn't cost us any-thing—just some USMC ingenuity!"[1]

Back on the European front, however, with the war in Europe inching its way closer to a conclusion and defeat of the Nazi reign of terror, one of the final dogfights of the war took place low over Germany with two very unique aircraft playing the role of adversaries. Inspired by the earlier exploits of Charles Carpenter, many liaison pilots secretly acknowledged they were "frustrated fighter pilots" itching for a fight. One of those was an L-4 pilot with the 5th Armored Division, 71st Field Battalion, by the name of Lt. Merritt Duane Francies, who recalled his mission on April 11, 1945, near Vesbeck, Germany:

I had named my new L-4 "Miss Me!?" for two reasons. One was that I wanted the Germans to miss me when they shot at me, and the other was that I had hoped someone was missing me back home. On today's mission, Lt. William Martin was spotting from the back seat as we flew out ahead of the advancing armored column looking for targets. We were flying at between 600 and 800 feet when we spotted a German motorcycle with a sidecar that came racing out of a tree line below. This guy was parallel to the front lines, and we assumed he was a messenger. Our plan was to see where he was going, then fly alongside him and "pop" a couple of rounds off at him from our .45s. We were all set to do just that when all of a sudden, out of nowhere, a German Fieseler Fi 156 Storch flew right below us at treetop level.

The Storch was the German observation equivalent of the L-4, but it was a lot bigger, weighed twice as much, flew faster, and was sometimes lightly armed with a machine gun. But, at the time, I didn't give any of that much thought because we had the altitude advantage—and, besides, he hadn't seen us yet. This guy was in a big hurry, skimming the treetops, and he must have thought his camouflage would blend in with the terrain below. He thought wrong; those German crosses were as clear as day as he headed east above the trees. I lifted the side-door window of the L-4 and pushed the door down to give Lieutenant Martin and me more room to shoot at him. I pushed the stick forward and the nose of the L-4 pitched down, diving onto the Storch.

We came up from the Storch's blindside as I tried to cut in front of him. While I was diving down on him, I yelled to Lieutenant Martin through the swirling wind in the cockpit, telling him that I was going to try to chase this guy toward our tank column so they could get a shot at him. Unfortunately, the Storch wouldn't go along with the chase idea, however, and instead, the German pilot cranked that big wing over and started going around and around in a great big circle. We circled above him, trying to figure out what we were going to do next; that's when I unholstered my .45 and pushed the L-4 closer to the Storch.

The Storch tried his best to outmaneuver us, but it is darn near impossible to outmaneuver a Cub! I flew at him head on, and neither one of us was changing course or altitude. At the last minute, I jinxed back on the stick and we flew over him, missing him by a few feet.

I remember thinking there were a lot of glass windows over the Storch's cockpit, and I realized that both the German pilot in the front and the guy in the back had seen us—their eyes were as big as saucers. Lieutenant Martin and I started to fire at him with our .45s as we passed overhead. The Storch was 30 miles per hour faster than we were, but instead of running, he tried to circle upward for altitude. I could turn tighter than he could, however, so it didn't take us long to get back into a firing position and let loose again with our handguns; this time I unloaded my entire magazine.

I had to hold the L-4's stick with my knees as I dropped my empty magazine out of the airplane; there was no way I wanted that to lodge under my rudder pedal. I continued to fly with my knees as I put a fresh magazine into the .45 and began to fire at the Storch again. I was getting close to him at that time, still above him, and I led him just a little bit. When I thought I had the right lead, I began to crank off rounds as fast as I could. I saw a small flash near his engine cowling and on his fuselage, so I knew I was hitting him, especially when I saw fuel streaming from one of the fuel tanks. The Storch began to turn left and climb, and then suddenly it made a hard right and dived into a corkscrew turn. I was still above him when I emptied my last magazine into him.

I had him pretty well boxed in from above as he tried to turn away from me. We were finally able to drive him into the ground as the Storch tried one last turn. Because his wings were much longer than mine, he misjudged his height, and his right wing dug into the ground. It was more of a controlled crash than it was a landing as the Storch plowed into a beet field, wiping out his gear and right wing. One thing was certain—that German pilot didn't want any part of us! A couple of minutes later, I set the Cub down as close as I could to the Storch, and Lt. Martin and I made our way over to the wreckage. I went for the guy who was still in the back seat while Lieutenant Martin went looking for the pilot, who had taken off running.

We saw that the guy in the back had been hit in the foot, so I tended to him. Lieutenant Martin had retrieved the carbine rifle that was stuffed in the back of the L-4 and went after the pilot, who had run north and was hiding behind a pile of beets. Lieutenant Martin yelled in German to him, "Hands up!" He stood up, and for a minute he thought Lieutenant Martin was going to shoot him.

Eventually, all of the troops in the area who had been watching our "dogfight" came racing up to our position. I turned over my prisoner, the pilot, to some MPs. One of my friends in a half-track jumped down and cut the tail number and swastika off the tail of the Storch and handed it to me as a souvenir.

In assessing our kill, we saw a few bullet holes in the cowling, one in the windshield, one in the fuel tank, and a couple in the fuselage. We also found a lot of paperwork and learned that this Storch had been based at a temporary field with a bunch of other Storches. Unfortunately for him, he was the tail-end Charlie guy, and all his help was fleeing eastbound away from the advancing allied troops. The entire duel lasted no more than 10 minutes, but it sure felt like an hour to me. Lieutenant Martin and I hopped back into the L-4 and completed our observation of the front lines. We had been told to cover a certain area, and that's exactly what we did—we went back to spotting artillery fire as if shooting down the Storch was all in a day's work.[2]

April 21, 1945 (*letter excerpt*)

Dearest Bunny,

My status changes almost daily. There still seems to be some question as to whether I really have Hodgkin's. The future of my health is of course uncertain. I never felt better than at present. However, I don't intend to risk any of my years from now on doing something I do not like. I was all keyed up at the thought of getting out of the army and being on my own again.

It must be hard on you to have my status changing so from day to day. Your voice sounded so fresh and eager yesterday that I wanted to reach across the hundreds of miles and hold you close—very close!

Charles was eventually deemed well enough to travel home as he arrived back at 724 221st St. in Moline in late April on a thirty-day leave. Charles shared his thoughts with a reporter from the *Moline Dispatch* on May 2, 1945, stating, "Home is just what I pictured it and hoped it would be." But when pressed to discuss his involvement during his battles with the Germans while in Europe and how he earned his Silver Star and Air Medal, Charles was not very forthcoming. Instead, he said, "I plan to let my almost-three-year-old daughter (Carol) entertain me while I am home."[3] That same day, the newspaper *Stars & Stripes* printed an extra with a large-print title that many in this world at that time had been praying for since the war began 2,190 days earlier: "Hitler Dead."

Less than a week later, on May 8, 1945, Maj. Charles Carpenter was the guest of honor at the Moline Rotary Club luncheon. While he was sharing his thoughts of flying his Cub, "Rosie the Rocketer," at treetop level, he stated to the assembled crowd:

Wes Gallagher hung the name "Bazooka Charlie" on me for some of my exploits with a Piper Cub with bazookas tied to the wings. I do not deserve as much credit as some of my buddies who are still over there, and our successes against the enemy were for the most part the result of indignation at seeing our comrades shot down, rather than from a spirit of courage or patriotism. When we saw our soldiers taking a beating, we would wait for the Germans to line up for chow and then let them have it from low level, where it was hard for the Nazis to get at us. At 500 feet it made the German antiaircraft (gunners) powerless against us. We had a definite advantage over other types of craft since it could come back full of holes, have them patched up, and go out for more.

The Piper Cub proved to be invaluable to observation work for artillery batteries as we could fly low, making a difficult target for them to hit. We could bank around a tree or turn on a dime, where the larger ships couldn't change their course so quickly and consequently were hit more often.

But war is discouraging to a history teacher. History books glamorize war. With what little I've seen of this war, I can reread battles of other wars and see a few things I didn't see before.

Most young people don't realize how fortunate they are to be in America as far as privileges and the future ahead of them are concerned. Especially those of the high school age. Over there the boys and girls are much more serious-minded because they have seen so much more.

Education, although slow, will be the answer to the problem of peace. The new generation in Europe, though, will be poorly educated because many teachers have been killed or are in prisons.[4]

But as Charles was sharing his tales with his attentive audience, his brothers in arms still based and fighting in Europe were told the Germans had surrendered. News quickly spread all over the world, with newspapers running special editions and people from towns and cities, big and small, spilling into the streets celebrating VE-day, Victory in Europe. But for Charles, the memories, some good and much more unspeakable, remained bottled up inside him as he prepared to return to the military hospitals for more treatments; the swelling in his neck had returned. Charles would continue to receive both treatments and temporary leaves but did not necessarily return home each time as he searched for some sort of normalcy.

June 15, **1945** (*letter excerpt*)

Dearest Bunny,
The days are still drifting by and I'm drifting with them. Each day my doctor tells me there is no news but that there should be soon. I am not impatient because this hospital is as good a place to loaf as the next one. The other night I went on a picnic up at Mildred's (oldest sister). Her school teacher friends and some sailors made up the group. There was an abundance of good food and I had a pretty good time.

June 25, **1945** (*letter excerpt*)

Dearest Bunny,
I've finished my fifth day at Percy Jones Hospital (Ward 23, Battle Creek, Michigan) I'm waiting now for some slides to come from Walter Reed Hospital. When the slides arrive I suppose some decision will be made as to further x-ray treatment.
   Letter-writing seems to be quite a problem with me these days. I feel good but can't seem to give a damn yet about anything much. Perhaps that may change when I get away from hospitals.

There was little to no reprieve for Charles as he endured test after test, continual (irradiation) x-ray therapy, and a relentless change of hospitals and doctors. For him, the days were filled with agonizing pain, boredom, and unknown futures—not only his own but those with his marriage as well. But there was also a mysterious side to Charles and his ambiguous relationship with Elda since returning home, unknown to Elda until 1995.

While receiving treatment at Percy Jones Hospital, Battle Creek, Michigan, Charles had written a letter dated Monday, July 16, 1945, to a woman named Miss Betty Young, who was residing at room 934 at the Chelsea Hotel, located at 920 Wilson Ave., Chicago, Illinois. No other reference to her was mentioned or uncovered by the family, and perhaps it was a woman he met while at his sister's picnic, perhaps not. Nevertheless, there were more questions than answers, unfortunately:

July 16, 1945

Dear Betty,
I've had two very nice letters from you since your visit. It made me feel very good to know that in retrospect your trip was as grand as it seemed while we were together here.

Elda's visit has not been a happy one, especially for her. There have been tears and some hysterics, and I have felt like a "skunk" much of the time. However, this too will probably pass away.

Yesterday the doctors told me that their recommendation for me is another operation. The fact that it is likely to come in the next week or so makes it difficult for me to plan more than a day or two ahead. It does appear now though that I'll probably be here at least for the rest of summer.

Your mention of Denver disturbs me. Yet I know that if you go there it is because it is a better opportunity for you. Knowing me should not influence your decisions in anyway because, at best, I represent instability during the foreseeable future.

I'll be calling you one of these afternoons. Things may be less complicated then.

Good-bye, for now,
Love, Charles

Charles's use of the word "complicated" was an understatement. On the basis of previous letters he had written to Elda, his admission of unfaithfulness was outwardly confessed and addressed with her. It was not uncommon for soldiers to find solace with other women during wartime conditions. These men, especially those in the frontline combat arenas, faced life and death and uncertainty daily. For many of them, physical attraction and interaction with the opposite sex was their only escape from the horrors of combat.

Many soldiers developed what early military doctors called, "combat fatigue." In modern terms, it is now known as posttraumatic stress disorder (PTSD).

But ironically and perhaps erring on the side of providence, this letter never arrived in the hands of Betty Young. Instead, this letter lay dormant behind a mail sorting machine in Battle Creek, Michigan, until it was discovered more than fifty years later on October 11, 1995, by the postal service. It eventually made its way to Ohio, where Elda was residing. A widow since 1966, Elda's first remark to her daughter, Carol, upon opening the letter, was "We have to find this woman and deliver this letter to her." She never did. Even at eighty-three years old, Elda Carpenter held no ill will for this stranger. Elda Carpenter was by all accounts a loving, faithful wife who had made peace with the ghosts of the past and forgiven her husband long ago.

July 25, **1945** (*letter excerpt*)

Dear Bunny,
I hope Carol Ann had fun at her birthday party. It's hard to realize that she is three years old already. It seemed only a short while ago that she was a tiny thing sleeping in a basket.

Yesterday I appeared before a board of doctors. They decided that a preliminary operation should be made to remove a lymph node from under my arm. If the pathologic report on that is negative, another operation will be performed to remove what is left of the swelling in my neck.

I hope you are not worrying about me. All of my health troubles are relatively simple and nothing serious insofar as operations are concerned. The future, though puzzling, is far from dark. My mind is in hibernation, I guess, until I'm called upon to use it again. Your letters sound bright and cheery—that helps a lot.

August 5, **1945** (*letter excerpt*)

Dear Bunny,
No further word on my leave. I will be notified when I can depart from the hospital. My own mind is confused more than a little, but I

do intend to go to New Mexico for a while. By doing so I may add to your disappointment in me, but I believe it is the best thing in the long run. I have hurt you so much that I am actually ashamed to face you. It seems I have few ties anywhere—even at home. In brutal frankness, thirty more days waiting in Moline for some decision on my case does not appeal to me as it should. Why, I do not know—only that it is so.

I'm still hoping to return to full active duty so that, possibly, I could return to a combat zone. Such a thing is rather unlikely, however.

Please keep your faith in things that are good if not in me. Probably the greatest wrong I have ever done has been the pain and worry I have caused you—but I do not seem to be able to help it and still remain what I am.

Charles's hope of returning to combat was vaporized the very next day as a lone, silver metal-colored four-engine Boeing B-29 Superfortress bearing the nose art "Enola Gay" unleashed a new wonder weapon called "Little Boy," an atomic bomb, from its belly over the city of Hiroshima, Japan. Three days later, this time over the city of Nagasaki, Japan, a B-29 Superfortress displaying the nose art of "Bockscar" dropped an atomic bomb called "Fat Boy." On August 15, 1945, Japanese emperor Hirohito announced to his loyal subjects, during a radio broadcast, that Japan was surrendering to the United States and its Allies.

**American Red Cross
Oklahoma City, Oklahoma
August 16, 1945**

Dear Bunny,

Temporarily I'm stranded here at Tinker Field. The end of the war has stopped a lot of the flying for a while at least. I had a chance for a plane ride west if I left immediately. I took it and got this far before the celebrations started. One way or another I'll be at Margaret's [Charles's sister] in several days.

Love, Charles

By the time Japan had officially surrendered in early September, Charles was in and out of military hospitals dealing with not only his x-ray treatments for his cancer but also trying desperately to pick of the missing pieces of his life and reestablish a relationship with his beloved and patient wife. As time began to heal some of his wounds, Charles still struggled, like many other returning servicemen did, with the horrors and atrocities they witnessed while in combat. Charles, whether he knew it at the time or not, was one of the lucky ones with a loving family waiting for him to return.

December 11, 1945 (*letter excerpt*)

Dearest Bunny,
This morning my doctor asked me if I preferred to be operated on after the holidays or as soon as possible. I told him that I preferred to have the operation as soon as possible. That may mean of course that I will be here at Christmas time.

I love you and my disposition is excellent again, but I do expect to be hard to get along with maybe for several weeks, and I don't want to be ashamed of myself again if I can help it.

I think we have lots of good times ahead of us, and I hope you are not getting discouraged by my present hospitalization. I certainly am not myself and feel glad to be getting this present treatment over and behind me.

Lots of kisses and goodnight,

Charles

December 15, 1945 (*letter excerpt*)

Dearest Bunny,
My face is badly swollen and I look like I had the mumps. Tomorrow the doctor is going to take all the stitches out. He says that if all goes well, I might be able to make it home at Christmastime.

CHAPTER 19

A Teacher's Wisdom

As a child, Carol, who was still under five years old, recalls that she didn't particularly care for her father when he returned home after four years of military service, and considered him an intruder and felt that her father was somewhat sharp with her. After all, with what Charles had to endure and his witnessing the atrocities of war, and the brutality from both sides, he felt more like a stranger in a strange land. Elda would regale the story to Carol of the first Christmas when Charles came home in 1945 as a relative stranger. Carol had all kinds of Christmas presents spread out before her, and as she was ripping through the packages gleefully, throwing away the ribbons and moving on from gift to gift, acting, as she recalls, "a little spoiled about it," her dad, visibly upset, just stormed out of the room in disgust. The contrast between life at home and what Charles had endured in combat was overwhelming. He had seen the limitless destruction of homes, lands, and people. He witnessed orphaned children scattered about the European countryside who were lucky to have the clothes on their backs, with little to eat and a hopeless future. The adjustments back to civilian life were extremely difficult for him, even more so with the compounded and added burdens of wondering when he would die from his cursed cancer.

Because of the uncertainties of his life and how much longer he would be around to enjoy it, Charles decided that he had no patience for death and was not simply going to sit in an easy chair and wait for the Grim Reaper to appear. Charles wanted to visit the American West.

With his most recent treatments completed in the spring of 1946, Charles Carpenter had been promoted to the rank of lieutenant colonel, FA (field artillery) Division Headquarters, 4th Armored Division, and honorably discharged from the Army of the United States of April 6, 1946.

The family home at 724 21st Street A in Moline was rented, a long silver Airstream trailer was purchased, and Charles packed his wife and daughter and headed out on the next Carpenter adventure. For the next several months, they visited Charles's sisters in New Mexico, and camped at the Grand Canyon and the Grand Tetons before visiting Yellowstone National Park in Wyoming. The Carpenter family was soaking up the sights of the American West, never questioning the rationale of Charles or his decisions. Elda knew her husband was dying, and as a faithful partner, she stuck by her man in sickness and in health.

But with a family to feed, and very little traveling money left, along with an uncertain future, Charles determined to head back to Illinois and surrender to his ultimate demise. But the old Carpenter luck had reemerged—death had decided to take a holiday. With his cancer now at a standstill, Charles took advantage of whatever time he had left with his life and accepted an old familiar job. For the third time in his life, Charles returned to the familiar grounds of the Roosevelt Military Academy. The April 1947 edition of the school's newspaper, *Rough Rider*, reported the following:

Famous Colonel to be Commandant!
Internationally famous Lt. Col. Chas. Carpenter, known as "Bazooka Charley," will return to Roosevelt next fall as Commandant of Cadets.

The colonel is a former student of Roosevelt Military Academy Junior College and also of Reynolds High School. He graduated from RMA's Junior College in 1934. Colonel Carpenter is replacing Maj. George D. LaMont, present commandant, who has resigned effective at the end of the school year.

After graduating from RMA Junior College, Colonel Carpenter completed his college days at Centre College in Kentucky, where he was outstanding in athletics. In 1936, he returned to Roosevelt as coach and remained here until 1938. In 1938, he resigned to take up a position on the Moline High School faculty as coach and history instructor.

As a pilot of a supposedly unarmed Piper Cub observation plane, which he armed with "Bazookas," Colonel Carpenter gained worldwide fame as the "Mad Major" for knocking out Nazi tanks and planes.

For the past month, Colonel Carpenter has been enrolled as a student in the University of Chicago.[1]

For the next year, Charles was back in familiar territory; surrounded by the military-like structure and discipline, he was content. But at some point in his tenure at RMA, Charles decided he wanted to obtain his master's degree in teaching. Knowing that teaching was a viable career for him, he once again pulled up the family stakes and moved to Champaign, Illinois, where he enrolled in the University of Illinois, Champaign–Urbana and became one of the "Fighting Illini" students.

While obtaining his master's degree, Charles wrote the following paper for one of his classes. As a history teacher who had lived through and directly experienced some of the world's darkest days, Charles did not need to rely on periodicals, newspaper reports, interviews, or official documents. As a combatant with a front-row seat, his only difficulty was trying to write faster than the memories flowing from his mind. Charles gives a rare insight from not only his own experience as a soldier during the war but also his perspective as a history teacher about the challenges of protecting democracy when totalitarian regimes are on the march. What he wrote shed a harsh light on the more glorified views of the Allied victory and the state of democracy in the years after the war.

The Problems of Education and Democracy Today
by Charles M. Carpenter. (*paper excerpt*)

The urgency of the times requires that nothing be too sacred for us to examine carefully. Doubt is the beginning of wisdom and symbol of maturity. The light of truth, unlike our love, warms us little, but it may be the price of freedom.

How fares our hero, the common man, amidst all this? … He votes the straight ticket because he doesn't know the candidates and regards his government as the source of most of his troubles. He is generally anarchist in his childhood, socialist in college, democratic in his sports, fascist in his office, and dies a reactionary. He believes in God but prefers golf, professes the highest moral code in history, but astounds his less puritanical neighbors with the depravity of many of his moral practices. He desires an education, not to know but to be known. He recognizes no nobility but wealth and places size high among his list of virtues. He likes to think that he believes in social equality, but religious prejudice, racial intolerance, class hatred, and snobbery are dominant features of his culture. Believing that

206

education is essential to democracy, he votes vast sums of money for buildings and reserves the bulk of his teaching for the unmarried daughters of the nations. … He is drafted to fight for freedom and caustically maligned by the envious Europeans he has unwillingly come to save as "over-paid, over-fed, over-sexed, and over-there." He decorates himself on the way to battle and deplores the blunders of allies whose blood and courage have bought time for him to decide whether or not to fight. If aroused sufficiently, he out produces his enemies to ride triumphantly into their fallen capital and returning home to make a career of being a veteran, leaving behind him memories of chewing gum and jeeps. Hog butcher and banker for the world, conquering, voting, preaching under the dollar sign—pal of Abe Lincoln, idolizing Babe Ruth, the suffering ages look to him for the shape of things to come….

The caricature is done, perhaps overdone. It would be unkind if it were not as old as Plato and as common as Babbitt and other exposures of this "generation of vipers" could profitably make it. We are often most cruel to the things we love. We, like God, must love the fellow or why would there be so many of him? Then, too, there is a disturbing fear that he is our brother, even ourselves. Tremble as we will, Democracy is the Faith and has chosen the popular vote as the rock upon which to build.

… A seeming defect of our type of democracy based on the equal popular vote is that it provides for the solution of only those problems that the intelligence of a cross section of the majority is capable of perceiving as being necessary of solution. This might be one explanation for the decline and disappearance of such representative governments as have appeared from time to time in the deep historical past.

… Most men have done as little thinking as possible since to the average man, thinking is more torture than a cold shower. It is one function of his life that he seems only too glad to delegate whenever possible. No amount of problem-solving activity in the classroom is likely to fit him to solve the problems of this era when the finest minds are taxed to attain even a basic understanding of them. The very fact that great minds are almost by nature democratic, and small minds can seldom be taught it, is ample cause for thought about democracy. The masses of American population are scarcely more democratic by choice than are those of Russia communism. Both nations had their political beliefs foisted upon them by revolutionary minorities, and both beliefs may die unless constantly propagandized and nurtured by those in control.…The power-drunk proletarian government of Russia masquerading under communistic ideology fears nothing so much as the truth.

It is conceivable that, if all nations were democracies, no nation would need to fear its neighbors. However, such is not the case, and history has not generally favored the unregimented, amiable product of civic equality over the lean and hungry, but more unified opponents.

In this postwar paper, Charles was unflinching about his views of the American soldier at war overseas. Such views are hard to ignore because he saw so much up close. In a preface to his paper, he wrote:

All impressions of Americans at war are either my own or based on personal conversations with German prisoners, medical officers and patients, fellow officers, and enlisted men, often before the shock of battle had worn off. Other limited associations with nations of England, France, Belgium, and Luxembourg offered opportunities for views of war from their standpoint. Much of the noble side of our military effort has been omitted because it seemed more characteristic of the innate comradeship and decency of the human animal rather than a derivative of any political or educational beliefs. Perhaps the problems presented are those of all mankind rather than peculiar to the political and educational philosophies at which they are pointed. If so, they are still great problems and challenge worth accepting.

These impressions may also account for so much of the anger he exhibited on the battlefield.

The truth of how we fought and acted in this last war will never be dwelt upon by anyone seeking election in this land. No greater blow has ever been struck to the wavering prestige of American democracy and education than that delivered by its own soldiers by their conduct and attitudes abroad in the war just ended.… It will take some time to buy our own way back into the hearts of the Europeans. For many of them, the arrival of the Americans marked the end of a myth. It was the acid test of our culture and our way of education, and it failed miserably. Only the worse conduct of the Russian savages has ame- liorated the attitude of the defeated toward us.

Democracy is bought with "blood, sweat, and tears." It is not so much inherited as it is learned. One thing is certain, if democracy perishes in our time, the hearts of the English people will be its last stronghold. Democracy is designed for peace....No nation, even a democracy, can fight well without discipline and respect for leadership. The same lack of respect that we have at home for the local mayor, the governor, and the traffic regulations was characteristic of attitudes in the armed forces toward superior rank and regulations. No nations in history had ever attempted, however blunderingly, to sift so much of its leadership from the rank and file.

Men do not fight well unless they have a desire to fight well. The importance of training is even secondary to this motivation. The attempted motivation of our troops in the recent struggle was humorous if it had not been almost tragic. It was a complete and acknowledged failure in spite of careful preparation of materials by trained psychologists. The great moral issues at stake had almost nothing to do with the outcome of any battle. American courage and resourcefulness rose to the highest peaks when motivated by pride in the outfit, former combat successes, anger at the bestiality of the enemy, injury or death of buddies, or a downright fatalism based on loss of hope. As desirable as these stimuli are in combat, they are not unique to any political philosophy, and they may not suffice in a coming struggle where the odds are less in our favor. The mythical initiative of the common man at war was never more conspicuous by its lack. The infantry motto of "Follow me" could better have been "point out the way" in the hedgerows of Normandy when lieutenants died faster than privates. Too much of our Saturday afternoon spectator and watch "John do it" attitude was carried over into our fighting for the freedom of mankind. It was accepted combat philosophy to "volunteer for nothing" and "let the boys drawing the big money do it." Courage was classed with stupidity and "eager" was a synonym of disapproval. Majors were messenger boys, colonels "kicked upstairs" for inefficiency, and West Pointers remembered by their willingness to cover up for a classmate.... Generals lied to save American technical pride in equipment whose design they had suggested. Europeans chuckled at American proficiency in awarding decorations for "being there," and many be-ribboned heroes are ashamed to read aloud their own citations.

One apparent result of American education and democratic culture observable abroad was the extremely high valuation placed on his own life by the American soldier. Our safety campaigns at home must have been more effective than we realize. It is a genuine tribute to the pleasures of the existence of most of us have known or expect…. The pictures of war painted by Stephan Crane and Tolstoy have not changed. War and democracy cannot travel together long.

The American approach to the problem is illustrated by this account witnessed by a fellow officer in the Battle of Ardennes. A dejected and weaponless G.I. strolling to the rear through an American artillery position was roughly collared and accused of dereliction of duty by an artillery colonel. Jerking a thumb in the direction of distant rifle fire and the thud of mortars he explained wearily, "It was getting' too hot up there for me."

So much of Charles's impressions of the Allies at war is in keeping with what more-recent historians have been uncovering and writing about.

Sir Max Hastings, a renowned author of twenty-seven books about war, writes in a 1985 *Washington Post* article, "Their Wehrmacht Was Better Than Our Army," that "most men of the Allied armies were openly contemptuous of the fantasies about themselves peddled…. This reaction makes it more remarkable that for a generation after the moment of victory in 1945, so many myths were perpetuated not only by popular historians, but within the military institutions of the West." Hasting reports that the great British military writer Capt. Basil Liddell Hart wrote a paper in which he reflected on the "reluctance of postwar military critics in Britain and America to draw appropriate conclusions about Allied performance." He said, "There has been too much self-congratulation and too little objective investigation." He states that Gen. George S. Patton himself wrote, "It is unfortunate and, to me, a tragic fact that in our attempts to prevent war, we have taught our people to belittle qualities of the soldier."[2]

Charles writes that "in this age of two world-crushing wars in the span of one generation and the next already looming darkly on horizon, we must be realistic, we must speak what is felt to be the truth." However, he also acknowledges, "the thousands of brave and sincere men, many dead or maimed, who though under no delusions as to the nobility of their mission, saw a man's duty and reacted to it like men. They were not common men and nothing can dim their glory except the passing of those who knew them.

For them, we repeat Turenne's soliloquy on the verge of approaching battle, "Body you tremble now, but you would tremble still more if you knew where I was going to take you today."

Charles concludes his paper by noting that our democracy during peacetime is becoming a society stratified by wealth not wisdom … and if students can learn to think:

We should kneel and thank the gods. Individualism is not synonymous with freedom and our nation must not, like classic Greece, perish because of an excess of individualism in times that cry out for leadership and unity.

(All impressions of Americans at war are either my own or based on personal conversations with German prisoners, medical officers and patients, fellow officers and enlisted men, often before the shock of battle had worn off. Other limited associations with nations of England, France, Belgium, and Luxembourg offered opportunity for views of the war from their standpoint. Much of the noble side of our military effort has been omitted because it seemed more characteristic of the innate comradeship and decency of the human animal rather than a derivative of any political or educational beliefs. Perhaps the problems presented are those of all mankind rather than peculiar to the political and educational philosophies at which they are pointed. If so, they are still great problems and challenges worth accepting.)

Eventually graduating from college in August 1952, with a master of arts degree, Charles accepted a position at Urbana High School teaching US history, a position he would hold for more than fifteen years. As a teacher he not only inspired and educated his classes; he went out of his way to treat his students as equals. Several of them commented in the *Rosemary* yearbook about how much he changed their lives:

Mr. Carpenter,
I have never met a teacher that would give a person a chance to make good in the subject that I thought least of until I had you! I think everyone thinks the same way on that too! Lots of happiness in the future. I thank you!
Jean Harlow "54"

Mr. Carpenter,
Thanks a lot for all the help and keeping me on the right track. I really enjoyed this course and I believe I got a lot from it.
Bob Watt '54

Sir,
Tho I may not have done my share of the work, I have learned more from your teaching, and your classes than from any other. I know you've started the "wheels of thought" turning for many people.
Thanks again, Judy

Mr. Carpenter,
To a wonderful teacher and especially wonderful person. I'm sure looking forward to having you for US History next year. Enjoy yourself this summer.
Until next year, an admirer "55"

Because of his teaching style, the yearbook was dedicated to Charles and contained the following dedication:

Although Mr. Carpenter has only been with us at Urbana High School for a little over a year, he has won his way into the hearts of many. Especially the seniors in his United States History classes have come to know, respect, and admire Mr. Carpenter.

And so, to you, Mr. Carpenter, in appreciation of your sincerity, patience, kindness, understanding, and helpfulness, we dedicate the 1953 *Rosemary*.

At school, whether in front of a blackboard with chalk in hand, at his lecture podium or in the hallways talking with students about sports, history, or life in general, Charles Carpenter was walking, talking, and living his creed he had written in 1929. While the scars of war were only a few years behind him, not knowing if he would ever completely heal from them, the one unfortunate constant that Charles and his family had to endure every Christmas break was for Charles to return to the hospital and endure painful surgeries where cancerous infected and enlarged lymph nodes would be removed from his neck and under his arms. With his neck carved open and scraped of cancerous infections, he would return home swaddled in bandages, healing and waiting for school to commence. But after each surgery, he never complained, never felt sorry for himself, and vowed to return to class with more vigor than he had before.

As his health blossomed and stabilized, so too did his relationship with his daughter, Carol. As a child, Carol knew that her father was sick and that her dad could die at what she thought was "any moment." But Charles, who had earlier been no more than a stranger to her, was now focused on making sure his daughter grew up fearing nothing. By the time she was eleven or twelve, the two of them would be found canoeing on weekends, playing tennis, or teaching her how to jump off a high dive. Carol recalls one incident as she stood frozen at the end of a diving board, suspended 30 feet about the deep-blue water below. With Charles motioning her to jump, Carol was beyond terrified. Having no patience for Carol's fears, he yelled up at her, "Jump, dammit, jump!" Concurring her fear of heights, Charles challenged his daughter once again on a hiking trip. Finding a "small 4-foot" snake, lying under the hot sun, bothering no one by molting away and shedding its skin, Charles encouraged Carol to pick it up by the tail and hold it. Before she fainted, Charles was able to grab a quick photo of his daughter, proudly holding the snake and ridding herself of yet another fear. The two, father and daughter, became close—as close as a Carpenter could get. Carol still encountered some of the earlier nonaffectionate, stoic traits of Charles's mother from her father,, but overlooked them as they grew together, whether it was learning how to play tennis, chess, or poker, or reading endless stacks of books on the world, its history and events, and poetry. They spent hours listening to operas and classical music and, enjoying their togetherness, Charles began to find his daughter interesting. One of the many things Charles taught her was the meaning of generosity and looking out for those in need of help.

Because the Carpenters resided in Champaign, they frequently traveled back home to the Moline area to visit with both Charles's mother and Elda's mother. During one of those trips, traveling south in a driving rainstorm as they headed back home on Illinois Route 150, Charles quickly swerved and slowed his car to a stop; a family, with heads hung low and soaking wet, were walking along the edge of the highway. Seeing the distress in front of him, Charles invited the man and woman, small child, and baby, into the shelter of the family car. With Carol moving up to the front seat beside her mother and father, the woman, with flowing dark hair and a dark-skinned complexion, explained that they had been part of a carnival that was performing nearby and there was "some trouble" so they decided to leave. The husband and wife were billed as the "Tattoo Man and Tattoo Woman." Carol, looking in the back seat, stared in disbelief as the woman, opening the front of her shirt, displayed a large American eagle tattoo across her ample breasts, all in vivid color, along with countless other ones running down the length of her arms and other assorted parts of her body. Her husband was like a bookend canvas, with a rainbow of colored tattoos spread across his body as well. The more Carol stared at the couple, whom she estimated were in their late twenties or early thirties, and she thought they resembled gypsies, the more she worried about how dangerous they might be.

With the man coughing in the back seat, at times uncontrollably, and the woman explaining they had no home and no money and that her husband was very sick, Charles decided to take the entire clan home with them. Charles and Elda showed them the upstairs spare room where they would be guests of the Carpenters until the man got well and back on his feet financially. For the next several weeks, Charles tried to help the man find employment. While the two of them were out searching for a job, Charles found him one at the Chanute Air Force Base as a tattoo artist. But back at home, Carol remembers her mother changing the sheets in their room and finding blood on the pillowcase and sheets. The Carpenters learned that the man had tuberculosis (TB), which meant he should have been placed in a TB sanitarium. Not wanting to be separated, the family fled the carnival as all they had was each other. And as quickly as the strange family came into their lives, they disappeared again into the night. No stranger to tragedy and heartache, Charles and his family knew that for a brief time, this wandering family felt joy and love in their lives and felt like fellow human beings in the Carpenter home.

By the mid-1950s, during the summer break from classes, Charles, who was still enjoying his time teaching US history, traveled south with his good friend Sam Drake. The two army veterans and fellow teachers were simply looking to get away for a while and find a good place to fish. Charles had long fascinated himself with the idea of opening a woodland camp where he could help cultivate young men and assist them in their life's journey. Wetting their lines in the various rivers of the Ozarks, the two fishermen became enamored with a place called Bay Nothing. But the more they observed their surroundings, the more enticed they were to turn this 400-acre hunting and fishing camp into a place where they could help turn boys into self-sufficient men. He had drilled this idea into the heads of his former mentor back home in Reynolds, J. H. O'Leary, along with countless conversations with Sam. Knowing that his time left on this earth was short, Charles, not one to "wish" about doing something, decided to act on his inspiration. By 1960, with the financial help of both O'Leary and Sam, the 400-acre site with 2 miles of river frontage on the Current River was purchased by the trio.

The advertisement in surrounding southern Illinois and St. Louis area newspapers was enticing to any teenage boy who read it, or for a parent that was looking for a summer camp to send their child to. Located 150 miles south of St. Louis, in the southeast area of Missouri, alongside the Current River in the Clark National Forest, Bay Nothing was open for business. Charles commented to one newspaper reporter:

When we were thinking of starting a camp two years ago, this country immediately struck me with its potential as a camping area. We're going to try to instruct the boys in skills their busy fathers don't have time to show them.

Our aim isn't exactly to turn city slickers into hillbillies, but that's close to it.

Newspaper Advertisement

"Calling All Campers"
Bay Nothing Summer Camp
For boys (10 to 16 years) on the beautiful Current River in the Missouri Ozarks. An unforgettable adventure into manhood for your boy.

Featuring: float trips, trail rides, woodcraft, fishing, swimming, boating, shooting, and summer sports.

All under outstanding adult leadership. For further information contact Charles M. Carpenter, Camp Director.

All inquiries were answered with a personal letter from Charles that stated the following:

Hi! Fellows:
Have you ever wanted to float down a beautiful river to camp by a fire at night on a gravel bar far from crowds and cities? Would you

thrill to cross streams and wooded hills on horseback or explore a cave as Huck Finn and Tom Sawyer did long ago?

For these and several other reasons, Bay Nothing might be your choice of summer camps. Our small enrollment in the middle of a big wilderness area makes it possible to promise memories like these to all campers.

Bay Nothing itself is a hidden spring-fed pool behind an old beaver dam near camp. We took its name for our camp because it suggested the backwoods adventures that we wanted our campers to have. The Current River is famous among sportsmen for swimming and fishing and floating. It is so wild and beautiful that the government is considering preserving the entire area as a national park.

Our program is built around the idea of having fun while learning some important things about nature and out-of-doors living that a fellow can use for the rest of his life. One of our goals is to train young fellows to take care of themselves under all kinds of conditions. We try to operate as one big happy family with everyone helping out and everyone having some responsibility. Our counselors are college boys of all-around ability and are the type boys will like and respect.

If you come to Bay Nothing, we only expect you to try to be a good sport and do your share of improving yourself and upholding the good name of Bay Nothing.

Sincerely,

Charles M. Carpenter
Director

Charles retained a longtime employee, Romey Cromwell, who was a former Mississippi River bargeman, farmer, deputy sheriff, and expert horseman. Described as a soft-spoken gentleman and the dean of woodlore at Bay Nothing, Romey had eighteen years of experience running the camp, knowing more about horses, dogs, and boys, as well as wild animals and where to catch the biggest fish. In the eyes of many outsiders, Romey may have looked like a long-lost hobo, but to Charles he was a guiding light on how to run a camp and he quickly became his right-hand man. As an Ozark backwoodsman, Romey was a guiding light on boating and fishing skills, and he quickly became a trusted, right-hand man.

To accommodate the young boys who began to sign up for two-week sessions of outdoor serenity, limited to twenty at a time, Charles enlisted the help of both current and fellow students from Urbana High School. These included James Hageman, Mike Russell, and Harold Wanless.

Bay Nothing was later described by the trio of camp counselors as "Camelot-like," almost magical at times and transformative in several important ways. This was the case both because of the place and situation and because of the force of personality of Charles Carpenter. Hageman recalls having Charles as his history teacher when he was sixteen or seventeen years old:

> Wearing a suit and tie, he projected certain confidence. As students we understood that there was no question about goofing off in class; it may have happened in other classes, but it never happened in his class. He was a natural leader and carried an air of respect. He appeared strong and muscular, a very athletic type of frame.
>
> I did notice that one side of his throat was indented quite a bit, more than the other side, and learned later as a camp counselor about his cancer treatments and surgeries. During my junior or senior year, my friend Hal Wanless encouraged both Mike Russell and me to become camp counselors. We had all been in Boy Scouts together, and after talking with Charles about his camp and our expectations, we became Bay Nothing counselors.

For the next three years, James spent his summers on the Current River, helping to turn boys into young men alongside Charles. And when the boys had been sent home as they awaited the new group to arrive, Hageman, Russell, and Wanless would have in-depth late-night conversations with Charles about his wartime experiences:

> As we sat around a roaring campfire, he shared his view on the world politics with us, and how the political system should be assisting those that need help, as they didn't always get a square deal. Mike had learned from Carol that her father was suffering from PTSD, from seeing so many dead people and the waste that war was with so many young men dying. None of us saw any side of that from him. But there was a residue of disgust from him about war. When he told us what he did in the war, it was not one of self-indulged boasting, but one of just the facts.

He told us he had flown spotter planes, a Piper Cub, and he had decided to put bazookas on his to shoot at the Germans. I remember him saying he would sit above them and could see them with their tank hatches open, opening themselves up as targets. He also told us he didn't like to carry a firearm with him because he figured, if he had landed next to a battlefield, and if the Germans saw him carrying a gun, they would shoot first and ask questions later. He told us the time he landed behind enemy lines to repair his plane or take a leak or something and several Germans came out of the woods with their hands up. He was standing there without any pistol and grabbed a rifle that was nearby taking them to other American soldiers. He told us how exciting and, at the same time, horrifying war was and that it should never be glorified.

All of us admired him—his integrity, his generosity, and his compassion especially for those less fortunate. He continually reminded us that "before I go, I want to create this environment for these kids, so they grow up to be strong, courageous, and ethical people."

Elda and Carol would also pay visits to camp and help out with chores and bookkeeping. Carol would stay for extended periods and help her father with the odds and ends of tending to a camp.

July 20, 1961 (*excerpt from a letter by Carol*)

Dear Mom,
The stationery isn't very fancy, but I have about ten thousand sheets of extra Bay Nothing paper, and I hate to waste it.

Today was sweltering. After I called you, I came back and went swimming. Daddy went up to the O'Leary cabin to do some work and fell asleep next to the air conditioner. Things have pretty well settled down now that the O'Learys have gone—it certainly means less dishes to wash. Although I do miss Helen, O'Leary's niece. I think that is what I miss most—some good old-fashioned girl talk!

My big project right now is making a butterfly net, and getting books and bills straightened out. Boy! Is Daddy ever behind! I've had to write two letters to Mrs. Chilton about her check. Daddy had stashed it away and forgotten about it. But really I do seem to be doing pretty well.

So don't worry about anything—least of all any broken hearts etc. I'm doing fine and plotted my course and am on safe seas!

Love to you and Pleumy

But Carol, who had recently graduated high school, plotted her next course in life. She did not see herself running a boys' camp and instead set her sights on college.

Carol eventually attended the University of Illinois. But it was a talk given by Robert Sargent Shriver Jr. about a new program that was about to begin that sent Carol's head spinning. Brother-in-law to John F. Kennedy, Shriver served as the first director for the newly formed Peace Corps. After listening to his electrifying speech, Carol decided to join the Peace Corp of her senior year. Her mother, Elda, was very fearful, pleading with her not to go. But Charles, who had instilled in his daughter to fear nothing and experience life, encouraged her, saying it "would be a wonderful thing."

In 1964, after graduating college, Carol was sent to Central Thailand, teaching English to Thai school girls.

But it was in January 1966, at only fifty-two years of age, the "Carpenter luck" was coming to an end. With three months to go before finishing her tour of two years in Thailand, Carol was contacted by her supervisor, Charlie Jenkins, who was a former Olympic runner. Standing in her little teak wood house she shared with four other Thai teachers, Charlie was somber according to Carol and said, "Your mother has contacted the Peace Corps, and you are to come home. Your father is dying."

Carol had earlier received a letter from her mother that told her about her father falling on a basketball court while playing and that he wasn't doing well. Carol knew her father wouldn't hear of her coming home, but her mother was persistent. Carol didn't know how bad her father truly was until she arrived back home in Champaign.

Charles had been admitted to Carle Memorial Hospital around February 8, 1966. Carol and Elda were both stunned that this "rock of a man" was dying. For the next month and a half, Carol sat with her father every day, talking and laughing and reconnecting.

"I told him about my time in Thailand and of my adventures. He was very sick, but he always had a book on his chest. The nurses would have to turn him often due to bedsores and I knew he was in anguish, but yet he never complained. He told me, "You know, I feel with all this suffering that I am purified.""

Carol and her mother were pleading with the doctor to do something to extend his life. The doctor caring for him became angry with the two of them and said, "Your dad is suffering, and there is no reason to try to extend his life."

It was then that Carol and her mother both realized that there were going to be no heroic efforts to extend his life. Peace came upon Charles M. Carpenter at 2:00 p.m. on March 22, 1966, his book of poems, resting on his chest, open to Thomas Gray's poem titled "Elegy Written in a Churchyard." It was a poem that Carol remembers her father reciting to her from memory in the past. According to Carol, the opening line reflected her father's thoughts of being a man and looking back on his life:

The curfew tolls the knell of parting day, the lowering herd wind slowly o'er the lea, the plowman homeward plods his weary way, and leaves the world to darkness and me.

CHAPTER 20

Remembered by Deeds Alone

The accomplishments of this division have never been equaled. And by that statement, I do not mean in this war, I mean in the history of warfare. There has never been such a superb fighting organization as the 4th Armored Division.

—Gen. George Patton

There was no denying that the 4th Armored Division was one of General Patton's paramount units during World War II. The 4th was one of only two divisions during the war to be awarded a Presidential Distinguished Unit Citation. Maj. Gen. John Shirley Wood—or "P" to his men—insisted that all would be recognized or none at all. Enduring ten months of almost constant combat, the 4th Armored Division accounted for over 90,000 prisoners taken, 13,641 enemies killed, 847 enemy tanks destroyed, 3,688 vehicles destroyed, 103 locomotives destroyed, and 128 enemy planes shot down.[1] Charles Carpenter is credited with a handful of tanks and vehicles destroyed while at the controls of "Rosie the Rocketer" during his more than six months in combat. Along with his medals earned (these include Silver Star with Oak Leaf Cluster, Bronze Star, Air Medal with Oak Leaf Cluster, Presidential Unit Citation, American Theater Ribbon, World War II Victory Medal, and European Theater Ribbon with four Bronze Stars), his fellow 4th Armored Division comrades were also awarded 3 Medals of Honor, 34 Distinguished Service Crosses, 802 Silver Stars, 3,031 Bronze Stars, 88 Air Medals, 11 Soldiers Medals, 92 Croix de Guerre, and 6,000 Purple Hearts.

But to General Wood's mandate, when it came to giving his outfit a nickname, he stated, "The 4th Armored Division does not need and will not have a nickname. They shall be known by their deeds alone."

And just like his commanding officer, Charles Carpenter was remembered too by those he had touched in life by his deeds alone. Although heroic in combat, Charles was just as heroic in his civilian life and touched the lives of countless young men and women, and strangers, treating them with respect and dignity, not as a superior but as an equal.

On Thursday, March 24, 1966, services for Charles Carpenter took place at the First Congregational Church.

March 24, 1966

The Personal Prayer for Charles Carpenter (*excerpt of prayer*)
In thy sacred presence, O Lord, our God, we remember this our beloved. We call him to mind in life and not death. We think of him as he would have us, as he lived in the fullness of health and vigor. In this hour we praise thee for memory—memory that gives strength to life as it moves on into thy future.

We remember and give thanks for the deep joy he found as a teacher, the easy wit of wisdom on so many subjects…the delight he found in seeing young minds dance with new ideas, explode with the power of knowledge…his curiosity about the unknown, his care for his students, knowing them as persons, naming them one by one. We praise thee that he had found his calling, that he loved each day because it was fresh adventure. His competence, his passion for excellence, his mastery of method, his unflinching integrity gave dignity to the calling of teacher and embodiment to the teacher as servant. For this we thank thee.

We praise thee for his love of music, light operettas, "schmaltz" stuff. In an age of metallic coldness, we praise thee that he warmed us with lyrics, brightening our barrenness with the beauty of ancient ballads recited by one who breathed the bards' spirit.

We praise thee for his dream of Bay Nothing, a dream that he dared to act upon. Bay Nothing, a place where one could enter a boy and leave a man. There under the Ozark moon, with the chirp of crickets and the rush of the river at the rising of the storm, there in the flickering glow of a dying campfire or the dash of fording a river on horseback, or the quite grassy place in the still on Sunday morning… there he spoke as the light shone through the mist which gathered in his eyes, there he spoke with eloquence, with fervor of his dream to help make me…men who could hold a hammer and saddle a horse and fish a stream, men who could stride a trail, and swim a rough place, men who would love all creation, and learn to serve and conserve…men who could control their desires, express their feelings, exude their concern, men, not of the fist clenched tightly, but of the outstretched hand of brotherhood. We praise thee for this daring spirit that lived a dream.

And Lord God, always in the background, the looming shadow of death…to be bent but not broken, to be burned by its pain and not to be bitter, to waste with its weariness and not to whine…to be loving and tender and humble because of peace..a final blessed peace…to walk lightly as though the burden were easy when we knew it was not…it takes a rare man, Lord, a man of valor.

We praise thee that his family was always a rich part of his life, that he loved and cared for them with a quiet tender loving and deep gay spirit. He gave his dreams and his ideals and himself to those who were near, Precious gifts for precious people.

After professional services were rendered by the Crummy Funeral Home, in Reynolds, which included a vault, two limos, a hearse, flower car, minister and organist, Charles M. Carpenter's final resting place at the Edgington Cemetery, bordered by rolling hills planted with soybeans and corn, near the place he grew up, and use to roam with his childhood best friend and dog Jack, would be familiar territory for his eternity.

His gravesite, marked with a flat gray marble stone, dug into the rich dark Illinois soil, etched with the following:

Charles M. Carpenter
Illinois
Lt. Col. US Army
WWII SS 1 OLC-BSM-AM 1 OLC
August 29, 1912, March 22, 1966

The thoughts, prayers, and heroic memories of an incredible man whose personal creed is an accurate testament to a man of high honor and ethics. The lives he touched by those who fondly recall him were everlasting and immeasurable. "Lucky Carpenter," an Illinois farm boy, teacher, husband, father, pilot, soldier, camp director, and guiding light to his wife Elda and daughter Carol, will forever be remembered as a man of unlimited resilience.

March 25, 1966
To the family of Charles M. Carpenter

Dear Elda, Carol, Mrs. Carpenter, and family:
For the past two days our flag has flown at half-staff in memory of one of the finest, most respected, and well-known Alumnus of Roosevelt Military Academy. News of his passing has brought sadness and sorrow to all who knew Charles.

It was our good fortune and privilege to not only have Charles as a student but also as a member of our faculty. He was dedicated to his work and his leadership was an inspiration to all cadets who came under his supervision. Because of his faith and confidence in youth, he was so successful in instilling within a cadet a sincere respect and love for his God and Country; a pride of his own being and a pride of accomplishment; the proving to a cadet that success in every area comes only through diligence and endeavors; and even more important, the creating within a cadet the true values of Honor and Integrity.

On behalf of the cadets, faculty, trustees, and the alumni of Roosevelt Military Academy, may I express our sincere sympathy to you. May it be some comfort to know that we share your sorrow in the loss of a loved one, and one who has been close and dear to all of us. We will cherish forever the many wonderful memories we have of Charles. It was God's will that he was permitted to remain with us on borrowed time in order that he might further enrich our lives through our associations with him

With deepest sympathy,
Glen G. Millikan
Superintendent

March 25, 1966
Mrs. Charles M. Carpenter

It is a curious feature of a man's nature that at precisely that point in his history when words are of no use—and convey no meaning—precisely then, he feels compelled to hold forth with a few thousand.

When Mike called and told me of Mr. Carpenter's death, I could only feel that great and awful void in the pit of my stomach, followed by recursing waves of sorrow. But a selfish sort of sorrow—grief for my loss.

As I have gone through this week, darkling hints and obscure references have appeared as though from nowhere. As if by some magical force, "those golden days and happy hours" have come filtering through my sluggish brain as afternoon light through the maple trees on the waterfront on a humid Sunday.

Schoolboys trudging suddenly become weary hikers slogging down Bagamaw Ridge, fallen oak leaves crunching beneath their step.

A traffic jam is miraculously transformed to a harried crossing of the current after dark—horses gnawing the water, boys shouting, beams of flashlights confusedly directed, seemingly without purpose—piercing the darkness first here then there, and the director with a grim sort of abandon getting on with adventure.

And a broken bum on a corner tiredly taking the last drags on a cigarette butt becomes an illiterate Bill leaning against the tool shed "rolling his own." "A totally worthless fellow" hired by the director for his infinite worth of being a fellow human—and therefore deserving of love and a hand up.

Then slowly crept into me a wondrous knowledge—only the physical perishes while the good of a man remains an eternal spring of joy in the hearts of his friends

Love,
Jim Hageman

"Rosie" Rediscovered

The exploits of Charles Carpenter and his mount, "Rosie the Rocketer," are nothing short of unbelievable. Over time, his feats of heroism begin to come into question as self-proclaimed "historical military experts" become doubters and the nonbelievers spewed their opinions on internet message boards. What they didn't expect was a well-deserved dressing down from Charles Carpenter's only living relative, his seventy-six-year-old daughter, Carol Apacki.

A few years ago, Carol was casually surfing the internet late one night and decided to type in the name of her father and his L-4H Cub, "Rosie the Rocketer," that he flew as a reconnaissance pilot in World War II. What popped up from The Great Planes Community Warbirds Forum website immediately caught her attention:

Hi, I've got a reference I've been curious about for a while. It concerns a Major Charles Carpenter of the US Army who reportedly went hunting German tanks in a Piper L-4 observation plane. I have a photo of the plane, called Rosie the Rocketeer [sic], with what looks like three standard infantry bazookas underneath each wing. Considering that the maximum effective range of the contemporary 2.36 bazooka was 650 meters at best, and wildly inaccurate at that range.... Well, sorry, but I don't believe it ever happened.

Others on the site added their own skeptical comments:

I also have my doubts but "The Fighting Grasshoppers" by Ken Wakefield has a photo of Carpenter standing in front of bazooka-equipped L-4 notes that he knocked out a number of German tanks, armored cars, and others vehicles. The complete lack of detail in the story makes me a bit skeptical.

I'm inclined to dismiss it using a highly technical historical term: "Complete Bollocks." During World War II, propaganda, both against the enemy and to bolster the Home Front was in high gear. Rosie appears to be the result of yet more "home-grown" hero wishes.... I'll put it down to propaganda and a bit of a laugh at the back sheds by some maintenance guys on some officer's liaison aircraft.

The more Carol looked, the more she discovered, and when she continued to search the internet, she encountered even more naysayers.

While Carol would later admit that she had never been very interested in her Dad's war record before, these comments of disbelief were rankling and she found herself unable to sleep one evening. Carol found herself consumed at one o'clock in the morning, going through a boxful of old yellowed newspaper stories that she had found in her mother's closet after her death and had stored in her home's basement.

During that short journey into her family's past, Carol learned more about her father's exploits. These included an article written by Marlene Gantt in *World War II* magazine and the numerous press accounts, found in *Stars & Stripes*, the Associated Press, *Popular Science*, the *New York Sun*, and *Liberty Magazine*. After spending the next several hours digesting information about her father, she had read about it for the very first time in many years. She paused to gather her thoughts and decided to take the naysayers on. At 3:00 a.m. Carol wrote back:

I happened to see your discussion about Major Charles Carpenter and whether it was possible for a Piper L-4 observation plane to knock out a tank. It was possible. As Charles Carpenter's daughter, I grew up listening to some of my father's experiences as Bazooka Charlie and his plane, Rosie the Rocketer. I also have a scrapbook full of World War II newspaper articles that describe in full detail some of my father's adventures in his little plane with six bazookas mounted under the wings.

Drawing on the information in Gantt's article, Carol explained that her father used the first bazooka model produced for the war and that it fired utilizing a battery igniter. Each bazooka was a one-piece metal tube 54 inches long, weighing about 13 pounds. While each projectile had a range of 500 yards, the sights were only calibrated for 100 and 300 yards. Barely understanding the details herself, Carol explained that her father had to launch his rocket rounds carefully to ensure that the back-blast wouldn't ignite the doped fabric on the flimsy craft's wings and tail feathers. Carol went on to explain that her father would dive within 75 yards of his targets, and use his little L-4 to knock out German armored vehicles and Panzer tanks. Carol explained to her bewildered audience that destruction was usually not necessary if the tank was set afire or simply immobilized; the Panzer crew usually abandoned the vehicle. To finish off her nonbelieving audience, Carol included a quote from the highly respected Associated Press war correspondent J. Wes Gallagher, who wrote to readers back home, "Carpenter is fast becoming a legend in Lt. Gen. George S. Patton's army where eccentricity is not unknown and bravery is commonplace."

In the following days, Carol answered the *Warbirds* forum readers' many questions with pictures and stories that she found in the clippings. To her delight, Carol received several responses from incredulous *Great Planes* readers:

Well, it looks as if some of us have a trace of hen's ovulations to wipe off our faces, but it's well worth it to uncover the real truth of an absolutely amazing story.

While another responded with this mea culpa:

Holy liv'n crimany!! Five-star thread! Moral: Never underestimate those damn Yankees! WOO-HOO!

For Carol, there was a certain irony in writing about her father's war record as "Bazooka Charlie." Some of the stories in the clippings portrayed him as both "mad, and as a legendary warrior"—an image that was very different from the person she knew. Carol's family and friends knew him as someone who was gentle, highly principled, articulate, and wise. He was a scholar, read widely, collected great books, loved and sang operetta in the shower, and carried on serious discussions about philosophy and history. He was a poet, a practical joker, an athlete, and a tender husband and father who patiently taught his daughter chess and tennis, and regularly took Carol, his only child, on nature walks, and on camping and canoe trips.

As a proud daughter, Carol also knew her father was a beloved high school history teacher who had the school yearbook dedicated to him many times. Carol remembers fondly the summer's her father ran Bay Nothing boys' camp in the Ozarks—a camp that focused on teaching outdoor skills and building character. But what Carol was trying to express to the world was the fact that his war deeds as Bazooka Charlie with "Rosie the Rocketer" were only a small fraction of who he was and the legacy he left.

One of Carol's most unexpected outcomes of discovering the World War II stories about her father was the opportunity to meet and develop a friendship with a man named Colin Powers, who restored an L-4 Piper Cub similar to "Rosie the Rocketer." Carol first met Colin at the Dayton Air Show in 2004, where he allowed Carol and her five-year-old grandson to sit in a real L-4 cockpit. Trying to imagine what it must have been like for her father, Carol was amazed at how such a small and lightweight plane could fly—let alone be fitted with six bazookas to knock out German Panzer tanks, as her father had done on several occasions. Colin's plane went on to win top honors at the 2005 National Aviation Heritage. Spending three years on the restoration, Colin even stenciled on the alphanumeric code that was used on planes bound for World War II service to expedite repairs.

With the memories of her father burning brightly and with newfound interest abounding around the world, Carol decided to write an article about her father's wartime experiences for *EAA Warbirds of America* (October 2017) that caught the eye of Joseph Scheil, of Jurupa, California. By day, Joe is an airline pilot for Alaska Airlines, and when he's not flying for a living, he can usually be found at the controls of his yellow and black lightning bolt J-3 Cub.

Joe is a serial number guy. When he sees an old picture of an airplane, he generally looks the serial number up to find out what he can about it. When he saw Carol's article with "Rosie's" serial number, he found it very interesting because, at first, the story sounded somewhat unbelievable. Joe was dumbfounded at how Major Carpenter could have survived in that environment. For Joe, it was nothing short of miraculous. Joe read about Major Carpenter expressing those dangers early into his campaign that, "they shot at Cubs now because they knew the Cubs had teeth."

It didn't take Joe long at all for his Cub hunting instinct to kick in. Within a few hours after reading Carol's article, he found out that "Rosie" had been surplussed in a German yard in September 1946. From there L-4H 11717 became HB-OBK with Heinz Wullschleger, Olten, and then moved to

Austria in 1955. By April 1956, sporting yellow Piper Cub colors, the registration changed to OE-AAB when it became part of the Oesterreichischen Aero Club in Vienna, where it towed gliders. From there the airplane flew as a civilian airplane for several years before it disappeared into the Österreichisches Luftfahrtmuseum at Graz Airport in Austria. Joe, who had done some prior research for the Collings Foundation, was aware that Rob Collings, chief executive officer and chief pilot of the Collings Foundation, wanted something from the 8th Air Force, a fighter that had actual combat history.

Fascinated by what he had discovered, Joe sent a letter to Carol, not knowing their own lives would soon connect:

Dear Carol Apacki,

Hello, my name is Joe Scheil, and I am one of the people that works for the Collings Foundation in the effort of creating the Living History Museum Collection in Stow, MA.

It was on a week at Rob's during an event that I discovered your article, Carol, and I was so stuck by the one photo of your father with his plane. His story was so consistent with the "American Ingenuity" unique to the way American soldiers went to war and the wartime photo of him with Rosie showed a defiance and determination that is rarely captured by a camera. That photo really put the hook in me to find out more. His expression connected to me very profoundly, and I could not stop thinking about him and the plane. It was a surprise to discover the connection you have with my wife and her family and a really great connection to your family.

Becky had not made the connection when we first looked at the article, and we were surprised and thrilled to find out you were the people she knew in Ohio. As you probably know now, Becky and I are both airline pilots and truly enjoy our lives together residing in Southern California and flying from LAX. I am so happy that Kathi and Jim are the greatest "in-laws" to have. I hope we can all meet in Oregon as the plane goes together. I have to think that Rosie wanted to be found after so long in obscurity. So many L-4 Cubs are restored to be presented as "combat" aircraft that I think Rosie was somewhat miffed in faraway Austria. For a time I could think of nothing else, and still feel that the plane or something aligned with her was calling me.

I had previously found several aircraft that were lost to time (however, I hiked to them on hillsides generally), yet that connection with Rosie was very similar. When I first set eyes on the pictures of the plane on the net, it was a very emotional moment for me. I knew that Rob would bring her home. My friend Rob Collings is my best friend in the world, and when it comes to understanding the real stories, chasing the real planes, and when needed rewriting history so that the story is correct, through him the Collings Foundation has been transformed and continues to evolve as the place where the most important artifacts and stories will be housed and most importantly exercised. These planes and vehicles are maintained alive and exactly as they were to honor their moment in history. It's a wonderful mission for all of us. This plane could find no better home to fly again in her original colors, and to be displayed alongside the tanks she once fought with and against.

Colin is the best Cub restorer in the world, and is equally interested in bringing Rosie back. We are all invested in this restoration, and returning this plane to the EXACT condition, as close as we can to when your father stepped into her on an "average day" in combat. Learning about your father and his modifications to the plane are now so important. Logbooks, or any notes he left, are what we are so interested in. We have contacted the Associated Press, and it was interesting to me that the original correspondent who interviewed your dad went on to run the Associated Press. We are looking to find his original notes and submissions if they are held on digital file there. Lots of threads. Also researching the way the Piper L-4 was made is so important to us, so that when the plane is presented she appears as she was, not better than she was. When people see this plane, we feel that the courage of Charles Carpenter is easier seen when the plane is as she was, a regular "GI" or Government Issue Cub. No frills.

A fighting machine that the US government paid $1,000.00 for. A tall order in retrospect. Lots to do. Please contact me at any time, and the pictures are tremendous. I am flying to Guadalajara next, and have to get ready. All the best, and can't wait to sit down over dinner and hear more about your father and your families' story since his return.

Sincerely,
Joseph Scheil

Joe knew there was no European theater combat aircraft that were obtainable. He understood that no P-47s from the Eighth or the Ninth Air Force that survived the war and weren't in a museum were available. Joe knew he and Rob had a better chance with the P-51 Mustangs; there were a couple around, but like the P-47, they weren't obtainable. Joe knew that the Collings Foundation was looking for something that could capture the fight from Normandy to Germany. For an aircraft that was doing air-to-ground work, unfortunately, there was nothing left that had survived. The B-26 Marauder "Flak Bait" (part of the Smithsonian National Air and Space Museum) has that distinction of being a medium bomber, but there's no single-engine aircraft that seems to have survived intact. So when Joe discovered that this L-4 Cub, "Rosie the Rocketer," not only survived the war but was also hidden in plain sight and showed up, with an unknown number of tanks and armored cars killed, he realized it was oddly enough the most destructive aircraft that the US Army had extant from the ground war across Europe. As such, it's probably the only intact surviving example of a single-engine ground-attack airplane used in the war. "Rosie" is credited for turning the tide in one battle and stopping a German counterattack. That was a very significant accolade paid in 4th Armored Division records to a liaison aircraft—the only time in history that's ever been done. There was only one thing to do; Joe needed to let Rob Collings know about the historic artifact he had potentially just rediscovered.

(Ironically "Rosie" had been resting comfortably in plain sight, at least since 1985. From a news article in the *Moline Dispatch* newspaper, it reported that a gentleman had been corresponding with Elda Carpenter asking if she had any of her husband's L-4 "Rosie the Rocketer" photos he could view as he was recreating that scheme on the L-4 project he was restoring. In the body of that article, it was casually mentioned that the original "Rosie" was located in Austria housed in a museum.)

Seizing the news of the discovery from Joe, Rob traveled to Austria to determine firsthand if Joe's suspicions were true. When Rob Collings first saw the L-4 in person, he confirmed the serial number and found that the Cub had recently been recovered and was being restored as a static display. Although Rob was curious about any visible battle damage, or other battle scars it may have carried, he would have to wait and see because the museum had just recovered it with fresh fabric and they weren't too keen to let Rob start cutting into it to verify its battle scars.

Because much of its life after the war was used as a glider tug, the fuselage was recently covered with an assortment of stickers and decals all over it. But Rob knew, underneath that gaudy exterior lay a true legend.

After lengthy negotiations with the museum, Rob was able to acquire the L-4 Cub and determined to ship it back to the states and send it to Colin Powers of Oregon for restoration. Rob chose Colin for several reasons. One was for his strong background with other L-4 restorations but the other more important reason was the personal connection Colin had with Major Carpenter's daughter, Carol.

"Rosie" was loaded in a cargo container in Austria, trucked to Spain, and put on a cargo ship. From there it traveled across the Atlantic, much like it had done in the spring of 1944 as it headed to England before being assigned to Maj. Charles Carpenter. In late 2018, "Rosie" arrived in New Jersey, where it was loaded aboard a train and rode the rails across the United States, similar to the one that Carpenter had taken in late 1943 going in the opposite direction, and was brought to Portland. The L-4 arrived at Colin's shop on January 8, 2019.

Once the L-4 was unloaded in Oregon, Rob and Colin had the new fabric stripped off. Both men were completely awestruck by what they discovered—bullet holes and combat damage just like Carpenter had described in some of his letters home. As they discussed the next steps and how the restoration was to proceed, Rob knew, based on what lay in front of him, that he didn't want to make everything perfectly new because what was underneath was in pristine condition. The original wooden spars still had great varnish on them. The ribs were bare aluminum, but they were all clean. Even the grease pencil handwriting from the Piper factory employees who had built this airplane in early 1944, with names and dates, was still found inside. "Rosie" was a true time capsule with items that could never be duplicated and needed to be preserved.

According to Colin, as Piper Cubs go, it was a relatively easy airplane to restore because much if not all the parts and pieces for J-3s are readily available. For flying, nothing beats a Cub on a warm summer afternoon with the right side window and door open, slowly watching the world float on by.

For Colin, "Rosie" is the third L-4 airplane that he had restored. The first one he finished, he got to fly quite a bit and was amazed at how defenseless they were. Most of Carpenter's missions were around at between 1,000 and 1,500 feet, and many more much lower, which was within rifle and pistol range.

Both Rob and Colin agreed that the Cub didn't look very pretty in that yellow fabric. But once it was bare they checked it over to see if there were any other bullet holes. A very obvious bullet hole had come up in a 20-degree angle, passed through the aileron and the front spar and then on through another rib and then through the steel plate hinge before passing on throughout the top of the right wing. That bullet hole was preserved during the restoration.

Colin also located a double patch on the front strut where a bullet had gone through both sides, and as standard practice, the army had patched both sides and sent it back to the line to fly more missions. Both Rob and Colin's intent was to bring the L-4 back so it looked exactly like it did in 1944. Because of that, Colin created a laundry list of items that he needed to return to the original.

Because the airplane had been modified, those parts needed replacing. The cowling and boot cowl and a lot of the instrument panel were all different and need to be replaced. While in Austria, the new caretakers had put Super Cub landing gear legs on it. Colin replaced those with a set of NOS (new old stock) 1944 Piper L-4 gear legs. Colin also found that they had replaced the engine at some time with a Continental C90 because they probably needed the extra horsepower as a glider tug and the power it took to coax a glider off the ground. Colin located a period-correct 65 hp Continental that was installed in "Rosie." The Austrians also replaced three of the instruments with German instruments which Colin removed and replaced. With an original bill list from Piper as to what original instruments were in it in 1944, Colin set out and located those. Keystone Instrument in Pennsylvania was responsible for refurbishing all the original instruments so that the L-4 is period correct. The bill list from Piper includes compass, tachometer, altimeter, and airspeed indicator. Other period-correct items include a new Sensenich wood 72C-42 prop and Scott 3-21 tailwheel along with modern fabric covering. The biggest challenge was locating six original M1A1 bazookas and then trying to figure out how they were mounted was another daunting challenge. With wartime bazookas in short supply, Colin fabricated six new ones that look period correct. Using old wartime photographs as a guide, Colin found that they were mounted on a piece of plywood on the struts. But figuring out the proper angles was trial and error, probably what the pilots and ground crew endured when they first mounted them in England in the summer of 1944.

When Colin finished his part of restoring "Rosie" to its former glory, he remarked that this restoration gave him a lot of pride and inspiration in helping to preserve our nation's history and especially that of a true American hero, Maj. Charles Carpenter.

But there was one last item that Colin could not perform and was quick to give credit to—the reproduction of the Rosie the Rocketer nose art. That honor went to Charles Carpenter's granddaughter, (Carol's daughter) Erin Pata of Lompoc, California, who duplicated the L-4's namesake in the exact location her grandfather had it painted seventy-five years earlier.

Erin, born four years after her grandfather had passed, had never had the honor of meeting him. Erin's earliest recollection of him was when she was in the second or third grade and did a short book report on him. According to Erin, that was her first memory of learning about him, and yet she recognized that of course, as a third grader, she didn't quite have the grasp of a war hero's exploits. Erin remembers her mom talking about him throughout her childhood. Since she never met him, Carol had a responsibility to give her children some memories of him, and recalls during one of those little teaching moments her mother Carol gave her, was telling Erin about a Piper Cub plane. Part of that early book report included writing about him putting bazookas on his plane, which Erin had no idea at the time what a bazooka was or how profound their use was. Erin also found it difficult, if not impossible, to elicit wartime information about her grandfather from her grandma Elda.

Growing up, Erin remembered Elda as very quiet. Even when Erin was older, as she read some of her grandfather's diaries and letters home, Elda wouldn't share any of those details with her. Erin could see that it must have been a difficult chapter of her grandmother's life, especially since her grandfather died at such an early age and half of Elda's world was completely gone. Erin's interpretation of her grandmother was that she wore her emotions close to her sleeve. She didn't share a lot. She kept things bottled up because, perhaps, it was just too painful to talk about. Erin could sense it was hard for her to relive those memories, and that's why she didn't connect with her about her grandfather.

In 2016, Erin remembered her mom being excited about an article she had written about her father and his wartime exploits. At the time, according to Erin, it was something that she didn't quite understand how philosophical it is until in mid-2019, when she received a call from her mother stating, "They're looking for somebody to paint the logo back on 'Rosie.'" And

Erin remembered thinking immediately, "Oh, well I've got to do that, that's what I do for a living."

One of Erin's talents includes painting things, at her rural California workshop she calls Butterbean Studios. Erin's tag line is "Where Art and Farming Collide"; her husband is the farmer in the family.

Erin learned through her research that the military did not use a lot of color choices. They had red, black, white, yellow, green, and blue so to keep the restoration true to form, Erin, stuck to those basic colors.

After physically touching her grandfather's airplane with her mother standing beside her, Erin was more interested in tracking what her mom was feeling at the time. Although Erin didn't necessarily feel a deep connection to her grandfather, a war hero whom she never met, she did feel that for my mother. Erin knew that this moment would be a profound thing for her mother, to touch something from the past that her father had touched, lived in, and survived combat in, especially since she had lost her amazing dad early in life.

As Erin's eyes tracked Carol, she saw that her mother was quiet, maybe a little nervous. But it was when she saw her mother become teary-eyed, and holding her heart with her hand, she knew her mother had made an emotional connection with her past as she laid her hands on "Rosie." Carol stated, "It's hard to imagine how this plane, so small and fragile, could have been shooting at tanks and survived."

As Carol stood back and observed, Erin set out to recreate the nose art on her grandfather's airplane. Using a color photo of Rosie's nose art as her main source, Erin taped it nearby, right next to the plane.

Erin began with the yellow color first which she admitted was "a little scary" because that's when you find out the paint's either dripping or not thick enough and then it's permanent. Satisfied she had the right colors, she began applying the rest of the nose art and rocket.

For Erin, she remarked that it was an honor as a fellow painter to trace the artwork exactly of the original artist, not knowing who he was, where he came from, or what happened to him after the war. Many unanswered questions were swirling around in her head, like, Did he survive the war? Did he too raise a family? Why did he make the rocket look like that? But as an artist, Erin knew that everyone has their little imperfections and style, so she felt in tune with whoever this anonymous artist was that her grandfather used to christen "Rosie the Rocketer."

Erin, Carol, and Colin sat around imagining the stories of how this came up. Was it the artists that everyone used? Or was it just a friend of a friend who said, "Hey, my friend so and so knows how to paint; let's get him to do it"?

For Erin, it was kind of fun to imagine the stories of how you get someone to paint your plane. But she also knew that names and art and sayings gave each plane its personality, and "Rosie" was no exception. But the whole time Erin was concentrating on painting the nose art, she was also focusing on her mother, Carol, and observing her. Carol was realizing that the clock was ticking and that this would probably be her only time alone, at least with a few people around, with her father's plane. Besides the letters and some other personal items, "Rosie" was the only thing left really that Carol could physically touch and feel the connection with her dad. For her, that was just as important as the final application of nose art. Erin also remembers that when her mom talked about Charles, she talked about the "sheep" part of him and never knew about the "wolf part" of her grandfather. Erin recalls fondly growing up hearing those kinds of stories about the wonderful man that Charles was and how he touched the lives of so many. There were never any conversations about the impressive heroic stuff from the war, but more about how Charles treated the students he taught and the boys at the camp, and the impacts on later life he had with them. Carol also talked about the kinds of things that he taught her in life, and to never be afraid of anything. With the painting work complete, "Rosie" was eventually crated and shipped to Rob Collings and the Collings Foundation Museum.

On October 19, 2020, after seventy-five years and countless hours of combat, a freshly restored "Rosie the Rocketer" took to the skies once again over the rolling, emerald green fields of the Hudson, Massachusetts, countryside. Piloted by Rob Collings, chief executive officer and chief pilot of the Collings Foundation, he described the first flight in "Rosie" with a very simple and profound account. "She flew perfectly."

And for Colin who witnessed the event via video, he proclaimed that "to be able to do this and see it take to sky's again not only for the Colling's Foundation but for the Carpenter family is one of my greatest honors and achievements in life."

About a month after "Rosie's" first flight, I knew I too had to see "Rosie the Rocketer" in the flesh. I arrived at a nondescript metal hangar in November 2020, as a bitterly cold northwest wind rattled the hangar doors. As the door slowly opened, I noticed a New England sun playing hide and seek behind fast-moving rows of oblong clouds. As my Collings Museum guide pushed and shouldered the heavy hangar doors open, he resembled a high school football player, during practice, pushing a three-man sled.

As the first rays of light streaked inside, chaperoned by gaggles of late autumn leaves, a flash of sunlight arched over the nose art, "Rosie the Rocketer" appeared illuminated by neon light.

As I stepped outside, oblivious to the bitter cold, I saw "Rosie" bathed in golden light as white flecks of snow spit at its olive drab frame.

I was in awe as I sized up and gazed upon one of the last World War II veterans to return home. My attention, however, shifted to the powerful sound of screeching to my left.

As if on cue, or perhaps well planned, a magnificent bald eagle made a headlong, winged run toward the open hangar. At twenty-five yards out, it pulled up into a 30-degree climb. With its dark black wingtips curled, it circled over "Rosie" and screeched once more before retreating westward.

As I tracked the big bird and watched it head for a far-off stand of barren trees, I couldn't help but wonder if perhaps Charles Carpenter's spirit was still patrolling the skies above.

So that's the remarkable story of a remarkable airplane named "Rosie the Rocketer," remembered in many ways as the greatest tank hunter that the US Army had during that time in history. But "Rosie" brought a very difficult and emotional piece of that to me in researching this book. Gathering all of Charles Carpenter's personal accounts through his letters and his diaries that his family had collected, preserved and saved, along with firsthand news reporter accounts and detailed books on the 4th Armored Division gave me a much-broader understanding of the ground war for what it was; plain and simple, it was just a horrific thing on both sides—a thought that I'm sure Charles Carpenter would never argue with after witnessing it firsthand both in the air and on the ground. But as historians have shown, like it or not, this war had to be fought. "Rosie" was certainly part of that devastation. And one of the astonishing and mesmerizing things about "Rosie" is the fact that she's definitely one of the last veterans to come home from World War II. We know she was built in April 1944 and she shipped out for England shortly after being constructed, with no thought whatsoever from any of the Piper employees who laid their hands on her or the soldiers who flew or maintained her that she would ever return, let alone survive the combat conditions of war. In essence, she had done her part as a war machine, left behind by an occupying army who no longer required her and was forgotten over there in Europe for many years, at least by those who participated in it firsthand. Most veterans wanted to quickly shove the horrible memories of the war into the past and forget about its worldwide devastation. By the end of the war, it wasn't known who she was or what her wartime accounts were. In all due respect, this 1944 L-4H Cub should be revered as not only a historic treasure but one that sheds light on the ingenuity of "common soldiers" whose main mission was to end all wars as quickly as possible and return to life and loved ones they left behind as they laid their lives on the line, ensuring that our freedoms would be forever protected.

Both Charles Carpenter and "Rosie the Rocketer" saw a war that we need to remember, study with great intensity, and demand that we don't fall into that fatal trap and repeat history. This L-4 is different from every other airplane extant because of that reason. The suffering that she saw is nothing short of dreadful. But she did it and so did Charles. And neither was born or made up to do so, but they both performed their duty honorably when they answered our nation's call to serve. She was an American invention as a Piper Cub, an airplane so welcoming and docile in its civilian livery of bright yellow with an attractive black lightning bolt running down its sides. It wasn't until the coat of olive drab paint was applied that this L-4 became no more than a "sheep in wolf's clothing." But the best thing that Americans do is to modify a product built for a consumer into something else and, in this case, something deadly. And Charles Carpenter and several of his fellow pilots did that and did that in an imaginative way. By all accounts, the exploits of Charles Carpenter and the use of his bazooka-equipped "Rosie the Rocketer" in an antiarmor role certainly hinted at greater possibilities with the use of light aircraft. This testament later proved itself true both in the skies over Korea and Vietnam. This is why these men, like Charles M. Carpenter along with those who paid the ultimate sacrifice, were the true heroes during our times of conflict and their heroic actions must never be forgotten.

Endnotes

Chapter 2

1. *Woodfield County Journal*, review of "Aviation Events Big Fair Feature," August 29, 1912.

Chapter 7

1. Günther Voltz (retired Luftwaffe pilot) in discussion with the author 2001.

Chapter 3–6

1. Edgar F. Raines, *Eyes of Artillery: The Origins of Modern US Army Aviation in World War II* (Washington, DC: Center of Military History, 2000).
2. Ibid.
3. Ibid.
4. *L-4 Grasshopper Wing Newsletter*, review of "A Chronology of Key Events." February/March 1987.

Chapter 10

1. Don M. Fox, *Patton's Vanguard: The United States Army Fourth Armored Division* (Jefferson, NC: McFarland, 2003)).
2. Ibid.
3. *Daily Dispatch*, review of "Race Riots in Detroit," June 21, 1943.

Chapter 11

1. Robert Pearson (retired US Army) in discussion with Mike Pearson 2011.

Chapter 12

1. Robert Pearson (retired US Army) in discussion with Mike Pearson 2011.

2. Ken Wakefield and Kyle Westley, *The Fighting Grasshoppers: US Liaison Aircraft Operations in Europa, 1942–1945* (Leicester, UK: Midland Counties Publications, 1990).

Chapter 13

1. *Stars & Stripes*, review of "1 Cub Plus 6 Bazookas Equals Bad News for Panzers," October 5, 1944.

2. *New York Sun*, review of "The Mad Yank in a Flying Jeep," August 14, 1944.

·3. Leonard Kiley (retired US Army) in discussion with Mike Pearson 2011.

4. Robert Pearson (retired US Army) in discussion with Mike Pearson 2011.

5. *Stars & Stripes*, review of "Besieged Germans Fight to Save Subs," August 1, 1944.

Chapter 14

1. *New York Sun*, review of "The Mad Yank in a Flying Jeep," August 14, 1944.

2. *Daily Dispatch*, review of "More Honors for Carpenter," November 4, 1944.

3. *L-4 Grasshopper Wing Newsletter*, review of "A Letter From Overseas," April/May 1992

4. *Stars & Stripes*, review of "Moline Pilot in Small Plane Wrecks Tanks," October 3, 1944.

Chapter 16

1. *Stars & Stripes*, review of *Now Comes the One-Man Air Force*, October 5, 1944.

2. *Stars & Stripes*, review of "Cub Ace Blasts Ammo in Snowstorm Flight," November 20, 1944.

Chapter 17

1. Don M. Fox, *Patton's Vanguard: The United States Army Fourth Armored Division* (Jefferson, NC: McFarland, 2003).

2. Robert V. Brulle (retired army air force fighter pilot) in discussion with the author, 2002.

3. *Des Moines Tribune*, review of *WWII Letter…I owan's Brush with Death*, December 24, 1964.

4. *Yank*, review of "Battle of Bastogne," January 21, 1945.

5. Oscar Boesch (retired Luftwaffe fighter pilot) in discussion with the author, 2002.

Chapter 18

1. Thomas Rozga (retired US Marine Corps pilot) in discussion with the author, 2008.

2. Merritt Duane Francies (retired army liaison pilot) in discussion with the author, 2001.

3. *Daily Dispatch*, review of "Famed Major Enjoying Home; Reluctant to Discuss War," May 2, 1945.

4. *Rock Island Argus*, review of "Nazi Nemesis Tells Value of Bazooka Plane," May 8, 1945.

Chapter 19

1. Roosevelt Military Academy, *Rough Rider*, review of "Famous Colonel to Be Commandant!," April 1947.

2. Max Hastings, "Their Wehrmacht Was Better Than Our Our Army," *Washington Post*, May 5, 1985.

Chapter 20

1. Don M. Fox, *Patton's Vanguard: The United States Army Fourth Armored Division*. (Jefferson, NC: McFarland, 2003.

Bibliography

Baldwin, Hanson Weightman. *Tiger Jack*. Ft. Collins, CO: Old Army Press, 1979.

Fox, Don M. *Patton*'s *Vanguard: The United States Army Fourth Armored Division*. Jefferson, NC: McFarland, 2003.

Daily Dispatch. Review of "Race Riots in Detroit." June 21, 1943.

Daily Dispatch. Review of "AP Man Says Moline History Teacher Is Making History on Western Front." October 3, 1944.

Daily Dispatch. Review of "More Honors for Carpenter." November 4, 1944.

Daily Dispatch. Review of "Famed Major Enjoying Home; Reluctant to Discuss War." May 2, 1945.

Des Moines Tribune. Review of "WWII Letter …I owan's Brush with Death." December 24, 1964.

L-4 Grasshopper Wing Newsletter. Review of "A Chronology of Key Events." February/March 1987.

L-4 Grasshopper Wing Newsletter. Review of "A Letter from Overseas." April/May 1992.

New York Sun. Review of "The Mad Yank in a Flying Jeep." August 14, 1944.

New York Sun. Review of "Charlie Fights Nazi Tanks in Cub Armed with Bazookas." October 3, 1944.

Raines, Edgar F. *Eyes of Artillery: The Origins of Modern US Army Aviation in World War II*. Washington, DC: Center of Military History, 2000.

Rock Island Argus. Review of "Nazi Nemesis Tells Value of Bazooka Plane." May 8, 1945.

Roosevelt Military Academy. *Rough Rider*. Review of "Famous Colonel to Be Commandant!" April 1947.

Stars & Stripes. Review of "Besieged Germans Fight to Save Subs." August 1, 1944.

Stars & Stripes. Review of "Moline Pilot in Small Plane Wrecks Tanks." October 3, 1944.

Stars & Stripes. Review of "Now Comes the One-Man Air Force." October 5, 1944.

Stars & Stripes. Review of "1 Cub Plus 6 Bazookas Equals Bad News for Panzers." October 5, 1944.

Stars & Stripes. Review of "Cub Ace Blasts Ammo in Snowstorm Flight." November 20, 1944.

Stars & Stripes. Review of "'Rosie the Rocketer' Plays Bazooka for German Tanks." December 26, 1944.

Wakefield, Ken, and Kyle Westley. *The Fighting Grasshoppers: US Liaison Aircraft Operations in Europa, 1942–1945*. Leicester: Midland Counties Publications, 1990.

Wakefield, Kenneth. *Lightplanes at War: US Liaison Aircraft in Europe, 1942–1947*. Stroud: Tempus, 2000.

Washington Post. "Their Wehrmacht Was Better Than Our Army." Max Hastings. May 5, 1985.

Woodfield County Journal. Review of "Aviation Events Big Fair Feature." August 29, 1912.

Yank. Review of "Battle of Bastogne." January 21, 1945.

Interviews

Carol Apacki (Carpenter) in discussion with the author, 2019.

Oscar Boesch (retired Luftwaffe fighter pilot) in discussion with the author, 2002.

Robert V. Brulle (retired army air force fighter pilot) in discussion with the author, 2002.

Rob Collings (CEO and chief pilot Collings Foundation) in discussion with the author, 2019.

Merritt Duane Francies (retiredarmy liaison pilot) in discussion with the author, 2001.

James Hageman (professor emeritus, New Mexico State University) in discussion with the author, 2019.

Leonard Kiley (retired US Army) in discussion with Mike Pearson, 2011.

Erin Pata (painter) in discussion with the author, 2019.

Robert Pearson (retired US Army) in discussion with Mike Pearson, 2011.

Colin Powers (aircraft restorer) in discussion with the author, 2019.

Thomas Rozga (retired US Marine Corps pilot) in discussion with the author, 2008.

Michael Russell (PhD, senior lecturer in Business Management, University of New Hampshire) in discussion with the author, 2019.

Joseph Scheil (airline pilot/aircraft restorer) in discussion with the author, 2019.

Gunther Voltz (retired Luftwaffe pilot) in discussion with the author, 2001.

Harold Wanless (PhD, professor of regional studies and geography, University of Miami, Florida) in discussion with the author, 2019.

Index

North American Aviation B-25 Mitchell, 54–55

North American Aviation O-47, 75, 77

North American Aviation P-51 Mustang, 9, 121, 133, 166, 174, 232

O'Hara, Maureen, 36

Okmulgee, Oklahoma, 67–68

O'Leary, John H., 24, 215, 218

Pata, Erin, 235

Patton, George S., general, 15, 93, 125, 132–133, 153, 163, 170, 171–172, 210, 221, 228

Peace Corps, 219

Pearson, Robert, 115–116, 129, 135–136

Percy Jones Hospital, 199

Philippines, 40–43, 45, 46, 48, 54, 72, 75

Piper Aircraft Company, 76, 101, 161

Piper L-4 (also known as Piper J-3 Cub), 9–10, 12–14, 68, 79–80, 96, 100–101, 109, 113, 115, 123–124, 129–130, 131–132, 134–137, 140–141, 170, 173–175, 183, 194–197, 226–239

Powers, Colin, 12, 229, 233

Republic P-47 Thunderbolt, 17, 30, 121, 133, 151, 173, 184, 232

Reynolds, Illinois, 22–24, 41, 108, 205, 215, 223

Rockets Inc. Flying Club, 40

Roosevelt, Franklin D., US president, 43–44, 78, 98, 171, 192

Roosevelt Military Academy, 26, 29, 140, 156, 205, 224

"Rosie the Riveter," 99, 141

"Rosie the Rocketer," 9–10, 12–13, 137, 141, 147, 150, 152, 173, 175, 184, 192, 198, 221, 226–227, 229, 232, 235–239

Rozga, Thomas, lieutenant, 192

Russell, Mike, 217

Scheil, Joseph, 12, 229–231

Seversky P-35, 42

Shriver Jr., Robert Sargent, 219

Sill, Joshua, brigadier general, 83

Smyrna Army Flying School, 69

Spaatz, Carl, general, 93

Stars & Stripes, 134, 135, 137, 149, 162–163, 167, 192, 197, 227

Stearman PT-17, 62

Stinson L-5 Sentinel, 9, 96, 174, 192–193

Stinson O-49/L-1, 76, 78

Stuttgart, Arkansas, 70–72, 105, 115

Swift, Innis P., major general, 78

Taylorcraft L-2, 68

Thomas-Morse O-19, 42

Urbana High School, 211, 212, 217

USS *Hornet*, 54–55

Voltz, Gunther, 61

Waco CG-4 Hadrian, 71, 126

Walter Reed General Hospital, 189–190, 199

Wanless, Harold, 217

Weaver, Dempsey, 60, 62–63, 67–71, 73, 105, 126–128

Women Airforce Service Pilots (WASPs), 113–114

Wood, John S., general, 15, 92–93, 96, 104–105, 112, 125–126, 134, 153, 164, 170, 171–172, 221

Wright, Wilber, 20–21

YANK, 178, 192